TOASTING THE BRIDE

Memoirs of Milestones to Manhood

Benneth Nnaedozie Okpala

TOASTING THE BRIDE

Memoirs of Milestones to Manhood

By
Benneth Nnaedozie Okpala

Eagle & Palm Publishers

ISBN: 1-890232-07-6
L.C.C Card Number: 99-48982

Eagle & Palm Publishers
1026 Welsh Drive
Rockville, MD 20852-1202

Printed in the United States by: Morris Publishing
3212 East Highway 30 • Kearney, NE 68847
1-800-650-7888

Dedication

To my ancestors, my parents, my family,
I lovingly dedicate this book.

To the many servant-leaders of our society who break a
bloody sweat every day striving to carve out a niche for the
Nigerian community in the Diaspora, thank you for walking
with me through thick and thin.

TABLE OF CONTENTS

AUTHOR'S STATEMENT

I can not change yesterday.
But I can make the most of today
and look with hope toward tomorrow.

We are living the two worlds and dying to belong! I present to you a culture-based social commentary with an invitation to think along.

Culture! — "The arts, beliefs, customs, institutions, and any other products of human work and thought created by a people or group within a time or era." Aren't we mostly what we acquired by heritage? Or don't we become what we program our minds to think or believe?

Many things, however, are not in our power to change. Obstacles don't disappear merely by our exercise of faith. Patience is learning to cooperate with the inevitable.

Milestones mark important dates in the event of one's journey through life, and memoirs capture the essence of the journey. One is process and procedure, the other is substance.

I believe there are three selves to any individual: The self as perceived by the individual; the self as perceived by those with whom the individual interacts; and, the true self, which is known fully only by God. Social and emotional dimensions of our lives are tied together because our emotional life is primarily, but not exclusively, developed and manifested in our relationships with

God and with fellow others. Integrity is a measure of the whole-someness of the combination of the three aforementioned selves. A practical understanding of the three selves is required by the individual to define character, formulate personal philosophies, and relate to human and superhuman realities.

I believe there is more to human life than is readily evident to the naked eye— more to oneself, more to one's neighbor, and more to the world that surrounds us. There is more to the past out of which we come, and more to the present— maybe infinitely more. There is more to the interrelationships that bind us together as persons and players on the Earth's stage; and, the further we probe, the deeper the mystery, or the reward or, even, the involvement.

We are both spectators and actors in a continuing performance where life is both author and producer, and for which nature serves as an ever-changing stage. Even in its simplest manifestations, [human] life is historical. It embodies the past and carries instructions for the future. [René Dubos][1].

ACKNOWLEDGMENTS

This work is a product of many minds. I am grateful for the inspiration and wisdom of my ancestors and many thinkers; and for other trans-generational sources and roots of this wisdom. I am also grateful for many friends and colleagues at work and in our community, and other people who have read this material and have given feedback and encouragement. More so, for the few special friends at work and in the community who have helped me maintain sanity through all these years of innumerous trials and temptations.

For the development and production of the book itself, I feel a deep sense of gratitude:

— to professor Ali Mazrui, whose solemn advice empowered me to trust my instincts and write boldly without reservations.

— to Mrs. Christine Okeke and professor Nkem Nwankwo for weighing in early with valuable comments on the rough first drafts of the book.

— to my publisher, Dr. Christiana Chinwe Okechukwu for taking my manuscript at face value and running with it, providing new ideas and new leads.

— to Dr. Mary E. Owens for her invaluable professional editing of the manuscript at a much reduced price to fit my meager budget.

— to Dr. J.O.S Okeke, Dr. Augustine Egbunike, Mr. Chibuzo Onwuchekwe, Dr. Youmay Ogboso, Mr. Ken Chinweze, Mr. Anthony Oji, Mr. Aloy Obiechina, Attorney James Okorafor, Mr. Matt Odili, Mr. Blaize Kaduru, Dr. n'Ekwunife Muoneke, Mr. Chukwuma Nwosu... for their financial contributions in funding the production of the book.

— to Henry Ihediwa and Mira Washington for their hearty effort in formating the text and lending the book a beautiful style.

— to the happy memory of my father and my childhood mentors.

— to my very good friend, Naeem Husain, whose sincerity consistently reaffirmed my belief that the human family can remain pure regardless of race, religion, or nationality.

My deep and sincere gratitude also goes to the many devoted acquaintances who read the manuscript and took time to write in some positive reviews: Paulinus Okonkwo, Atlanta GA; Chudi Anwusi, Houston TX; Festus Okere, Houston Tx; Youmay Ogboso, Houston TX; Mary Owens, Rockville MD; Carlos Zapata, Katy TX.

PREFACE

More than once, my wife had said to me: "Ben, you ought to write a book!" I had finally impressed her with the many "Honey do" term papers I had helped her write, and the few here-and-there articles I had gotten published in local newspapers and organization newsletters.

I have always known that as far as communication goes, I am better at relating my ideas, feelings and thoughts in writing, than in speech. But writing a book was the farthest thing on my mind. I was a very busy man and, from what I have found out writing this book, authoring a book, any book at all, is one heck of a laborious undertaking.

In early 1997, I had just come to the painful end of my long, drawn out, two-phased legal war against the City of Houston. At the climax of this war along with a challenging full-time job and part-time law school attendance, added to a continuing dose of painstakingly-tough service to my community, I noticed a rather big bulge at the back end of my head — very much like a backyard addition to a house or room, or a memory upgrade to a computer motherboard. I had then joked with my wife that my brain was finally filled up, and it had desperately added some new space as needed. I knew something had to give.

I was right! Because as soon as I discontinued law school, the bump disappeared without fanfare.

But my brain continued to seethe with mega amounts of information, thoughts, worries and emotional pain. These needed to be packaged and neatly filed away in some physical space outside my head, to free up some usable space for me to mentally move on with life. So, I picked up my pen and paper and started writing. Sure enough, the more I wrote the easier and freer I felt. But what type of book and for whom?

In the matter of personal experience, I am uniquely qualified to write about Africa and about America as well. In me, the phrase "African-American" is alive with vivid experiences. I have spent equal halves of my hitherto eventful life in Africa, and in the United States of America. I have citizenship in both and have been uniquely impacted by both through bouts of traumatic experiences. Presently and continuing, one—America—gets to house my body; the other—Africa—my soul. In the ensuing strange marriage of the two cultures, the line between the bride and bridegroom is fluid at best. I can, therefore, constructively praise and/ or criticize both, interchangeably, with civilized equanimity; and without fear, favor, or shame. I can "Toast" or "toast" the Bride, circumstance warranting.

INTRODUCTION

This is NOT a look-it-up book! Neither is it a simple autobiographical novel. Rather, the book is a selective assemblage of natural philosophical wisdoms; the cultural basis of personal beliefs and identity; and, the living story of personal experiences. Thus, in effect, a practical commentary on our modern man's politico-economic social culture.

Realistically, and for cause, I have subscribed to, and accepted as basic, the view that the context of "life" is at its highest where it involves man's consciousness and free will; and where it refers to the deep realities of the world within—the affirmation of the individual self under unique and prevailing circumstances of nature, politics and culture—a situation where the choices of the individual may uniquely determine that individual's Fate, and the fate of human life in tandem.

The reader is not to equate the different chapters as simple matching titles of the knowledge they contain. Although these chapters are meaningful and intelligible in themselves, the reader is persuaded to accumulate them progressively as the background necessary for understanding the relation of each to the whole. The "whole" is my insight into what is known and can be conjectured as the total sweep in the life experience of a spiritual, metamorphosing Igboman turned Nigerian, turned Biafran, turned Nigerian-Igboman, turned Nigerian-American in perpetual emotional exile.

My book is to inform and to query alike. It is meant for any inquisitive mind that wants to know and know more. First, to know my total person as molded by my past and remolded by my present. Then, to imbibe some universal lessons of life by partaking in the more vivid accounts of my personal experiences, and by pondering on the harder questions of living, in general, which are progressively generated herein in the book.

Chapter I— "WHAT'S IN A NAME?"— uniquely introduces my person to educate the reader on the fundamental basis for the author's mindset, and on the overriding context of the book itself, whereby, get this, the actual person of the author is unabashedly employed as a canvas for painting the more difficult but necessary social pictures involved. Chapter V—"THE DAWN OF EXPERIENCE"(with a must-read Appendix)—presents the raw information sufficiently challenging the involved reader to know more about certain naked hypocrisies of the American legal system, in terms of its strengths and weaknesses, and to formulate educated personal opinions about the American social culture. The rest of the Chapters fill in the voids in-between—partly informing and partly entertaining. Ultimately, in compendium, we have a uniquely dynamic discourse.

I speak in this book my own voice, and the voices of its contributors, from and with authority of the educated mind and serenity of the emancipated soul. Although the material presented is predominantly a product of the African culture, it is not parochially African in its view of human life and Nature, nor in the content of the personal experiences presented.

The book draws heavily from the literary wisdoms of philosophers — both old and new — to articulate the language and extract a body of knowledge suitable for describing, and coincidental to expressing, the deeper side of personal life experiences. It also juxtaposes traditional African spiritual idealism with modern American material realism to establish context. In this view and in the context of personal life experiences, "success" is relational and its measure, necessarily, subjective. The quality of human life is, therefore, dependent upon the value system of the individual; and upon one's total exposure to cyclic circumstantial experiences, that cycle of living experiences which occur in the universal continuum of birth, death, and rebirth as determined by fate, and as sustained through faith in God or any other applicable symbol of human common beliefs.

In writing this book, I have not tried to become a perfectionist. ("No writer has a monopoly on correctness," says Professor Ali A. Mazrui, a prolific author of more than twenty books.) Rather, I have tried to be open and brave, and to publish a continuous discourse. The language of the book is essentially poetic, because poems strike the deep chords of human thinking and inquiry. The lyric poem has more to tell us, or at least deeper ways of touching us, than the most tremendous tragedy in many acts; or the subtlest comic novel in a thousand pages. Poems paint pictures! And, "[a] picture is worth more than a thousand words."

It therefore behooves the average reader to strive to peel the veils of inquiry to see the literary and philosophic thinking at work; and, ultimately, to imbibe universal knowledge enough to participate effectively in this life's continuing symphony of muted indulgences.

Welcome!

1

¥¥¥

WHAT'S IN A NAME?

*N*gozi, Nneka, Ogechukwu, Ogbonnaya, Ozoemena, Nnaedozie.... All Igbo names, all packed with meanings in language and culture. One of them is mine — Benneth Nnaedozie Okpala — for I am rooted in my culture, and defined by the spiritual language of my people. I was destined to suck it all in from an early age, for I was born a man, growing up to die a child. My father called me Dad! So, if it all goes well, I'll die a child — finally, the son of my father-son whom I have dutifully buried, and the father of a son I shall yet meet, who will dutifully bury me. It's all in the name, the culture, the people. *Benneth Nnaedozie Okpala*, the son-father of *Amos Ukokweremuo Okpala*, and the grandson, reincarnated person of *Azakochuba Okpalakoronkwo Nwambuba* — the official patriarch of our surviving family tree growing on the sublime roots of our past ancestors and linking their Spirit world to our present and future generations.

As far as the family tree goes, my grandfather, reincarnated in myself, was and still is the trunk that bears the spreading branches of my living, and recently dead, chain of uncles, cousins, nieces and nephews; feeding off the deeply buried ancestral roots of long dead, but yet living, spirits of preceding family patriarchs who are culturally recognized in their own rights as deities, saints and guardian angels, and whose perpetual presence in and over the family is represented by the family land, or compound, as documented by the surviving worship symbols and traditional oral literature from as far back as memories can hold. Culture evokes their revered presence in ordinary daily prayers with kolanuts, and with ceremonious libations and sacrifices at more elaborate grand occasions.

The Igbo people inhabit the large and fertile region of the lower Niger river and its adjoining territories. The current population is estimated at around 30 million people. This area probably has the highest population density, compared to any other area on the continent of Africa. Archaeological evidence and other research support the view that it was from this region that pioneering groups of Iron Age people spread the knowledge and use of iron to far and distant lands.

Historically, Igbo people have a complex and very sophisticated form of political life. Governmental power and governance were much more diffused in this region than elsewhere in Africa, owing to the strict representative and republican nature of the people. At the lowest level of governance or community life, Igbo people adhere to a strict "No representation, no support" form of community involvement. Representation evolves from Elders, through Chiefs, and then to the general populace.

Igbo people are predominantly Christians. It is estimated that they constitute the largest block of Christians found anywhere on the African continent. Before the advent of Christianity, the Igbo belief system revolved around one God, "Chi". Because Chi is an omnipotent and omnipresent God, symbols or sanctuaries representing Chi can be found in every home, compound, or village square. These sanctuaries are called different names in different parts of Igboland due to the dialectical wealth of the people. The fact that Chi can be personalized as well as shared by the community may explain the Igbo acceptance of and affinity for the Christian religion.

The Igbo language is said to be one of the most difficult languages to learn, mainly because it is not spoken anywhere else in the world. It is, however, one of the richest languages in Africa: from the Owerri-Ngwa-Umuahia variation or dialect, the Onitsha-Awka, Enugu-Abakaliki, Orlu-Okigwe to the Opobo-Ikwere variations or dialects. Igbo people are as diverse as these dialects, but they share a common tradition of independence and dynamism. Prior to the amalgamation of Nigeria, Igbo people were involved in iron work, farming, and commerce. Communities were organized in trading blocks for the exchange of goods and services. Movement by people was minimal and largely unnecessary. However, there are groups that had a need to move around, such as native doctors, blacksmiths and ceremonially titled people.

As people moved around, it was mostly out of character to resettle permanently outside of one's place of birth. This may explain the Igbo penchant for general "returns" during special occasions. Communities often encourage their sons and daughters from far away to return, and as much as possible, bring their offspring back to the ancestral home. Recent Igbo history in Nigeria has made this custom much more compelling, as communities dedicate these returns to general stock taking, as well as establishing societal priorities.

Igbo society is very patrilineal. The husband is the head of the household, and the well being of the family is the man's foremost responsibility. Not only to his family, but also to the larger community. The extended family is commonplace and has been perfected by Igbo people for community development and through every facet of life, including commerce. In recent times, as the Igbo people have left their ancestral homes, we have striven to maintain these values which have sustained our people for generations.

My family land sits defiantly, but for a reason, on the plain narrow boundary between my small birth town, Okoh, and her much larger town-neighbor to the West, Nanka.

These are not friendly neighbors. They were warring neighbors in the days of my grandfather, land-disputing neighbors in the days of my father, and non-socializing neighbors in my time. At present, the crystal ball is spinning, and the gods of civilization are working hard for these two town-neighbors.

It was different in the days of my grandfather, understandably different! Tribal wars were not unusual in my culture a century or more ago. Growth and expansion of one domain happened only at the life-and-death expense of some lesser other. Towns marched through and over towns; villages swallowed up villages. Nanka and Okoh were two such towns; Ifite, Nanka, and Ezioko, Okoh, were two such villages. Nanka town, by and through the people of Ifite Nanka, sought to expand and dominate the people and town of Okoh through and over Ezioko village, my village. (Igbo towns are made up of distinct quasi-governmental entities called villages, which are themselves made up of extended family groups called clans).

There are five villages in my town. Ezioko village is the largest in both population and land area.

As the name states, Ezioko people take pride in themselves as the true aborigines of Okoh, since literally in Igbo language, _ezi_ means real or true. Hence, _Ezioko_ means real or true Okoh. It was this type of sense of trueness, perhaps, that forced the village's generation of my grandfather's to see the defense of their village as inseparable from the defense of Okoh town at large. This feeling of total and general obligation by my village towards our town continues today.

Ezioko village, like most other villages, is comprised of clans or groups of blood relatives in an extended family system, which is the hallmark of the Igbo social culture. Culture forbids marriages between members of the same clan or _Umunna_ — meaning offspring of the same father. Indeed, the Igbo culture holds the clan of family sacred, and it includes aunts, uncles, cousins, grandparents, and other distant blood relatives. The extended family system creates a bond among its members, which is beneficial both in its function as a corporate system in which family groups rely on each other for survival, and act as an educational setting in which children learn the lessons of life through daily experience and oral instruction by their elders.

My family clan — Akulu family — has a special history in Okoh and a close link to another town, Isuofia, not very far from Okoh. Long ago, Akulu was an organized town of its own, comprising nine villages. It was so organized, powerful and progressive that it became a concern to her neighboring towns, which not only felt threatened, but also grew envious of Akulu town and sought ways to destroy it. Lacking the ability to engage Akulu town in a local war, however, these towns connived and brought in foreign powers to aid them in their cause. The story has it that they brought in notorious war mongers from Ohaofia and Arochukwu to invade Akulu town on the town's holy day, thereby employing the element of surprise to catch the citizens of Akulu town when they were most vulnerable.

That element of surprise worked! The foreign invaders struck on a ceremonial day while my ancestors celebrated at the palace of *Udo-Akulu*, their town's spiritual deity or *Chi*, and the seat of their social organization. The invaders devastated Akulu town, killed most of its able men, plundered the town, and drove the citizens into exile to any of the neighboring villages and towns that would accommodate them.

The fleeing Akulu citizens took aspects of their deity with them and established parallel worship stations round and about their new places of residence or domicile. Hence, even today or until the recent past, we have aspects of *Udo* (deity) in neighboring villages in Ekwulobia — *Udo-Uhuokpala*; and in Nanka — *Udo-Ifite*, Nanka (*Oye-Udo*, Nanka). But in these towns, my ancestors were not settled enough to establish their own villages in their original town's name, Akulu. Only in the town of Isuofia, farther to the west, did these Akulu refugees settle down completely in a village of their own and retain their original name, Akulu. Hence, today, we have *Akulu Isuofia* as a village in the town of Isuofia.

As time went by, some of the Akulu refugees made their way back to their homeland. But they were too few and too weak to reestablish themselves and survive as an autonomous town. Most of the well-settled refugees, such as those in Isuofia town, did not migrate back, but they have maintained cultural links with our clan to date. The returning Akulu indigenes resettled only a portion of their original land area and joined the town of Okoh as Akulu family in Ezioko village. History has it that most of the land area constituting the present-day Ezioko village originally belonged to Akulu town.

My great grandfather was one of those who came back from exile. He and his diminished number of kindred resettled the western tip of Okoh town, at its boundaries with the hostile town of Nanka to the North and further West, and the much bigger town of Ekwulobia, to the South. This move could have been strategic, because of their proven capability in defending against local invasion. Or, it could have been social, because they wanted to collect themselves as distinct a family as possible under the circumstances of their loss of autonomy and their new citizenship in Okoh town.

The Akulu family settled in Ezioko village as blacksmiths. In Igbo culture, blacksmithing is an exclusive trade or profession relegated to a special clan or extended family group in a town or geographical area. Like such other revered professions and crafts as native doctor and witchcraft, blacksmithing is a special endowment handed down from generation to generation within a family group or clan.

Blacksmiths worked the iron metal and made farming tools, such as hoes and knives; tools of war and hunting, such as guns, spears, machetes, and traps; and kitchen utensils, such as pots, pans, knives and spoons. In the old days, blacksmiths played a vital part in the survival and advancement of the Igbo culture and, indeed, African culture. They were the machine that drove the equivalent of the industrial revolution for the African people, in the context of their indigenous ways of life and eventual civilization.

Over the years, my clan, Akulu Okoh, has maintained a special link with its sister clan, Akulu Isuofia, both in the practice of their trade, blacksmithing, and in other necessary rituals of social and spiritual connections. They still maintain the inalienable "right of passage" into each other's domain and use of tools of trade. Traditional practice holds this to be true for many other fields or professions in Igboland, and, indeed, in many African cultures today.

The two neighboring towns of Okoh and Nanka fought numerous battles in one prolonged war of aggression and survival. Only the very brave dared to stay in the path of this war—a narrow path indeed, very plain and very well defined; a path bounded to the North by very deep and wide canyon (Mbuze), and to the South by the large and more formidable town of Ekwulobia. Nanka people knew better and knew enough to keep away from Ekwulobia. Okoh had a much friendlier association with Ekwulobia, her neighbor to the South. My grandfather had as many as eight (8) wives at certain time in his long life. Most of them were from Ekwulobia, including my grandmother on my father's side. My father followed suit and married his only wife, my mother, from the same town.

Only the unflinching spirit of ancestral continuity could fire the human resolve of one   patriarch to protect and propagate the symbols of family identity handed down and entrusted to him by another as a matter of cultural duty.   Only my grandfather, Okpalakoronkwo, could risk everything and live that resolve and responsibility in a family land that had become the only established channel of war between two enemy-neighbors. His only option was to dig in and fight to block the frontal advance of the invaders, at all times and at all cost.

Tactically, Okpalakoronkwo ingeniously constructed underground bunker residences to shield his many wives and children. He then established defensive sniper positions on yet other ingenious   constructions of towering mud houses. Within the compound, he set up shop and manufactured his own weapons of war — guns, spears, machetes— and with the help of a few courageous indigenes, my grandfather's compound became and remained a constant war zone through many assaults by the invading neighbors who constantly sought to take home his head on a stick.

But civil conflicts are riddled with politics of convictions! Because war is a political conflict, there were two sides to my people's convictions about the ideologies of Right and Wrong, and about the order of priority of the many elements of their social needs at the time and the proper organizational action to address those needs. Both sides of the ensuing social conflict produced overt and covert proponents of differing preferred ideologies, and of the acceptable enforcers of the preferred actions. My town's organized resistance against the invading army of Nanka neighbors was therefore not without its detractors. There were saboteurs who sold out to the enemy and joined them in several plots to assassinate my grandfather. They acted in expectation of favors from the Nanka people after their expected eventual defeat of Okoh town. My grandfather was not interested in the politics as much as he was in the people. His convictions and leadership were challenged and tested to the limits by his detractors, some of whom acted out of mere jealousy because they were hungry for the leadership position, others were motivated by selfish interests contained in their thinking that Okoh town did not have a chance against Nanka town and, therefore, acted in ways that would guarantee them safety and prosperity at the hands of their eventual masters. Among these people came traitors and double agents of the wars who went as far as plotting to kill or deliver my grandfather to the enemy.

The frustrations, disappointments, and deeper emotions of my grandfather, which combined to establish his life philosophy and define his personal character, can be deciphered from the names he chose for some of his sons. He named his first son *Aka-jeonye*—a phrase-question literally asking, "Whom else could they talk about?" My grandfather was aware that people talked secretly and spitefully about him. Another son he named *Iloegbunem* — meaning, "May I not die at the hands of my enemies." Iloegbunam was kidnapped as a young boy (presumably by slave traders) as he traveled alone to Ekwulobia market to meet his mother. The third son was *Enemibe* — meaning, "I can only sit in awe and watch the actions of my people." In naming my father *Ukokwerenmuo*, my grandfather expressed his personal philosophy of life: "Only the gods and Spirits deserve to be given credit and adoration for any human successes". Okpalakoronkwo was a humble, self-denied man who was willing to serve and sacrifice, but unwilling to pursue personal glory. Hence, yet another son he named *Ezeado*— meaning that "a natural king or leader does not scramble for material possession, personal glory or public recognition."

Okpalakoronkwo prevailed in his duty against all odds. He not only succeeded in preserving the family name, but also in preserving the integrity of his town. He lived and died as a true symbol of human bravery, and of principled human determination to protect and preserve one's spiritual ancestral identity. He did that, and did so with remarkable results, thus earning himself the attachment, *Nwambuba*—meaning, "the great one," to his real name, Okpalakoronkwo. Hence *Okpalakoronkwo-Nwambuba*.

To define his person and his deeds further, and more completely, yet another precursor attachment, *Azakochuba*— meaning, impliedly, "The one they couldn't arrest"— was added to his name. Hence his full titled name was *Azakochuba Okpalakoronkwo-Nwambuba*.

Our present family name, Okpala, is a short form of my grandfather's real name, Okpalakoronkwo, without the two attachments, and the 'koronkwo' ending, which actually attached to the name to indicate that my grandfather was born on the third market day (Nkwo) of a four-day traditional market week. Of course, the core name, *Okpala*, meant literally, and in fact, that he was the first son of his father and, therefore, the heir to his father's estate.

It is significant that the 19th and 20th century generations of my family established the *Okpala* name as the earthly reference point in the language and the spiritual definition of our family identity. The cultural definition of this identity is another! And it is deeper, resigning and relicing the predecessors of my grandfather to spiritual patriarchs and custodians of the family destiny — ofo or spiritual staff of life. Ancestors are powerful departed souls whose hostility could be dangerous, whose favor could be beneficial, and who should therefore be propitiated. They enjoy a cult in the narrow circle of their family of descendants. We humans can only connect with them through libations and, ultimately, in death.

Ofo is a symbol of worship and prayer. The typical *ofo* is a pair of 10 to 12-inches long, approximately 2-inch diameter, soft, white wood carved out of the stem of a special evergreen tree-shrub called *ogirisi*. *Ogirisi* is a sacred shrub usually planted in shrines and other places of traditional religious worship: on human graves as grave markers and personal shrine of the buried person and, on land boundaries, fences, and other places where permanency is desired and trespass forbidden. *Ofo* passes down the generations from one elderly male-leader of a clan, upon his death, to his successor, or from a father to his first son (his *okpala*) in the case of a single family subsystem or compound. On some rare occasions and for a reason, a father may pass over his first son and award his *ofo* to another son. This act would permanently confer authority to the recipient son and often create deep resentment in the disinherited son.

Ofo is never washed in water! Therefore it retains, and passes on, all marks of history from generation to generation, such as chewed-and-spat kolanut and sprinkled blood of sacrificial chickens and animals.

Ofo is a permanent item in an Igbo elder's cowhide tote-bag, which he carries to all public functions and other serious meetings, as a constant symbolic reminder of the presence and supportive companionship of his dead ancestors in all matters of life and society, and as notice of his duty as an elder to always speak the truth and maintain honor and dignity as a trusted person. Also, always in tow in the elder's bag are such other items as *Nzu* or white chalk, used in marking off line-strokes during prayer or libation; cow horns or gourd cups, used in sharing palm wine in public; other trinkets of meaning and decoration; and, of course, kolanuts and hot pepper. A traditional doctor's bag would contain many more items of traditional medicine. *Ofo* and *Oji* (kolanut) are the two most important traditional symbols in Igbo culture.

A Matter of Life, Death, and Rebirth

My ancestors practiced a traditional religion, which was dominant in southern, central and west coast Africa.

The chief elements of the traditional religious outlook are the perpetuation of history and the rejection of profane, mundane time. Religiously, traditional man is not interested in the unique and specific, but rather, exclusively, in those things and actions that respect and restore transcendental models. Only those things that participate in and reflect the eternal archetypes or the great pattern of original creation by which cosmos came out of chaos are real in the traditional outlook.

The religious activities of the traditional man are the recurring attempts to return to the beginning — to the Great Time; to trace again and renew the process by which structure and order were established. Traditional religion finds the sacred in any aspect of the world that links man to the archetypes of time in the beginning. Its typical mode of expression is, in consequence, repetitive; its understanding of history, cyclical.

In Igbo culture, activities that relate to survival are believed to have their origins with the gods. All education is related in some way to this sacred context and is, therefore, religious. The worldview is communicated through myth, ritual, and other ways. Its importance to group survival is made evident by various devices. Every activity is communicated to children by means that tend to emphasize its proper performance and to insure its continuation. Dramatic and colorful ceremonies are used to re-enact significant episodes in the religiocultural history of a tribe or people. These have both religious and educational value, and young people may observe or participate in them. Seasonal festivals, such as Iri-ji Ndigbo (Igbo New Yam Festival) or Okponsi (Masquerade Festival), cooperate with events in nature to communicate and reinforce the individual's understanding of the natural cycle of death and rebirth, which is basic to survival and religious consciousness of the traditional person.

A masquerade is many things to many people; even to scholars and experts in the matter, wives and children. To those schooled in the arts, it is the oneness in theatre and ritual. It is intrinsically religion, theatre, and culture. To the traditional Igboman, it is a manifest of Spirits of some kind—dwellers beneath the earth on whom no dust can stick. Perhaps it may sound emotional, but hardly does any other cultural institution touch the heart of an Igbo person as it is stimulated by the community's masquerade.

Before a masquerade appears, those who have a stake in its traditional performance— be it an age grade, cult or gild, family group, community, a town—mobilize for various preparations which add up to what is known as *Icho-mmanwu*. There is no uniform formula among all Igbo communities, but preparation there must be. The more important the masquerade, the more elaborate the preparation.

Icho-mmanwu literally means searching for the Spirit masquerade. Therefore the Spirit does not appear while the search lasts. It is still in the Spirit land and, at the appointed time, will appear through an ant-hole which leads directly into the bowels of the earth, where it resides and where it is cleansed by the ants and sewn up and decorated by the spiders. Or so the tradition tells the young, the uninitiated, and women. *Icho-mmanwu* is a male activity, and it readily occurs in many Igbo communities. Appropriate rituals for purification and invocation of the masquerade from the Spirit land, underline the masquerade as part of the cast in a mystic drama. Whatever form the rituals take, they are for the honorable performance of the masquerade and the well-being of humans associated with it.

When you have seen one masquerade, you have not seen them all. There are many which symbolize many things and perform different functions in the community. Some are representatives for law and order. They enforce the Dos and Don'ts the people live by, and when there is a breach, show what happens to the transgressors. Here the masquerade performs the function of a disciplinarian and security agent. Yet, as a symbol of law and order, it is a powerful feature in Igbo community life.

There are those that appear to be instituted to please at festivals and ceremonies that are open to all, and by their looks and their dancing, they indicate the community's far definition of beauty and joy. There are those which mirror the passage of time and experiences of the community which they have met and seen in their slow parade of years. In another class, there are the qualities the Igbo people admire in men—valor, agility, action and achievement—the masquerades that symbolize these things command great respect.

Eze mmuo, the oldest masquerade of the Ojoto community, for example, is a manifest of the Spirit of the elder ancestor. It invokes the goodwill of our ancestors—goodwill on men and spirits alike. *Ekpe* masquerade of Ugwuaji is used to execute laws made by the traditional government of the community. They perform functions, such as collecting levies and fines, and administering punishment for failure to perform specifically assigned community duties. There are masquerades famous for their dancing. They employ idea, form, time and space, the unseen world and the invisible, what is heard and what is imagined, to take the Igbo dance culture to its latest height. Perhaps the dancing masquerade is more popular than any other type because it touches both children and adults by actively involving those who may join in the dancing and those who may only watch. It is found in virtually every community for cultural definition of joy and happiness and, it provides meaning to a festival.

Finally, there is the *Ijere*. The *Ijere* is not only the biggest Igbo masquerade but also the greatest. It is the complete Igbo masquerade alphabet, the universe in motion. When the *Ijere* appears, a fully commited populace is in motion. It is the climax in beauty and majesty, bigger in meaning than can be seen; the king and father of all Igbo masquerades. Anything or any masquerade the Igbo has made, heard of, or can imagine in their spiritual or cultural realms, can become a part of *Ijere*. So, the *Ijere* is always current in beads and trinkets of decoration. No masquerade takes preference over *Ijere*. None performs in the same arena at the same time the *Ijere* is performing, and none may perform after it has gone home.

When some masquerades step out, the collective will and commitment, spirit and action, pride and admiration of the whole community are aboard in spirit and in deed. As focuses of community mobilization, they have few peers. They are what the community says they are: masquerades beyond masquerade, the universe of reality and fiction in beauty, mystery and sheer size—all rolled into one. They are not only invariably community-owned;

they are the community. Whatever befalls them befalls the community, whether it is honor or shame. All members of the community are involved. According to Igbo culture, there are social strata in the land of the Spirit just as there are in the land of mortals. Therefore, society's respect accrues upwards just the same and, by the way some masquerades look, both lands use the same status symbols. So when the *Irekpete* masquerade appears, for example, to entertain or admonish, we can conclude from its ivory horns that it manifests the wealthy hierarchy of Spirits. When *Ngbadike* performs, either a big festival is holding and young men in their prime are bubbling over with the joy of living, or a heroe, a powerful man, or a young man in his prime of life has passed away and ceremonies and rituals are on, to assure that he goes with full honor to the land of the dead.

The masquerade show is to the Igbo what Opera is to some cultures of the world— the highest of the arts— rolling into one the artist and the art, the idea and its expression, time and space, plastic and the visual arts. Masquerading as an art has always been an important aspect of the Igbo culture. It is used not merely for entertainment during ceremonies. Instead, the functional dimensions of masquerading include its roles as a disciplinarian and security agent in the society, performing functions of induction, sanctions enforcement, burials, feasting, worshipping, mass education, mass mobilization, and information dissemination.

Rites of passage also perform a religious educational function. I was initiated into the masquerade society or cult when I was about ten years old. It was a major event in my young life. The sacred nature of the rite generated curiosity in me, along with fear and a desire for acceptance, all of which heightened the impact of the material presented to me. At that midnight-hour ritual, the secrets of the masquerade cult were disclosed to me. I was told about the exploits and travails of the ancestral gods and the cultural heroes who provided the knowledge. I was commanded by the older adults not to divulge any of the secrets of the men to women or uninitiated boys, and, ultimately, to live up to the tribal code.

code.

The belief in life after death or reincarnation is a fundamental part of Igbo culture, if not the very basis of it. Igbo culture recognizes life as a necessary part of death and vice versa. Therefore, it celebrates both, with equal reverence and enthusiasm. In my Igbo culture, "Even the corpse has its own beauty"—[Ralph Waldo Emerson]. Good people died with a smile on their faces, knowing that they would come back to life to continue their good deeds. Often, they would verbalize their intent to come back after death by indicating the preferred manner and time of their reincarnation. Some of these verbalizations are made as promises to certain individuals by the dying person, who is often an elderly member of the family or distant relation, that he/she would come back as a son or daughter to them. In some cases, the promise is plain and unqualified. Yet in others, the promise may be covert and conditional. However, in all cases, the promisees take them seriously and look for signs and other pointers to the arrival of the dead promissors in new born babies, whether shortly or long after the death of their respective promissors.

Whenever this happened as expected, the receiving couple would acknowledge the arrival of the reincarnated person in their new born baby by jubilantly announcing the same to the general public and close relatives as a matter of fulfillment of the cultural ritual for reaffirmation of their belief in reincarnation. Normally, people would anticipate, speculate, suspect, and use other means of common sense and intuition to correctly identify any incident of reincarnation within an immediate family.

It happens that on many occasions, younger members of the family can be identified as obvious favorites of an aging relative and, therefore, possible candidates for the surprise gift of reincarnation by the said relative after death. Also, some individuals work towards such a reward by treating elderly relatives especially nice during their lifetimes, not only because the society requires that they do, but also because they expect a return on the investment in the way of a reincarnated good son or daughter.

Often, failure to properly recognize the arriving life after death would cause the newborn infant to be sickly. The child may even die not long after birth. Hence, parents and relatives of a newborn baby who is always sick would seek the services of a native doctor to find out, as part of the routine diagnosis, the true identity of their child with respect to reincarnation. This is because certain reincarnations come unannounced as a surprise gift (or sometimes, punishment) by the reincarnating dead relative to the receiving family or couple. In these cases, the identity of the reincarnated person becomes crucial in determining the cause and/or intent of the sickness of a new baby for the purposes of performing the right ritual, either to jubilantly appease the arriving relative, or to relieve the punishment on the couple or family by seeking out the appropriate cure for the illness.

My parents were recipients of three fulfilled incidences of reincarnation from relatives over the course of the births of their eight children. Two were fulfillments of plain and overt promises; one was not so plain but nonetheless anticipated. I am a product of the latter.

Back in the late 1940s, my farther had lost a younger sister, Ugwunwa—meaning, "The dignity of child bearing"—whom he and his older brother, Enemibe, raised by themselves without their parents. My father, Ukokwerenmuo, his younger sister, Ugwunwa, and their oldest brother, Enemibe, were the three surviving siblings on their mother's side of the big Okpala family. Their mother had died shortly after the birth of their youngest and only sister, leaving the immediate care of the young baby to the two brothers, who themselves were also children at the time. Not long after their mother's death, Okpalakoronkwo, their father, also died, thereby rendering the three siblings orphans in their early ages. Although there was the extended family safety net, the three siblings were a separate family unit in an agricultural economy, and the responsibilities of that family unit rested squarely on the tender shoulders of my young father and his brother. Therefore they suffered, scratched, and searched to fend for themselves and raise their baby sister.

They would search for and gather palm nuts, crack and extract the kernels to eat, sell part for money, and crush and extract kernel juice from the rest to serve as baby milk for their baby sister. To these two young and very determined brothers, anything that looked like milk was milk. And indeed, when given with sibling love for their baby sister under the circumstances, palm kernel juice turned into a perfect and exact substitute for a loving mother's milk to a needy baby girl. Together and with the help of the extended family system, they raised themselves and their younger sister, who became the female mother figure of this special unit of the larger Okpala family. She later went off into marriage in another village of our town where she bore three daughters.

Earlier, the eldest brother, Enemibe, had gone away abroad on apprenticeship to a trader, with the hope of learning a trade and making enough money to help his brother, my father, go to school and 'take care of things' at home. He lived in Imilike-Ani, Nsukka, as a trader in palm products; and he was also a trans-porter. He was very successful and never forgot his brother and sister, nor their childhood experience growing up as orphans. He knew that good things would eventually come if he struggled hard and trusted in God, a philosophy he published widely on the face boards, back boards and side panels of all his many transport trucks and buses with the word, OKECHUKWU — meaning, "GOD'S WILL". The mere site of those vehicles gave us goose bumps when we were growing up. They would all come home with my many wonderful cousins during Christmas and take us places. They made us very proud!

My father and his only sister grew up close and remained very close even after her marriage. They were mother-father, brother-sister, one to another, both at the same time. My father finally got married and started a family of his own. Three children later (of which I am the third), Ugwunwa took ill and died. She died rather young, probably in her late forties or early fifties. Her remains were brought back and buried in the Okpala compound because she did not bear a son at her place of marriage.

But, at sometime prior to her death, Ugwunwa had promised my father that she would reincarnate as a daughter to him. And she did! She documented her arrival with a remarkable incident at the birth of my immediate younger sister, Edith Chinwe Ugwunwa Okpala.

On a very sunny, ghostly-quiet *Eke* market day, the fourth and biggest day of the four-market-day week (the other three in order are *Orie*, *Afor*, and *Nkwo*), my mother kept a hopeless vigil over a very sick baby girl she believed would die at any moment. The baby had been sick since birth and was not responding to all kinds of conventional medical treatment.

As the baby got even worse in the middle of the afternoon— which is very unusual according to traditional beliefs; deaths usually occur in the wee hours of the late nights and early mornings when the Spirits are believed to be most active— my mother had called out to the neighboring family and beckoned another woman, Victoria Ezeike (or Mgbeke Kwaja, as she was also known), who was older and therefore presumed wiser and more experienced than my mother was. Whatever the reason, my mother needed a crying shoulder under the impending tragedy of losing another child. She had lost one daughter earlier before I was born.

My immediate older sister, Monica, had died from an overdose of penicillin which was injected into her by a quack local medicine-man to whom my father had taken her when she suddenly took ill while my mother was off at the market one *Eke* market-day afternoon. Three-year-old Monica was dead by the time my mother got home in the evening.

The two women sat hand-on-the-jaw and talked very little. They looked out in empty consternation through the open northern end of our two-room-and-parlor, mud-walled, thatched-roof bungalow. This typical vernacular construction known as *Samanga* comprised of an enclosed bedroom, which opens into an open parlor; which is, in turn, connected to a semi-open kitchen; all for an average total living area of about 600 square feet. Security was not an important design consideration since there were no thieves and not much to steal from one another anyway. Moreover, pride and honor was more important than material things!

Usually, the open end of the parlor is covered with straw mats just to protect the inside from rain and occasional dry air during the night. But, on that sunny mid-afternoon on the fateful *Eke* market day, the mat was rolled up and the view was clear to distant trees and domestic animals resting in the shade.

Nonetheless, for my mother and her neighbor-friend, it was all but an empty view into an empty world. They took occasional looks at the sick baby lying near a small fire my mother had made in one corner of the parlor. The visiting neighbor, upon her arrival and assessment of the situation, had exercised her presumed wisdom and good judgment and covered the entire body of the dying baby with dry-fried palm kernel oil mixed with other medicinal ingredients to produce a concoction believed to ward off evil spirits. The burning of certain medicinal plants and pods over an open fire is an essential part of this recipe. She was doing her best to try to assure my mother that every hope was not lost. They waited and waited!

My mother knew enough not to cry over a breathing child, however shallow those breaths might bè. It was common wisdom that crying over a living person constitutes an invitation for death to come to that person.

Suddenly, out of the bedroom end of the open parlor wall, a smiling face appeared, looking into the parlor but with the rest of the body intentionally concealed behind the bedroom wall. Both women saw the face clearly at the same time, and it immediately spoke to them saying: "For three market-weeks (12 days), I've been here and nobody has cared to bid me welcome!"

Immediately, my mother's friend recognized the voice and the mystery behind the voice and advised my mother accordingly. She quickly turned to the sick child (then about two weeks or 14 days old) and jokingly called her by the name of my father's dead sister, Ugwunwa. The child broke into a loud giggle, and that was the end of her sickness.

By the time the two women turned to look outside again, the face had disappeared. They both dashed outside, looked behind the wall, around the house, far and wide but to no avail. The baby accepted breast milk for the first time in three days and carried on fine from then on— playing, giggling, and kicking.

My father was not surprised. Rather, he was ashamed because he "should have known better." "It shouldn't have come to that dramatic ending!" He quietly lamented. For the three daughters of my late niece, Ugwunwa, my younger sister, Edith, is "mother Ugwunwa" to the present day. My sister has retained that name as part of her remarkable identity.

My youngest sister, Ifeoma, is believed to be a reincarnation of my grandmother on my mother's side. She was a fulfillment of a promise made by my grandmother to my mother at the tail end of her life. She was very old and frequently ill at the time I was about eight years old. My mother, Comfort Ukanwa Okpala (nee Ezenwa), is the baby of their family, the youngest of five.

I was a constant companion of my mother in the countless trips we made to Ekwulobia, her home town, to be with her mother during the many times she became ill in her old age. Mostly, I looked forward to the trips because, just as my grandmother was very fond of her daughter, she was also fond of me. She always insisted that my mother brought me along, probably because she equally valued me as the only son of my mother at that time. She would give me great portions of the special meals my mother always prepared for her in effort to nurse her back to health.

We spent many nights with my grandmother when she had become seriously ill. On one of those nights, about two days before she finally died, my uncle from my mother's side and every one of his four sisters sat around the raised portion of the floor of the small hut where my grandmother lay close to the fire. (This time, I was asked to go out each time I came in to stay with my mother. I could see that they were very sad as they whispered to each other and to their mother who could hardly talk back.) The last time I checked, my mother's sisters were hugging her and they were all crying, but not openly. My uncle stood up and left the women alone, taking me with him.

We finally left for home that night, but my mother was asked to come back at cockcrow the next day, as she told me on our way home. It wasn't until we got home, while she was talking with my father, that we all knew that it was almost over for our grandmother and that she had told my mother, in the presence of all her other children, that she would come back to her after she died. My youngest sister was born about one year after my grandmother's death, and there was no gainsaying who she is. Uncle Eugene still calls her Mom 'till today, and an enlarged picture of my youngest sister hangs on his living room wall, a visual testimony to his ardent belief in reincarnation.

My Father Called Me Dad

My father was not a superstitious man. Rather, he was known for his ability and willingness to argue "until the cows come home" against anybody that would not present him with concrete and tangible evidence to convince him on any issue in contention. Circumstantial evidence was never enough to convince my father, throughout his life.

The fact that my father lived and died with the conviction that I was, indeed, his reincarnated father was a rare example of his conviction not based on direct evidentiary proof. He just simply called me Dad and deferred certain adult decisions to me from a very young age.

It was both exciting and confusing to me at the same time. Every adult person in my village seemed to know everything about me while I was growing up. Most seemed to admire me as a young boy and would always call me out from among my play-mates to rub my head and say things to me.

How could they have been so sure about who I am since I was born some thirty years after the death of my grandfather?

One man named Nwankwo Emenike, alias *Nwatakwue* — the meaning implying that in my culture, the opinions of children are almost always disregarded—was most persistent and enthusiastic about who he was sure I am. He would never call me by any name other than the precursor attachment to my grandfather's name — *Azakochuba* — which meant, impliedly, "The one they couldn't arrest." This grown man of about my father's age would make all kinds of respectful remarks at me and would remain frozen in one spot, uttering a barrage of praising adjectives as I usually broke his grip to continue my walk home from school or run away in youthful exuberance to rejoin my friends at play. I think he, Nwatakwue, told me more than my father ever did!

Old wounds heal ever so slowly! It is said. On a certain Oye market day, at the command of a visiting friend of my father's, I was running to the market to call my father. He had gone there to catch an early sale of the morning palm wine from the palm wine tapers who sold their take on their way home from the orchards at the early session of the market. We lived not quite one-fifth of a mile from this small Nanka market, of which we could always tell the crowd size of the market from my house merely by listening to the intensity of crowd noise coming from the market. My mother was in her regular business of producing palm oil and palm kernel at her local factory, some five hundred yards from the same Oye market. She and some other women, mostly from Nanka, owned the palm produce factory as business partners. My sister was their financial secretary at the time, and she kept the records of clients' leased-use of the factory for the purpose of collecting monthly fees. The fees were charged per drum of palm fruit processed by the partners and their other lease customers. Once a month, the three women would gather in our house to divide up profits and make other business decisions. They would always give some money to my father for snuff (or ground tobacco) and kolanut, in recognition of his status as the man-of-the-house, and some to my sister for her services. The amount of money varied according to the size of the proceeds for that month and upon how well my sister kept the books. On occasion, they tossed me some coins, if I hung around long enough and rendered them some, sometimes unwanted and unsolicited, help. I later took over from my sister as financial secretary when I came of age and my sister had begun to somehow feel too big for the job. In short, she was "fired" by my mother, and I took over! This duty would finally go down the line through my younger siblings as the years rolled by, and as we left home for college and into other endeavors, one after the other.

As I ran to the market to get my father, I was interrupted by a familiar old man, Ozuruonye. Actually, this man's name is his alias or title name, which, itself, is a question. (In my culture, people cease to call older men of a certain age by their real names as a matter of respect.) Ozuruonye means and asks the question: "Who on earth can claim to have everything?"

The old man was in the field adjacent to the road leading to the market, feeding his pregnant cow. We all knew this cow well enough to always keep a distance from her because of her usual tendency to pull on her tie-rope in attempt to "get us" with her horns.

He called me by referring to me in association with my grand-father and my father: *"Okpalakoronkwo nwa Amos, bia kana!"* Meaning, "Okpalakoronkwo (being my grandfather) the son of Amos (my father), come here!" Immediately, I took a ninety (90)-degree turn and ran towards him. We were taught to always respect our elders, especially the titled ones. Ozuruonye wore a thin rope around his ankle as an indication that he had taken the Ozo title in his town, Nanka. He was already reaching into his tote bag as I ran closer to him. "Hurry!", he urged me again.

I came to an acrobatic standing-halt right at his feet and greeted him in a panting breath, while looking at his hand to see what was coming out of the bag for me. He pulled out a big head of pear. A head of pear is how we would refer to the native fruit delicacy when it unusually exceeds its average size of two-and-a-half inches in length by one-and-a-half inches in diameter. A ripe pear at that time of the season was really a rare delicacy, even for adults. He took time to sink his long dirty fingernails into several places on the pear while he talked to me in a low tone and kind of nervously looked around the field. He then handed it to me and told me to show it to no one, but rather, to hide it in my pocket and go to the palm oil factory to roast and eat it all by myself because it was especially for me. I greeted him again by his title name and ran off to the market to complete my errand. I located my father, gave him his message fast and ran off to the palm oil factory, where my mother was.

My mother immediately greeted me with a chore at the factory. There was always something waiting to be done at the factory and we avoided it like the plague whenever we could. But this time I was not thinking because my total attention focused on the pear I had in the right pocket of my one-size-fits-all khaki overall jumper. My catapult pellets always occupied the left pocket within ready reach of my left hand, as needed, while I simultaneously would take my catapult from around my neck with my right hand, all for a swift aim-and-shoot at a bird, lizard, or other objects at any stroke of opportunity. At my age, a quick sharp-shooting skill with the catapult or slingshot was a desired virtue.

My assigned chore was to hoe up grass and sweep up a circular area in the field for the hired workers to start a new heaped-mound of palm nuts. My mother had decided that the newest heap was just the right size to get the best deal from wholesale buyers who came every once in a while to the palm nuts and then take them to the next level of processing, extracting the kernels and selling them for profit. Sometimes, however, my mother would process the palm nuts herself for increased profit, but that always meant a lot of extra work for us after school. We would always pray that she would go for the quick-and-ready cash and sell off to the wholesale buyers.

The chore was a tough one. So, I immediately took off my khaki jumper and its contents. The only piece of clothing left for the job was the catapult hanging from my neck and unceremoniously mimicking the swinging rhythm of another more precious element in the middle of my four foot frame, in between my legs, as I bent down and hacked away at the tough overgrown grass. But nothing mattered, so long as some girl didn't show her sorry face in the vicinity. My brain still remembered the goodie in my pocket, waiting for the right moment my mother forgot about me long enough to let me go for the fire. But that didn't happen!

I finally finished my chore and boldly went for the fire. Just as I ducked behind the huge metal drums used in boiling the raw palm fruit for processing, my khaki jumper (which I was now carrying over my left elbow) flipped upside down, spilling all its contents. The pear rolled farther away than the other articles and, worse still, towards the area my mother was standing. She leaned forward and picked up the appetizing fruit and immediately queried me about how I managed to come in possession of such a delicacy at that time of the year. It would have amounted to a major crime if I had spent my money on such an adult treat.

I promptly explained otherwise. But then she took a very close and suspicious look at the fruit and started shouting and running towards the market, apparently to get my father or something. The man who gave me the pear had taken off and gone home rather abruptly for a man who came to feed a pregnant cow. (It usually took all day to feed a cow in the field, and that's why I was glad my father never owned one. We used to pity some of our friends whose fathers owned cows, because they never had time to do the more fun things than stand out in the open field and watch ungrateful cows eat and drag the boys to different areas of the field as they wanted.)

My mother confiscated that pear in order, as I came to understand, to preserve the evidence for when they would charge Ozuruonye before the combined panel of the elders of both towns for attempted poisoning of their son — me.

Strange world! I thought. What did I ever do to this old man to deserve death in such a cold way? I suppose old wounds heal too slowly, or not at all. Ozuruonye obviously had not given up on the old pursuit of my grandfather, who, he was sure, came back to life in me.

I never crossed paths with the old man. He died about one year after the incident. My father had strictly commanded me not to carry out my boyish intent to hunt the old man down and use his gray-haired, partially bald head for a target demonstration of my catapult marksmanship. I regretted mentioning my intent to my father.

Years later, his sons brought a he-goat, yams, palm wine and kolanut and apologized to the entire Okpala family. In their town as well as in ours and, in fact, in the entire Igbo culture, it is an abomination for a titled man to harbor an intention to kill, such as their father had done. They had to appease the gods. Their father had confessed his intentions to them shortly before he died.

Proof Of The Pudding

If my grandfather meant for his reincarnation to be a puzzle by waiting for so long, he did not fool his first son, *Akajeonye*, alias *Isiebu*, who was my most senior uncle. The title name *Isiebuhunwoke* — meaning that a man does not accept his mortality until his head is cut off — tells the personality of my first uncle. He was a very strong and agile man who, in his seventies, could still run faster than most young men in our village and, in his eighties, was still climbing the tallest palm trees. He was the heir to the Okapalakoronkwo extended family and the holder of both the

Okpala family and Akulu clan *ofo* until his death in 1992, at the conservative estimated age of one-hundred-and-seventeen (117).

Although my uncle had grown-up sons of his own, he held me close to himself from an early age. He would take me to traditional functions and clan rituals at the shrine. On such occasions he would make me sit among the elders and brag to them about me in riddles and proverbs which I was too young to comprehend fully.

Igbo riddles are for the wise and experienced. Proverbs are special embellishments to Igbo linguistic expressions, as in most African conversational languages. They bring to life and personify the universal saying: "A word is enough for the wise." Oftentimes, the wise, the crafty, or even crazy people can decipher a proverb. Some are easy to decipher, but most are complex and difficult.

In all African countries in their myriad languages, proverbs are used to emphasize a point or two, to tell a story, to denote love or hate, or to warn of imminent danger. Generally, proverbs portend good tidings and woes, as applicable in their respective connotations. Their importance is linguistically obvious. They form an intricate mesh of information and communication in the language's vocabulary and, ultimately, they help the society to imbibe and impart knowledge. Adults in Africa use proverbs profoundly to convey important and sometimes confidential information from one party to another. Hence proverbs are often utilized as secret codes. In the presence of children, proverbs are applied to conceal sensitive words and information. What is true of proverbs is also true of all fables, parables, and allegories.

My uncle also talked to me plainly and taught me a lot about the family history. As I grew older, the episodes began to look and sound to me like discussions among equals. Then, gradually, he started to seek my opinion on adult matters. He talked to me about family land, and sometimes lodged any complaints he had about my father and certain other adult members of the Okpala family.

Most of the time, I was unable to address the situations, but he continued to press my intelligence and to solicit my input, no matter how childish I thought that input seemed. For example, at the time he divided his portion of land among his three sons, he consulted with me and insisted upon what amounted to my symbolic approval of his fairness in establishing the individual plot boundaries. Much later, at one time after I had finished college and gone off to work in the township, my uncle sent for me to come home. It happened that one of my first cousins, Henry, had approached him for a portion of land to build a house since his own father's portion of land was not enough for all the males in their sub-unit of the Okpala family and that my uncle's first son, Edwin, was vehemently opposed to his father's willingness to oblige and had threatened violence.

Upon my return, I had simply told my uncle to give my first cousin the portion of land he wished to give him and instructed his first son, Edwin, to accept the situation without further incident. Much to my dismay, that was the final solution to the problem. Obviously, there was some kind of ultimate arbitration authority in me, recognized even by the elders in the family who often, if not always, accepted my opinion at face value, even and especially on hot adult issues of land ownership and distribution. My father also responded without further questions to my solicited opinion on a similar issue of land re-apportionment between himself and his older brother sometime during the war.

One time, while I was in boarding school at Anglican Grammar School, Aguluenu, many miles away from home, a young suitor from Nanka came to ask for my sister Ngozika's hand in marriage. My father came on his bicycle to my boarding school to ask me if it was okay with me for my sister to marry into Nanka town. Without hesitation, I looked up and said an emphatic No! My father obliged, went back home, and called off the marriage. I was about twelve years old at the time. In all these and other occasions and situations, I found myself thinking of, talking to, and treating my father and my uncles as my own children and, most amazingly, they willingly allowed me to do just that.

Sometime in the late 1980s, during one of my visits home from the United States, my uncle, Isiebu, called me over for a midnight, private talk with him in his *Obi* or shrine. He wanted to let me know that he was being persuaded by certain members of our clan to "convert" to Christianity because, he said, it made better sense to make things a little easier for the family upon his death. Christian burial ceremonies are much cheaper than traditional ceremonies, he explained, and, also, the crowd of remaining traditional religion followers had dwindled to a handful of old folks, as they died off into history. He was very concerned about what to do with the family ofo and the clan gods or idols in his possession. He wanted my opinion or, should I say, my final decision on the matter.

I did not ask any "Why me?" questions, but I also did not have a ready answer for my troubled uncle. However, I told him that whatever happened, he should preserve the traditional worship items in his possession until I had figured out what to do on my next visit. I knew that wouldn't help in any way because the Anglican Church, I supposed, would not let him "have it both ways". They would not let him "serve two masters at the same time."

Christianity came to my people in 1857. Upon their arrival, the Christian missionaries saw a difference between the God of my ancestors and the God of Abraham, Isaac, and Jacob; I find no difference! The Christian missionaries preached that there was conflict between worship practices of sacrifice and libations by my grandfathers and Christian meditational prayer; I beg to disagree that there is a conflict. Rather, I find congruency!

My ancestral traditional religion addresses and reveres the *Osebuluwa* — the almighty, unseen God, maker of heaven and earth. They revered the earth and nature because it was their understanding that God put them in charge as caretakers of His creation. Their understanding of the original commandments is remarkably in sync with the biblical Jewish Old Testament ten commandments. For example, the rest of the tribal code of conduct to which I pledged allegiance at that event of my initiation into the masquerade occult read as follows:

"Respect your father and your mother."
"Never steal or tell lies."
"Do not run after women who do not belong to you."

My people believe in life after death — a higher Order! The Supreme Being my ancestors worshipped through gods, symbols and rituals is one and the same God as in Christian religion. Their methods are not different from Judeo-Christian religious saints or prophets, symbols, and rituals. The Christian missionaries saw chaos and condemnation in the spiritual life of my people; I see harmony with nature and eternal peace! They saw much foolishness in the ways of my fathers; I find great wisdom!.

By 1992 when I came home to bury my father, *Isiebu* had already transferred the traditional worship items in his custody to a clan member and become a Christian. He had also suddenly become blind in both eyes. As I stepped into his hut to pay him homage and to confer with him first as a matter of respect and tradition before I could see any other person in the family, he recognized my voice and immediately started to cry. He regretted that he could not wait until I came back, because he "wasn't sure it would not be too late." At this point his wife, Mgbeke, cut in. We called her *Nne* — meaning mother, because at her close to one hundred years of age, she was the matriarch of the Okpala family and had been the only wife of Isiebu for more than seventy years. Nne (who is the one that went out and heard all the rumors) whispered to me that, rumor had it that Isiebu had gone blind because he abruptly started to go to church without permission.

But, whose permission? Could that be me? Was Isiebu actually asking for my permission when we had had that midnight-hour talk in late 1980? Even today, a part of me still feels that, somehow, I had failed my great uncle. I still grapple with thoughts about how best to atone and make amends.

I still also grapple with certain proven realities of my life which seamlessly coincide with my grandfather's known personality and life philosophy. I possess the same sacrificial drive to protect and serve my people. I take little or no interest at all in some aspects of politics—the cynicism, manipulation, the selling that has nothing to do with real substance— and I shy away from the open scramble for wealth, material possessions and personal recognition. I believe totally in fate. I am very humble, resilient, confident and competent. I can deal with conflict, handle anger, and manage stress.

Yet, certain physical attributes of my grandfather didn't quite come true for me: My grandfather was a huge man — a giant in his own right. And so was my father. In fact, it was the remarkable resemblance of my father to his father and the preference my grandfather showed towards my father that formed the basis of my people's expectation, almost to the point of certainty, that my grandfather would pick my father to reincarnate into his household. Conversely, I remained a surprisingly short person (under five feet tall) through most of my teenage years. But then, suddenly grew to my present height of six feet in less than eighteen months at age 18.

But I proudly accept the person I believe and was told that I am. I dutifully embrace my fate and the responsibilities attached to it. My father named me Nnaedozie— meaning: "Father has set things right or straight." I have since thoughtfully picked out an alias for myself — Ome-na-nwayo — meaning among others, "The smooth operator" or "Mr. Cool", as certain friends choose to call me. Or maybe you'd prefer the meaning and/or wisdom in the old African saying, "Talk softly but carry a big stick." In all, I believe it is simply a universal matter of life, death, and rebirth. It's all in the name!

2

MAY YOUR WAYS BE ROUGH

*P*erchance we are associated in adolescent and adult life with some persons who, like sky and water, are coextensive with our ideas. Such persons who, each answering to a certain affection of the soul, respectively, satisfy our desire on that side. We lack power to put them at such focal distance from us that we can mend or even analyze them. We cannot choose but love them. "Good things don't last," it is said, but why?

I started college (or secondary school, as it is called in Nigeria) as a young lad of that unstable but important age when one begins to ask: Who am I? Why am I here? What is the nature of my kind? What is growing up? What is the world? How long shall I live in it? Where shall I go afterwards?

The late Dr. Clement Agunnwa, the founding principal of my alma mater, Anglican Grammar School, Aguluenu, had a tremendous influence on my adolescent life. A firm and dedicated mentor, he always admonished the school assembly at the close of morning prayers with this rather unusual wish to us: "May your ways be rough!" Posthumously, reality has proved him very wise and loving. I am who I am today mostly because of him.

My father had once told me that it took a long, long time to become a man. "You will learn in time that there is much pain here," he said. "Men will give it to you, time will give it to you, and you must learn to bear it all." "But you'd be better for the wisdom that may come to you if you watch and listen and learn." Then he added, "Remember you are an orphan despite having   me." "Orphans are eternal seekers," he said. "Try to see better."

"Yes, papa!" I had responded. And that was how, I believe, I started to study life — the self, the hope of future to come, the history of ancestors past. It is, essentially, to these basic words of wisdom passed down from father to his son that my college principal, Dr. Clement Agunwa, added significantly as he had continuously drilled in a chapter into our young heads, exhorting:

> You are human, the only creation in the universe who knows to ask questions. Now you must go on asking questions. Intelligent questions! You must find your way, yourself. You must be willing to assume the risks of the uncompleted journeys of your fathers' stories. May your ways be rough!

Dr. Agunwa died not long after the Nigerian civil war. Although his impact on me was brief, it was very effective and everlasting.

"You Refused To Grow"

When it comes to how tall we stand, inherent genetic factors establish a ceiling that limits our height. Regardless of diet and exercise, physical growth ceases at a certain point. No matter how hard we may try, once that limit is reached, we can't grow anymore—vertically that is, since many of us have a tendency to continue to expand horizontally.

Anglican Grammar School, Agulu (renamed Agulu Boys High School after the war) was noted for its excellence in discipline and academia. For decades, the institution maintained a perfect pass record in the West African School Certificate Examination — a general certification examination taken by all graduating students from five-year (presently six years for Nigerian students) secondary schools in participating West African countries. The school motto was simply, "Distinction", and we lived up to it exactly. During my time, before the war, we had the best staff of lecturers money could buy and competition for admission was tough. Every parent wanted to send his boy to Agulu Grammar School.

I started young and tender in January of 1964, having skipped two classes in primary school education (Class two and Standard five), both because of exceptional academic performances and, later, also because of a National transformation of the primary school system from the Class/Standard — a eight-year school classification program to Elementary— a six-year program. I was, therefore, at the least, two years ahead of most of my age grades at the time I commenced my secondary school education at Agulu Grammar School.

But there was a price to pay! I was too short and too small for most of what it took to be a "big boy" in areas other than academics — girls, sports, and due respect from "junior boys".

The junior boys were the "toads" or "tadpoles". Fresh students were called toads or tadpoles all through their first year in the boarding school and until their "tails" were cut in a grand ceremony on the closing night of their first school year. After that, and upon the arrival of the new "tadpoles" the following school year, it became their turn to expect and demand services and unconditional respect from the new "junior boys."

The junior boys never gave me any respect. There was this chain of service, command, and respect accruing upwards, in regimental order from class to class, the control of which ultimately belonged to the "senior boys" in classes four and five. It is in the matter of this due respect that I never became a "senior boy" because of my height handicap. I was many inches under five feet tall up to and including, my fourth year or Class four. Very unfair indeed!

Mr. Egbe (we never knew his first name), our chemistry and biology master, took me in and also took my "handicap" personally. This wonderful man would take me home regularly and make me eat unusual doses of beans or black-eyed peas. He had promised me, and himself, that he would see to it that I grew taller. Therefore, he would tease and force me to eat this high protein diet almost to the point of ridicule. But all the time, he was doing it with nothing but love and admiration for his "little wonder boy", as he often called me. I loved him too! Just as a father, which he was indeed to me, for he protected me as though he were.

As part of the boarding school activities, students did yard work and fetched water for the school kitchen, among other chores. The only source of our school water supply was a stream about two miles away. Through Mr. Egbe's protective influence, I was exempted from much of the hard labor activities. And to protect me from water fetching assignments, he helped to appoint me the school timekeeper, or more appropriately, the school Bell Ringer. He had reasoned that since we carried those buckets of water on our heads, he didn't want anything to shorten me further.

The rather prestigious post of School Bell Prefect accorded me some much-needed respect as a senior boy. But, of course, it did not cure my height problem. Later on, envy became part of my problem with some of my classmates and some of the senior students.

Earlier in my first year when we studied the Latin language, I made many enemies among Class Three boys, who were the most senior boys in our young school at the time. It wasn't really my fault that I was very good in that dreaded but required subject. Because I could translate as fast as anybody could read English or Latin in both directions, the Latin master, Mr. Ezeagu, would always take me to Class Three Latin sessions and make me "Show them how it is done." He would "mount" or stand me on the table in front of the class and sing praises as I did my thing to the bewilderment of the entire class of senior boys.

"That's my boy!" Mr. Ezeagu would shout and shout again. He loved me, but they hated my guts— the senior boys did, moreso because the teacher made them file past my temporarily tall, table-mounted person and individually receive a knuckled-blow on the head, by me, at his command. I did this part of my job with mixed feelings. While some part of me was afraid, knowing that I was dealing with senior boys — "enjoying senior joke", as it was said then, a silent part of me actually liked the temporary respect it accorded me. I thought it was a well-earned respect, but that didn't sit well with a lot of those senior boys who constantly looked for any opportunity to skin me alive.

I was called by all kinds of nicknames in secondary school. Most of these names had something to do with my height and one of them, "Chocho", finally stuck.

But for the sound of this nickname and the way my schoolmates used it interchangeably for both praise and ridicule of my person, I do not have the slightest clue as to its meaning. All I know is that it was given to me by one senior boy who lived in my dormitory, Quintus House, in my first year. (The five houses in our school were named by Latin numbers— Primus, Secundus, Tartius, Quartus, and Quintus). That senior boy spoke many Nigerian languages. Therefore it is difficult to trace the language origin, if any, of this rather weird nickname.

Boys usually picked their own nicknames, but not me! This one nickname was just assigned to me one evening as everybody laid on their beds after evening studies, before the final "lights- out" bell, and as I walked outside to actually ring the "lights-out" bell. That boy stood up and blurted out the nickname at me and everybody applauded, everybody but me!

I never really liked that boy because he was one of those senior boys that gave me a hard time for showing up in their Latin language classes. He had stated emphatically that I was not welcome in their classes "no matter what and why!" Nonetheless, the nickname spread like wildfire in school and literally took over my real name. Everybody called me Chocho, and there was nothing I could do about it.

Mr. Egbe (the chemistry and biology master) was not left out of the fun. Somehow, this man thought he could ridicule me into a forced extension of my physical height overnight. His "wonder boy" had "refused to grow", all the protein diet he fed me notwithstanding.

We usually got to the classes, prepared and seated, before the teacher walked in. Then, at a command tap-signal by the class prefect, everybody would stand up and greet the teacher as he/she positioned him/herself in place at the front of the class. The class would only sit down again at the behest of the teacher. It was at these times of his grand entries into our chemistry or biology classes that Mr. Egbe would almost always make his favorite joke of me, always to the delight of the entire class.

Normally, I sat in the front row by virtue of my height. Taller boys sat in the back. Of course, I would always spring up to my feet with the rest of the class as the teacher made his entry. But Mr. Egbe would stand in front of his table, look directly at me and say, in pretend annoyance, eyes blinking (Mr. Egbe stuttered): "Ch-Ch-Ch... Chocho, wou-wou-wou...would you s-s-stand up please!" Automatically, the whole class would burst out into a choking laughter at my expense while I pleaded my case that I was in fact standing up already. I knew it was stupid trying to explain, but ignoring the teacher would have constituted a serious offense of its own.

Then, after the laughter subsided, he would look at me again and say: " Stand up!" "Mount your desk! Again, I would have to obey. But usually he stopped me as soon as I started to climb upon my chair to mount my desk: "Co-Co-Co Come on, sit down!" "You-you-you...you refused to grow! You must grow! S-S-S-See me after school!" — to feed me more beans, no doubt.

Another of Mr. Egbe's favorite, not-so-funny classroom jokes on me was that he would write on the topmost portion of the blackboard during lessons. But then, in the middle of the class period, as he got ready to set the quiz for the day, he would stop, look directly in my direction and beckon me with all ten fingers to come to the board. As I got to his table, he would stare at me in mock seriousness with a puckered face, fling the duster in my hand, and ask me to clean the blackboard. The joke was always clear. Usually, wiping the board clean during and after lectures was the job of the class monitor, and the class knew it. My classmates would always burst out into synchronized laughter. "What's funny!" he would shout at them sternly; which really meant, "Shut up or else...!" Of course, everybody knew there was no way I could reach that portion of the blackboard despite my standing on my ten toes and all. I would then stand there and look pitifully at this teacher-friend of mine, literally pleading in silence that he would give me a break for Christ's sake! and that he would understand that I never personally made the choice to be a short boy. In fact, I wasn't the only short person in class but that didn't matter to him.

Then again, there was one remarkable man who worked as a cook in the school kitchen. We all called him "Major" and never really bothered to find out his actual name. Major was probably in his forties and about as short as the average "short boy" in the school, myself included. However, he asserted himself quite effectively and got along fine with everybody. This man was plainly a jolly good old fellow. Major was very popular with the boys. Apart from his generosity with food ("extra ration" as we referred to meals over and above regular dishes) which he would hand out to voracious students who hung around the kitchen before and after meal times, and the leftovers he saved in his house which he would willingly spare anyone, for the asking, when hunger bites hard in the late hours of the night, or for one to feed an illegal visitor to the school, especially female visitors, who must be concealed from the school authorities. This man was simply an all around nice guy who was down-to-earth (literally that is) and who would even play around with us in a big dog/small dog kind of way. Everybody loved Major.

But there was another function inadvertently served some of us by Major. Often, some of us vertically challenged boys hung around this short man to measure how far we were doing in the growing tall department, or to console ourselves that all was not quite lost yet. He provided us hope in knowing that we still had decades to give before we would have caught up and surpassed his adult-man short height. I was additionally comforted by the fact that both of my parents were tall and the natural odds couldn't remain against me for the many more years I had to go before adult manhood. Nonetheless, the urge to physically measure off against this adult man was always overwhelming. Most boys would sneak into the kitchen, mark off their heights on the kitchen walls, and hang around to see the result whenever Major unknowingly stood against their mark. Some bolder boys would run or walk past him and take a flash visual checking-out as they passed by.

I got desperate one day and actually touched Major's head as I tried to take a measuring level from the top of his head to mine. This time, to my greatest surprise, Major quickly turned around, grabbed me by the belt on my waist, and pulled me back to himself. Then he picked me up with one hand, turned my face around to his with the other hand: "Chocho!" he yelled angrily, "You are too wise for your age and that's why you don't grow any taller!" He then rudely put me down, and I wobbled away very shamefully. I had never before seen Major that angry. It bothered me immensely that this short man could be right. After all, he should know! Although his statement to me was rather an odd twist to the going paradigm in my culture on height and wisdom, it sounded logical nonetheless. In my culture, very tall people are usually presumed stupid. In that context, lanky heights much above six feet are suspect and the individual is often said to have "grown away" his or her wisdom. It seemed logical in my case, therefore, that a reverse occasion of "wizening away" one's height is possible. But then I thought, "Why me?" "Must I unlearn things and become foolish in order to grow taller?" I hoped not.

Unfortunately, Mr. Egbe was sometimes actually frustrated at my not responding to all his efforts at getting me to increase in height, by virtue of all the black-eyed beans he fed me. This man felt that I had "refused to grow" despite all his efforts. Most of the time, it wasn't funny to me at all, especially when he would call for a volunteer to come up and pick my short person up, to provide me the much-needed reach to the top of the blackboard. Some naughty boys would actually jump up to comply, but he would always scold them and say to me: "G-G-Go and sit down, Chocho!" But then, of course, the class would join in and shout in chorus, "You refused to grow! You must grow! S-S-S-See me after school!"

Actually, with this preemptive mimicking of the last stuttered statement, the joke would have turned on the teacher because he stuttered. Many a time, students had gotten punished for that. But they would always risk the punishment to enjoy the ultimate joke when they had the rare opportunity to do so. Not very often would a teacher open the door for good class humor at his/her expense. Once upon such a free-for-all class joke occasion, I had mustered courage and shouted at the teacher: "E-E-Excuse me Sir, b-b-b-but I am trying my b-b-b-best!" The entire class erupted in a wild laughter. Then, I thought loudly to myself, "Yeah, suits you fine! I too can play!"

But I knew he loved me. Mr. Egbe was very proud of my academic capabilities. I missed him when the war came and we all went different ways, trying to survive the war as a matter of first and only priority.

My shortness served me well during the war by effectively delaying my active involvement in the actual fighting until much later in that three-year ordeal. When we came back to school after the war, I was a different person, standing at just under six feet tall. My dear teacher/mentor was pleasantly surprised. "What a great return on investment!", he must have thought to himself. But there was not much to celebrate from the bitter experiences of war — all the wasted years and wasted lives. We remained close friends until I passed out of school after one year of accelerated studies. Mr. Egbe had already left his mark on me for life. And I had not disappointed him either.

The Designated Worrier

Fate dictates that I am my family's designated worrier. My everyday thoughts are preoccupied with concern for the welfare of the family as a whole. I often find myself crying internally at thoughts of how things could have been but are not: The children that could have gone to college if only there had been funding, the apparent divisive actions of certain family units that eroded the needed spirit of oneness; the nonchalant attitude of some members of the family, much older than me, towards our collective responsibility as the current generation to propagate the family name with utmost integrity.

A significant portion of my personal philosophies or paradigms is family centered. My security is substantially founded on family acceptance and fulfilling family expectations. Part of my feeling of self worth is based on the family reputation. My decision-making criterion is mostly "what is good for the family?" not necessarily "what do the family members want?" My actions are often limited by family models and traditions. It follows, therefore, that when it comes to family— the large extended Okpala family— I am emotionally vulnerable.

But I have a heart to run! I have come to become as emotionally tough as tough can be. This is possible because I subscribe to an adage in my language which says: "The God who gives an orphan the luck to find a wild yam will also give him the tool to dig it up." *Chi nyere nwa ogbenye ji, ga enye ya mbazu o ga-eji gwuputa ya.* Just like the often advertised commercial tough-guy claim of TIMEX watch, I can still "take a lickin' and keep on ticking".

And I'm not unlike most other Nigerians, and indeed most other Africans, in similar family and extended family situations far away from home. We are always in emotional limbo for being domiciled here in the Diaspora, against all hopes, but actively preoccupied with nostalgia and concerns about home folks and family matters. We are in perpetual emotional exile. We do not have to read our letters from yonder to know their contents. And it is seldom good news, for we are all harbingers of bad news. No joke!

It is no joke when one almost falls out of the bed whenever the telephone rings in the wee hours of the early morning. Almost always, such phone calls have strings of bad news attached to them at the other end. They do not come cheap, emotionally or financially — a death in the family, sad news of other deaths around the family, an "emergency" demand for a sum of money you don't have in all your many bank accounts, or in your dwindled credit line if you have any at all. Or they just called to say hello, but you must hang up and call them back because you deserve the bill not they.

After such phone calls, you worry and think and worry and think. You can't go back to sleep because your heart is now doing a one-hundred-yard-dash on you. Your other half—whom you must have awakened by mere shouting on the phone just to get through the static line connection to Nigeria—also wants to know who called and what happened. He/she is not immune. It could be from his/her own side of the extended traditional family. You are exhausted, but it's time to go to work. You can't eat breakfast for lack of appetite. Moreover, there's no time for food — just the time to think and worry. You are emotionally at home in the thick of the problem because it is expected of you. You have no time for self, spouse, or fun; no time for "luxury".

It is easy to get carried away by all these, easy to drown!

As much as I am a planner by profession, and a good one at that, I still constantly find myself putting out fires— operating on "emergency" mode. I am afraid I may have become too "responsible" for my own good. Because of the inflated urgency of these messages from home, they act upon us, not us upon them. They constantly press upon us, and so we worry, worry at our apparent inability to deal with them effectively.

My younger brothers, especially, seem to have noticed this soft spot of mine. In fact, I'm sure they have! And so have my sisters, cousins, nephews, nieces, uncles, aunts, in-laws, all in the family, all in the village, friends, acquaintances, and so on and on. Everybody seems to have my numbers. And I don't mean my ordinary phone number. I mean specific accounting numbers pressed to work in their individual studious calculation of my dollar-worth at any time of the year, meticulously extrapolated from their individual estimations (or more correctly, assurances) of my earnings and earning capacity in dollars, converted to daily rates in Naira, the Nigerian currency. From these numbers, they figure out percentages which you and I, the typical "provider" in the Diaspora, should be able to spare for this, and for that, and this and that.

There's something common and strange about these extrapolated percentages; they always add up to more than a hundred percent on the individual tallies, exclusive of all others, and, they never include the source provider's (typically a relation in the USA or so) personal needs and living expenses. They could care less if you have other must-dos, like taxes and emergencies, which you do.

Nonetheless, in every extended family member's book, the "provider" is judged a failure if he does not perform up to expectation, either with respect to these fictitious numbers or to the family members' comparative measurement of their "provider" against some other "provider" they know or have heard of. Strangely too, nowhere in these extrapolations and dutiful assignment of family responsibilities to the typical "provider" are the personal efforts of the assignors considered. They all presume and assign total immunity to themselves and their significant other from providing some of the needed funds.

The enormity of this problem notwithstanding, it is unbelievably true that monetary pressures are not the worst of our worries. For example, I do have to conduct court, in absentia, for all family and extra-family disputes. But I don't have the liberty to summarily dismiss any of the many disputes for lack of merit. Because, in the family court of uncles, cousins, sisters, brothers, in-laws, nieces and nephews, everybody is a judge, and every "case" is pre-judged meritorious by its owner. I only have the lucky but overwhelming privilege of being the only empathetic ear open for all feuding parties at all times. I literally have no choice! On those occasions when I must take a leave of absence from work to travel home, pretentiously on vacation, I cannot but hold my breath through the two days it takes to get home to the village, only to find out that the fire in the 'urgent message' for me to come home immediately, was not burning at all. Then, I would exhale, but my brain would have been rattled and would remain rattled for the duration of my stay with all the earfuls from all and sundry. So much for my use of vacation time that will not accumulate enough again for another year or more. But who needs a real vacation after all? Definitely not the extended Okpala family's designated worrier!

One court I held in early 1996 paid dividends. I had traveled home unannounced, partly because of security reasons, but mostly because I needed a mental escape from the tumultuous ordeal of my litigation against my employer, the City of Houston, four years running. I needed to get very far away from the United States to try to feel human again. Plus, I wanted to seize the rare opportunity to begin work on the new family house I had been putting off since my father' s death in 1992. I deliberately picked the quiet month of April to travel home, away from the hustle and bustle of Christmas or any other popular public events that would have brought many people home to the villages. April was also suitable because the holidays were over and the supply of construction workers, abundant.

I pulled up to the family gate with my younger brother, Chika, who had brought me home from Lagos. He was the only one that knew in advance about my trip home. As he sounded the familiar horn of the Mercedes Benz, my mother hurried out to open the gate because she recognized the horn. But she did not expect to see the other occupant of the car, me.

She was pleasantly surprised but not amused to see me. Very quickly, the house was full of neighbors who had also hurried over, having been alerted by my mother's joyful expressions and/ or by the sight of the yellow Mercedes. We said our long hellos well into the early part of the night and sat up rather late into the night with immediate family members, catching up on things. Mentally, however, I was sizing up the extent of my duties during the planned one-month stay in my village.

A soft knock on my bedroom door very early the next morning confirmed my fears that all was not well in the extended Okpala family. Talking with my folks late the previous night, I could sense my mother was not at ease at all with the presence of my eldest cousin, Edwin.

The bedroom door was not locked, so she opened it slightly and peeped in. "Nna, (as Mom always called me) are you still sleeping?", she asked as she stepped in and sat at the head of the bed, "It is very important that you know something before we all make a deadly mistake." I was listening as she stroked my back.

But my younger brother asked, rather angrily, whether mother could not wait until daybreak for whatever it was she wanted to talk about. "After all, you did not know Bene (a short for Benneth, as I am also called) was coming home last night!", he reasoned. But that didn't help. Mother wanted to talk to me about her concern with the activities of Edwin, my eldest cousin.

After all my mother had to say and upon her recommendation, I decided to call a family meeting of all members of the extended Okpala family, home, and abroad. Judging from the gravity of the allegation of voodoo (the misconceived Black magic) practices, among other things, by my said cousin, Edwin, there was serious problem in the family. (The misconception upon which the attendant concern is based, unfortunately, is that voodoo, in African context, has to do with Black Majic, conjuring and witchcraft. This is far from the truth. The fact is that voodoo is a good thing but badly portrayed. Voodoo is derived from the word Vodum. Vodum is the tutelary deity in the Fon language of Benin, the former Dahomey in West Africa. Voodooism is a traditional religion in Africa, which is now widely practiced in Haiti where Vodum is called loa. In its true African traditional meaning, Vodum or Voodoo or any other African tutelary god can be invoked and the symbol used only for good purposes. Any misuse for evil acts is believed to bring disastrous consequences to the perpetrators.) The allegation against cousin Edwin was collaborated by his younger brother, elder sisters, and some of his sons. An emergency meeting was needed to address the situation and keep the extended Okpala family from falling apart under our very eyes. We all knew that cousin Edwin joked and boasted much, but this was a serious issue. In my culture, when it comes to very serious matters such as voodoo, "There are jokes and there are jokes", the saying goes. Of course, Edwin insisted he was innocent of all allegations of wrongdoing and was supportive of the need for a family meeting.

We had an expensive three-day family reunion which, on its final day, expanded and transformed into a family clan celebration at my expense. We achieved a brokered peace agreement supervised by the Church and some of the elders of the community whom I had invited to help. Every male head of a family sub-unit signed off on a three-page affidavit for his unit of the extended family, swearing to maintain peace in the family and to unconditionally look out for the physical well-being of all members of the extended family. Edwin was assigned the extra duty of convening another meeting within six months to service the agreement and keep the confidence level up among family members who had reasons to be afraid of one another.

With that, my job was done. Or was it? I had very little money left for the building job I had planned to do, so I did very little. Two or three weeks after my flight back to the United States (two or three weeks is the fastest time for letters to get to the US from Nigeria), I started receiving a string of letters from everybody everywhere—letters I had to take time to reply to immediately, lest I be accused of selective neglect. Some were encouraging, most of them discouraging. All came with more concerns and more demands for my action; none with the prescription or a recommendation that I deserve a break — a mental break!

But I am happy for what I can do for my family as long as God allows me to keep going. I am happy for the limited synergetic relationships I've been able to generate and put to bear among the extended Okpala family members. Meanwhile, in all these, I've figured out what it is I shall NOT be in my next life as a member of the great Okpala family, or any other Igbo extended family at that: I shall not be a first son. So help me God!

3

¥¥ ¥¥

THE PACE OF HISTORY

A Any human story is history. Therefore history is necessarily as divergent as fates and faiths, in content and origins. "Nothing in history is truly compatible." [Jacques Barzun.][2]

The experience of history renews itself into infinity and, thus, is always a mystery by Divine intentions. A story, if properly told, is a whole, to be understood as a whole — synthetically rather than analytically. There can be no final statements in history because the perspective forever changes.

One thing about history is that it is always silent. Usually, changes happen so slowly that one would hardly notice them. The greater our interest in the facts and truths of human existence, our own existence included—the greater, necessarily, is our concern with the past. History is a part of consciousness. Everyone is a historian! Everybody finds occasion to say: "I was there." "I saw it." "I remember it very well." "It happened to me." Everybody remembers pieces of other people's pasts. Everybody, whether he/she means it or not, finds that he/she has learned about his/

her country, town, street, people, or many other things that came to pass well before his or her time.

The story of life is told in plain words, as it deals with ordinary human relationships. A reader of history is one who follows, with his/her mind, the steps another took on that other's voyage to discovery, achievement, or failure. History deals with particulars. Most recorded particulars contain puzzles, contradictions, enormities that spark curiosity: How did things come to be as they are? How was it when they were different? Is it true that once upon a time men did thus and so? Any curious search for the answers to these questions must, in effect, be inherently slow. Hence, history progresses at a very slow pace, quite unfortunately.

It is one of the illuminations of history for us not merely to know abstractly but, by learning the vernacular shape of things, to feel how the reality of each time and place differs; and how faiths diverge in content and origins and, thus, in persuasiveness. It follows, therefore, that a wise person should stand away from his or her prejudices and biases and satisfy his or her historical curiosity by sympathizing with what is farthest away or most alien. In so doing, 20th century Western man will find that he has no warrant for looking down on other people, cultures, times and places solely on the basis of unanalyzed human conduct over time.

All In The Pot

.

Human memory is man's richest possession. My people— indeed, African people—perfected folk memory through which they kept their myths alive, sustained their thoughts and feelings, and guarded such transcendental wisdoms as enjoyed by the world today. Folk memory is the basis for language. Without this earliest of all arts language, the world would scarcely know its essence nor appreciate the privilege of expressing satisfaction (or dissatisfaction) with present experiences. Without the intellectual arts of speaking, singing, listening, thinking, counting, and measuring, we could not assess or repossess the experiences undergone in space and time.

After all these years, the modern world is just beginning to comprehend the full meaning of African sounds— sounds of the past influencing the music of today — they provide the myth, the power, the foundation. The African drum was, and still is, a very important tool for sending messages. This cultural basis for unity set in the most basic form of communication has been in use in Africa for centuries. The nature of languages amongst tribes necessitated the use of the talking drum to relate messages almost verbatim — a musical language that knew no boundaries.

Then, there is African dance — the claps, the body movements, the steps— all basic and fundamental to African music, and also used for healing and communication. There are dances for birth, for death, for war, for peace, marriage, celibacy, love, self-esteem. The basis of all of these being always the worshipful reverence of God and the Spirits. Upon this basis, the music and the dancer marry. The abiding mutual influence is clear and deep.

The modern world still has a lot of catching up to do. The influence of African musical beats exists everywhere popular modern music and dance are found today in the Blues, Jazz, Reggae, Gospel, even Rock-and-Roll. Today's dance tells the story of a time long past and the future yet to come, a perpetual African story sadly very slow in coming.

What if the fundamental musical beats were patented by their original inventors and owners? Imagine the degree of universal control the African man would have exerted on the global business of development and marketing of musical products today. Indeed, all aspects of music!

But, in the wake of modern definitions of intellectual property and the piracy of the same by Western civilization's business corporations, there are no ethical boundaries and no people's demand for corporate responsibility. Western big businesses wallow in rampant appropriation of African indigenous knowledge and natural resources, such as music, medicinal plants, and animal husbandry. Big businesses now own patents on natural commodities in manufactured drugs, seed production, and, yes, animal cloning. The pace of history is ever slow in bringing back the African farmer and the African medicine man into the original and only human equation for man's ingenious survival in his natural environment. It has taken history and modern man too long to realize and accept the fact that innovation has existed as long as man (African man) has interacted with nature; not when modern mega-corporations entered into the business of production and appropriation of past knowledge and past labor for present and future unshared gains.

Generally speaking, according to Asa G. Hilliard, III. in his book *The Maroon Within Us*, Black Classic Press (1995):

Africa is the home of Black people and Europe is the home of White people. There is nothing inherent in those two realities that generates tension or confusion between individuals or among peoples. However, place a great civilization on the African continent; place native Africans at the root and branches of that civilization; show that that civilization occupied a leadership role in the world for centuries; do that in the context of a European White supremacy belief system and world view that has for centuries painted Africans as inferior beings, and you then have the makings of a situation in academic world where truth becomes a scarce commodity.

Objectivity and neutrality is a scientific ideal. However, it is seldom a social reality. Historians have been proven to have been too tentative and cautious in describing Africa's place in world history. When scholars come exclusively from one ethnic, racial or national group dominating a field, the likelihood, and in fact, the reality of ethnic chauvinism in both science and history is magnified. Add the economic and political self-interest—the enormous profits of slavery and colonialism—of such groups to the mix, a prudent person would approach the resulting scholarship with caution, even with extreme caution. But when the picture is drawn properly, the prominence of Blacks in the antiquity of infant civilizations of Greece and Rome (the accepted birthplaces of White Europe) will come as no great surprise.

The surprise is that few of us in the modern world have any idea just how intentional, systematic, intensive, prolonged, and widespread was and still is the defamation process directed at African people and their descendants all over the world. Martin Bernal in *Black Athena, The Denial of the Afro-Asiatic Roots of Greece* (1984) cited a few examples of grave scholarly racism and misinformation by some of world's most notable writers, historians, and philosophers. For example, David Hume (1711 - 1776), an English empirical philosopher, historian, and economist advocated both separate creation and innate inferiority of non-White races:

> I am apt to suspect the Negroes and, in general, all the other species of men—for there are four or five different kinds—to be naturally inferior to the Whites. There was never a civilized nation of any other complexion than White, or even any individual eminent, either in action or speculation. No ingenious manufacturers among them, no art, no sciences. [Serfontein, 1978].[3]

George Curvier, who is widely hailed in France as the Aristotle of his age and a founder of geology, paleontology, and modern comparative anatomy, referred to native Africans as, "The most degraded of the human races whose form approaches that of the beast, and whose intelligence is nowhere great enough to arrive at regular government." Thus he wrote:

> This compact continent of Africa exhibits a population which has been in constant intercourse with the White race; which has enjoyed the benefit of the Egyptian civilization; of the Phoenician civilization; of the Roman civilization; of the Arab civilization; and, nevertheless, there has never been a regulated society of Black men developed on the continent.... [Wilkins and Strydom, 1979].[4]

Arnold Toynbee (Joseph), an English historian (1889 – 1975), wrote in 1934:

When we classify mankind by color, the only one of the primary races given by this classification which has not made a creative contribution to any of our twenty-one civilization, is the Black race. [Bernal, 1984; Durkeim, 1977].[5]

And from George Wilhelm Friedrich Hegel, a German idealist philosopher (1770 - 1831):

This is the land where men are children, a land lying beyond the daylight of self-conscious history and enveloped in the black color of night. At this point, let us forget Africa not to mention it again. Africa is no historical part of the world.... [Jefferies (in Van Sertima), 1982].[6]

Samuel Baker (1821 – 1893), an explorer looking for the source of the Nile, stated:

Human nature viewed in its crudest state as seen among African savages is quite on the level with that of the brute, and not to be compared with the noble character of the dog. There is neither gratitude, pity, love nor self-denial; no idea of duty, no religion; nothing but covetousness, ingratitude, selfishness and cruelty. [Diop, 1978].[7]

And in Putnam's Monthly (author unidentified):

The most minute and the most careful researchers have, as yet, failed to discover a history or any knowledge of ancient times among Negro races. They have invented no writing, not even the crude picture-writing of the lowest tribes; they have no gods and no heroes; no epic poems and no legend, not even simple traditions. There never existed among them an organized government; they never ruled a hierarchy or an established church. [Rashidi, 1988].[8]

Asa Hillard, III. continued to write that one of the more curious academic debates of our time deals with the origin, the race, and the influence of the ancient Kemetic people — the Egyptians. In this debate, he said, there are two kinds of scholars:

> There are those with integrity who attempt to report the truth as they see it; there are those who deliberately distort the human record for explicit political purposes. Politically powerful nations and groups are in a position to impose their view of the world on the entire world. But while this may make political sense, it does not make scholarly sense.[9]

Speaking at an annual meeting of the Organization of American Historians, Leon Litwark, professor of history at the University of California, Berkeley, indicted past historians for perpetuating racism. He called on his present-day colleagues to heal that wound and charged them thus:

> No group of scholars was more deeply implicated in the miss-education of American youth and did more to shape the thinking of generations of Americans about race and Blacks than historians.... [W]hether by neglect or distortion, the scholarly monographs and texts they authored perpetuated racial stereotypes and myths.[10]

The great thing about classic work is that it reaches from the long past to have relevance to today's situations. Classic literature has enduring value. The Bible (the writing of which, it is believed, was inspired by God Himself) is one old book that stands above the rest and speaks clearly and accurately about the human condition. So, *The Book of Hope*, published by Life Publishers International in 1994, writes that "The second greatest lie— spiritual lie— ever told to Black people is the statement that 'the Bible is the White man's book.'" "The greatest lie", the book states, "is that the Black race was cursed by Noah." Thence the writer argues further and makes the following points succinctly:

The Bible is the White man's book, just as the lie about Noah's curse distorts the truth of the Bible. The first geographical areas mentioned in the Bible (Havilah and Ethiopia) are located in Africa (Genesis 2:11-13). Majorities of the people mentioned in the scripture are people of color. The two major European nations talked about in the Bible are Greece and Rome. These two nations are referred to by name less than 60 times combined. The two major African nations talked about are Egypt and Ethiopia. These two nations are referred to almost 900 times. [11]

More than 2000 years later, the modern world still grapples with the social and academic acceptance of the true history of the Bible. Shame!

In the final onslaught, and on the religion arena, Jordan K Ngubane commented in his book Conflict of Minds: Changing Power Distributions in South Africa, that missionaries sought above all things to impose ideological destinies on the African.

"... Missionaries were interested mainly in forcing or persuading the African to define himself in forms that served their interests. Naturally, the missionaries were not interested in preserving harmony in the African's personality. They wanted to fill the African's head with ideas that would enable him or her to be exploited and manipulated by his or her own consent." [12]

But also very readily on our part, we falter. Psychologists say that one aspect of culture is a matter of pace of life. The modern man's business culture is fast paced, but to differing degrees. For example, it is fast for Japanese, Americans, Italians, and Indonesians, presumably in that descending order. It has been said that Italians give long answers to questions, and Indonesians don't care a fig about setting their bank clocks. So, what about Africans? Did our original ancestors manage and define time? Or did they see it as an empty vapor? Was there any African cultural significance to the cradle of life, time and civilization?

Attitude soaks into the definition of our culture with respect to time. Science has established that, as humans, we respond automatically to certain body signals that occur quite regularly at timed intervals just like clockwork. That the human body has an inner timing mechanism called the circadian rhythm. The control mechanism for this body clock is believed to lie in the brain's hypothalamus, that part of the brain that regulates automatic activities. Thus, this inner 'alarm clock' is responsible for waking us up everyday around the same time and for telling us when to go to bed at night. This inner clock also tells us when it is time to eat or go to the bathroom. It synchronizes the human senses with bodily functions and with human actions, both voluntary and involuntary.

Time itself is intangible. Yet tangible things, such as money and contracts, are inextricably assigned to units of time. Time is unseen, a gossamer enigma to the average person. Yet, "Time rules all things." Time! a derivative of circumstances warranting the individual to desire to do something; a phenomenon of motion in relation to the sun or other heavenly bodies. Value attaches to action or inaction within time. Over the centuries, many cultures have tried to harness and define this thing called *Time*.

When we travel back in time, we can see that our African ancestors in the Southern half of mother Africa utilized the birds (especially the cock or rooster), the sun-shadow of physical objects, other natural phenomena and plain ol' human intuition to identify and manage time. The practice worked for them, so much that when the town-crier announced the commencement of a scheduled event in time by utilizing either his trumpetic voice, or the sound of the wooden gong, *Ikoro*, there was an instant synchronized response of human action relative to time. Simultaneously, in the Northern half of Africa, the Egyptians started the earliest known forms of modern scientific time telling with the invention of the sundial and the water clock. We Africans can very rightfully, therefore, claim that our African ancestors not only had a controlling grip on the value of their time and on synchronized human actions during their time but, also in fact, gave the world its sense of time as we know and employ it today. History is very slow in recognizing this phenomenon when the modern world, with help from us Africans, chooses to dub any human laxity in response to time the "African-time Syndrome," a practice that amounts to an orchestrated insult to Mother Africa, very despicable indeed.

It has taken the modern world so long to realize that early man —African man—gave the world the fundamental art of committing things to memory. A memory without which the world would have been worse than invisible, inaudible, ineffable, and intangible. It would have been a world without temporal dimensions, a world that human minds could not remember.

Of all the arts, none is more intimately ours than story telling. There are treatises and discussions of everything under the sun, but a story is our first and last entertainment. This is evident when we are children and then, when we have become too old to care any more what truth is, unless it comes in the past tense in a story with persons, reflecting in their lives the peculiar radiance that attends the accidents of time and character. Nature does not tell stories, only people do.

So, Africa bleeds and hurts. Very often, the wailing cries, the emotional pains and pulse of Africa are captured vividly in the more fundamental rhythms and lyrics of good Reggae songs. One such song by a Houston-based Wazobia Raggae Band soliloquizes the painful truths about elusive accolade and freedom for Africa, the continent. In simple rhythmic reggae lyrics, the singers cry essentially the following verses:

Oh No!
We have to fight, to free Continent Africa
We've got to fight, to free Continent Africa
See how long we've been fighting, to free Continent Africa
So many are dying, to free Continent Africa
See how long we've been striving, to free Continent Africa
We have to fight, to free Continent Africa!

All we are asking—
Political Adjustments, Equal Rights,
Democracy Rule in all the land, all the land
See how long we've been fighting, to free Continent Africa
So many are dying, to free Continent Africa

We 've got to fight, to free Continent Africa!

I don't want to live in the past
In trust of the shadows of the dark, No!
So, people, I wish that you can see
Like a bird in the tree, People must be free
See how long we've been fighting, to free Continent Africa
We have to fight, to free Continent Africa

Down in Soweto,
They're killing my people:
Mass murder, Funeral bands
In all the land, all the land
So many are dying, to free Continent Africa
We have to fight, to free Continent Africa

Down in Nigeria:
Soldiers took over
We need some food
To even fight, to free Continent Africa
We have to fight, to free Continent Africa
See how long we've been fighting, to free Continent Africa!

In the same album, the Wazobia Raggae Band delves into the limited history of the African struggle against White domination, by Africans, throughout Africa and the entire world. They state the facts and pose the pertinent questions:

Oh now! Tell the children the truth.
Black, for the color of the People they stole;
Why did they, why did they really, really have to steal us?
Green, for the color of the Land they stole;
Why did they, why did they really, really have to steal?
Yellow, for the color of the Gold they stole;
Why did they, why did they really, really have to steal?
Oh No!
All that we know is not what they tell us;
Jah knows you can't keep a good man down.

It's like—
Fella Ransome Kuti; He said, "Stand up for your right!";
Why did they, why did they really, really have to jail him?
Nelson Mandela; He said, "Down to Apartheid!";
Why did they, why did they really, really have to jail him?
Steve Biko; He said, "Africans Unite!";
Why did they, why did they really, really have to kill him?
Marcus Garvey; He said, "Repartriate!";
Why did they, why did they really, really have to kill him?
Martin Luther King; He said, "I have a dream!";
Why did they, why did they really, really have to kill him?
Malcolm X; He said, "Give man a chance!";
Why did they, why did they really, really have to kill him?

Tell me why!
Why did they, why did they really, really have to kill us?
Why did they, why did they really, really have to cheat us?
Why did they, why did they really, really have to steal us?
Why did they, why did they really, really have to cheat us?
Why did they, why did they really, really have to jail us?
Why did they, why did they really, really have to cheat us?

Marcus Garvey; He said, "Repartriate!";
Why did they, why did they really, really have to kill him?
Kwame Nkuruma; He said, "Africans Unite!";
Why did they, why did they really, really have to kill him?
Patrice Lumumba; He said, "Free the Congo!";
Why did they, why did they really, really have to kill him?

Tell me why, O Jah!
Why did they, why did they really, really have to kill us?
Why did they, why did they really, really have to cheat us?
Why did they, why did they really, really have to steal us?
Why did they, why did they really, really have to cheat us?
Why did they, why did they really, really have to jail us?
Why did they, why did they really, really have to cheat us?

History moves very slowly, if at all, for my country, Nigeria. It has taken my country decades and counting, to begin to realize the true meaning of the failed Biafran revolution: that being the need for Nigeria to learn how to give accolades and respect to people with exceptional, positive, mental reasoning, irrespective of their tribe, sex, religion, and political background. Nigeria continues to fail woefully today because it continues to abandon the principles of the Biafran revolution as articulated and presented in the Ahiara Declaration of 1969.

Then, in his comment on the attitude of the civilized world toward the Nigerian conflict at the time, the Igbo (Biafran) revolution leader, Emeka Odumegwu Ojukwu, expounded his conviction that "[o]ur disability is racial." "The root cause of our problem lies in the fact that we are black." Ojukwu reasoned that "if all the things that have happened to us had happened to another people who are not black; if other people who are not black had reacted in the way our people have reacted these two long years, the world's response would surely have been different." Excerpting the relevant portions of that 1969 Ahiara Declaration, the deposed Biafran leader stated:

The Biafran revolutionary struggle had far-reaching significance than the desperate action for protection of life and property of the Igbos from the genocidal tendencies of the rest of the Nigerians, especially the Northern Muslims, against them. The struggle was not a mere resistance, but rather, a total and vehement rejection of all those ills that blighted and continue to blight Nigeria— the three traditional scourges of the black race: racism, Muslim expansionism, and white economic imperialism. The Biafran struggle was a positive commitment to building a healthy, dynamic, and progressive state, such that would be the pride of black race the world over.

Indeed, our struggle was a movement against racial prejudice, particularly, against that tendency to regard the black man as culturally, morally, spiritually, and intellectually inferior to the other two major races of the world — the yellow and the white races. Our disagreement with Nigeria arose in part from a conflict between two diametrically opposing conceptions of the end and purpose of the modern African state. It was, and still is, our firm conviction that a modern Negro African government worth the trust placed in it by its people must build a progressive state that ensures the reign of social and economic justice, and the rule of law. Our struggle, in an even more fundamental sense, was the culmination of the confrontation between Negro nationalism and white imperialism. It was a movement designed to ensure the realization of man's full stature in Africa.

It is recorded history that ever since the 15th Century, the European world has treated the African continent as a field for exploitation. Their policies in Africa have for so long been determined by their greed for economic gain. For over three and half centuries, it suited them to transport and transplant millions of our people for the purpose of exploitation in the Americas and West Indies. They justified slave trade by making reference to biblical passages violently torn out of context. Later, out of necessity, they decided to install puppet African administrations to create the illusion of political independence, while remaining in control of the economy.

Nigeria was and still is a classic example of a neo-colonialist state. The crises that rocked Nigeria, beginning from the morning of her qualified independence from Great Britain on October 1, 1960 were brought about by the efforts of certain progressive nationalists to achieve true independence for themselves and for posterity. It is in the learning and implementation of the important lessons of these efforts that my country needs to hasten the pace of its history in the collective interest of its people and, indeed, all the black people of Africa and the African people in the Diaspora.

My people, the Igbo of Nigeria, and indeed all peoples and cultures of Africa may not have been exclusively barbaric as a human race. It has taken history 2000 years (since man started counting) to make the sobering observation and find, in both past and present, the evidence that inhumanities, for example, have been, and are being, committed by the brutish and the civilized alike; by the ignorant and the educated, the cynical and the devout, the selfish and the heroic; by the African, the European, the Asian, the American. There could have been no "monsters of error" in my people's past and present, in their time and place, beliefs and manner of worship, culture, and social survival mechanisms. For them and for me there can be no final statements because the perspective forever changes, and with it, the experience of history renews itself to infinity.

Unusual Places

Unusual places beget unusual experiences. Usually, the first response of the average human to an unusual experience is that of shock — mental shock, culture shock, etc. In the experience of culture shock, the individual is temporarily demobilized by something, such as an event or encounter that jars the mind or emotions as if with a violent, unexpected blow causing a disturbance of function, equilibrium, or mental faculties. This is a condition of severe anxiety and confusion that can affect an individual who is suddenly exposed to an alien culture or milieu.

The Israelites were in an unusual place and apparent state of shock when they soliloquized as in a song composed by the legendary Reggae superstar, Jimmy Cliff, in his *Songs of Babylon*, the lyric of which reads essentially as follows:

By the Rivers of Babylon
There we sat down
And there we wept
When we remembered Zion
    When the wicked,
Carried us away in captivity
Required from us a song
Oh! how can we sing our Lord's song
In a strange land?
    May the word of our mouth

And the meditation of our heart
Be acceptable in Thy sight
Oh Lord!

Usually, when one is in a state of shock — culture shock, as I have found out, life freezes momentarily, and special effort is needed by the individual to reassure him/herself that he/she is indeed still alive. Such reassurance may be totally mental, or it may include actually touching oneself for physical reassurance that the seeing of the eyes is not an aberration and the hearing of the ears is not a mental illusion. At such times, the mouth is shot dumb, and the functioning of the nose and heart merely a matter of automatic reflex, in the real sense of the phrase.

As soon as we were airborne in the DC 10 jet that brought me to America in January of 1977, the whole universe suddenly became an unusual place for me. When we touched down in Boston, Massachusetts, in the cold winter morning of January 10, 1977, America was certainly a very unusual country to me. Both unusual experiences of take off and landing of the airplane and the intervening fourteen (14) hours of air travel got me rethinking my youthful paradigms about the total concept of life.

In that flight, literally and in fact, I was all on my own. More so because a few minutes into the flight, the European man (In Nigeria, all white people are simply referred to as Europeans) sitting beside me unbuckled himself, stood up, left his seat, and never returned. I didn't make much out of that man's action, but it created a major problem for me when the crew started serving meals. It would have been much easier for me to discretely watch him and feel my way through the strange menus and the requisite proper table mannerisms of international travel. But the man was gone, and I was really on my own in all the strange realities of that on-flight experience.

Much thanks, however, to those air hostesses (flight attendants, to be more politically correct): they took extra time attending to me, asking at regular intervals if they could help me, even when I didn't give away any signs that I needed their attention. And they were often right in asking, because I was actually nervous and too ashamed to ask as many questions as I had problems, and, of course, I never really comprehended their brand of spoken English.

By the time we prepared for landing at Boston International Airport, I had gotten rid of most of my on-flight butterflies and was looking forward to my first walk on American soil. I was beginning to anticipate the enormous respect the other "Ekwueme students" would accord me for my manly feat of traveling alone to America, rather than being bundled up in a group on the presumption of immaturity. "Ekwueme Students" is the collective name for all the students sponsored by one Dr Alex Ekwueme, a great philanthropist who sent out batches of prospective students to colleges and universities overseas, mostly to the United States and Canada. Not only had I traveled alone, there was no prior arrangement for the College to pick me up from the airport since I traveled on short notice and the school was not expecting me as a late arrival for the spring semester.

The "big bird" lowered itself, dipping and swaying at intervals. I tried to look out through the window at every opportunity when the plane tilted to my side, but there was nothing to see, nothing but cloud, no trees, no buildings. When the plane got much further down to touch down, I still could see no land and no greenery. But I could make out what I knew must be silhouettes of buildings. Everywhere and everything was completely a different kind of white cloud, which I came to understand was snow. Strange! I thought.

Soon there was erratic movement of the passengers in the airplane. They were standing up, reaching into overhead compartments, and pulling out heavy coats and body wrapping materials. And they were actually wrapping themselves up completely, except for little provisions for the nose and eyes. I did not know what to make of this latest happening. So I sat still and looked and wondered.

Instinctively, one hostess approached me, leaned forward and asked if she could help me. "No, thank you!" I responded. "But Sir, you should be getting ready to transfer to your connecting flight to Nebraska," she explained. A bit angry and not understanding the reason for her concern about me, I made no further comment. She waited for a while and left towards the cabin.

She came back in a short while with two other crewmembers. They conferred with each other quickly, and the same hostess leaned towards me again and specifically asked me if I had a winter coat with me. Immediately confused, I thought, Winter? Coat? What could those mean? Why do I need them? "What do you mean?" I inquired. She swiftly withdrew herself, looked around, and pointed to a male passenger wrapped up in a heavy woolen overcoat. "That!", she said, "a heavy coat like that, do you have one?" But then, again, seeing the confusion in my face, she didn't wait for my answer. "Never mind!" she added. "Stay right there in your seat until I can make proper arrangements for you to exit the airplane." She left with the rest of the crew toward the cabin.

I had on a black turtleneck shirt and a pair of dark-gray bell-bottom (bongo) trousers, with a state-of-the-art 4-inch platform shoes to boot. I was well dressed by all standards. Those were the cool fashions in Nigeria at the time. I had paid good money for that outfit in preparation for the special occasion of my going to America. Actually, the pair of trousers was part of a two-piece suit, but I had forgotten the coat at my first cousin, Dr. Eric Ok-pala's house in Enugu, while I routed through the city on my way to Lagos to apprise him of my rather impromptu travel abroad and to solicit some spending money in case of any eventualities during my scheduled four-day stay in Lagos leading to my flight overseas. Nonetheless, I was beginning to think that the hostess must be crazy. I was just fine without a so-called heavy coat. The airplane was nice and toasty enough for me. Just then, the exit door opened, and some passengers started to hurry down the staircase and across the snow-white tarmac to a smaller airplane some one hundred yards away from ours. It was the breezy feeling of the outside air that reached my seat which told me, without words, that all was not well with the temperature outside. In fact, the hostess returned with a bundle of blankets and a wheelchair and told me that the temperature outside was minus ten (-10) degrees and that there was no way she would let me out of the plane without adequate protection. So, having wrapped me up like a log of wood, she put me on the wheelchair and wheeled me to the waiting plane. I felt very humiliated but undeniably very thankful.

At the Lincoln, Nebraska, airport, there was a connecting chute from the airplane to the airport building. So I walked off the plane on my own power. But I was immediately intercepted by a man, who, obviously, had somehow been advised about me. He checked me through and asked me to wait in a holding area. I sat there and, once again, wondered what was next.

After some thirty minutes, the man walked up to me and asked if I knew anybody in Lincoln. Of course, I said No! He started to ask if there was any prior arrangement for my school to pick me up but he stopped when he noticed I was already shaking my head to say, No. "Okay wait here", he said, while leaving in a hurry as if to say, "We have a problem here!"

There was a sign on the wall opposite the holding area, which read: "Public Telephones". There were some big books hanging down by each phone. I walked over to the phones and picked up a phone book. By then I had sensed that a public telephone book might contain names of people who lived in the town and that if there were any Igbo names I could recognize them. I was very right!

The listing was organized alphabetically by last names, so I quickly searched the "O" listings. Last names beginning with "O" are common in my culture and are very easily discernible. Behold there were several Igbo names! I wrote a few of them down and continued to leaf through the pages to "N", another common letter in Igbo last names. Among the "N" listing I saw a name, Borniface Nsofor, which is obviously Igbo and which also immediately rang a bell in my head. There had been a story at home about one Borniface Nsofor who had gone overseas before the civil war in Nigeria. I quickly wrote down his telephone number and went back to my waiting spot.

The same man came back to me and told me that he had called my school, York College, but that they could not pick me up until the next day because of bad road conditions. It was not safe for them to make the fifty-mile trip from York to Lincoln under the icy-road weather conditions. That I may have to "hang around" with them in the airport until the next day unless I had somebody in town to stay the night with. I immediately told him about the names I had copied from the phone book and asked if he would help me make the call to Mr. Nsofor. He did.

We walked over to the phone booth, and he put in some coins and dialed the number. He listened for a moment and handed me the phone. "Hello!" "Hello!" a man answered. "Hello!", I replied, " Is this Mr. Nsofor?" "Yes", he said, "Who are you?" As I started to introduce myself, he was already shouting in excitement, "Oh my God! Oh! Oh! Where are you?" he asked. Before I could answer, the man with me took over the phone from me and explained the situation to Mr. Nsofor: "You should come with a coat and a pair of sneakers", he concluded. Then he handed the phone back to me to talk some more with Mr. Nsofor. Indeed, he was the very same man from my town, and he assured me he would be there to pick me up in about forty minutes.

As we talked on our way to his house, Mr. Nsofor could not believe the coincidence of my coming in and locating him at first chance. He explained that he worked two jobs and went to school for his doctorate degree, and that it was a very rare occurrence for him to be home at the time of my phone call. Ordinarily, he said, he would have been gone with the only driveable car in his family. The second car did not have snow tires and his wife would not have been able to pick me up from the airport if she answered the phone at all. He further told me,that it was a good thing the man at the airport told him to bring a pair of sneakers because I would have been sure to fall down and break an ankle, or so, if I had ventured out onto the dry snow with the 4-inch platform shoes I was wearing. Mr. Nsofor asked many catching-up questions about home and told me quite a few things about life in America. I was very happy to meet him, as much as he was delighted to receive me. The next day he insisted on driving me to my school for the added chance of meeting with the other "Ekwueme students". Everybody was happy to see us and very eager to hear all about my bizarre experience coming to America, all by myself. I did not spare a tale.

York College had its own set of surprises: a three-credit-hour course on dating in a Christian college? free 24-hour access to the female dormitory, all-you-can-eat food service in the school cafeteria, multiple-choice test questions, take-home exams, and on-the-road class lectures while our tennis team traveled and played competitive tennis for the college. Definitely, some students learned much more and took their "homework" very seriously with regard to the dating lectures because, on many occasions, abandoned brassieres and other private articles of female clothing were discovered in the remote areas of the basement in the student center cum chapel building. For good or not-so-good, in my new-comer mind at the time, there were many other things quite unusual about that cold and remote school environment in my first six months of stay in the United States.

My world in Huntsville, Alabama, which began in the summer of 1977 was quite different. A car and home outside the school premises brought social freedom and some of the harder lessons of life in the United States — some very rewarding, many of them traumatic and very unusual. It was in Huntsville, Alabama, that I saw a sign displaying a church for sale and my spiritual life was forever changed. "Only in America, the modern cradle of civilization, would anybody sell a church, just like any other business or market commodity!" I have always replayed this in my head.

By the time I came to Alabama, I was already a man, with all the inherent need for female companionship. I felt I'd got to find somebody to love me. With newfound opportunities of a car and social freedom, I ventured out into the American social universe to try out my wings. A few outings later, I landed a beautiful young lady, Lisa, who became quite a friend with a twist.

Lisa did not live with her mother, but she always had me pick her up from her mother's house. Her reason, the few times I asked, was that she did not want to risk losing me to her room-mate who she was sure would go after me at any opportunity. Besides, she said, they lived very far in the outskirts of town and it would be inconsiderate of her to make me come that far for her. She told me many intelligent lies. Strangely enough, each time I picked Lisa up, as soon as we got to the house and my room-mates had expectedly removed themselves from the house, she would immediately lock herself in the bathroom, emerging in about fifteen minutes abnormally excited and "ready for some good time", as she would put it. I never really figured out the cause of her sudden mood change until she let me in on her secret one Wednesday afternoon and insisted I must "party" with her.

She re-lighted a stump of what looked like a big half-smoked cigar and took a l-o-o-n-g puff. Blowing out heavy smoke in my face, she extended her hand with a smile, meaning to hand me the thing. I refused, but she insisted. After she had persisted for some time, I took one puff like I saw her do, and the rest is history.

The story, as one of my housemates, Sunday Ekwueme, told it, was that I went nuts. He, Sunday Ekwueme, had come home and found the front door bolted from the inside. He had to knock very hard before I came to let him in, but I was dressed, strangely, in my "birthday suit" (I was butt-naked as the American would say). Sunday narrated that immediately he stepped through the wide open door, I grabbed him and loudly begged him to take Lisa home because I was in no shape to drive at all. He said that he broke off my grip and jumped outside, ready to leave. But he came back when he saw I was about to chase after him, birthday suit and all, and that he agreed to drive my girlfriend home only if I would go back to the room and go to sleep.

Well, I never tried to refute Sunday's story, nor did I try to figure out how I managed to take and pass a mid-term differential equations examination later in the evening of the same day. But one sure thing I figured out was that Lisa was a bad influence and I must 'dump' or part with her, forthwith. I did exactly that, more so because a near-death experience from a vehicle accident I had been in was still too fresh in my mind and too close in time for me to have forgotten why I must stay alive in the United States. Lisa was gone for good! Or so I thought.

I went cold feet and gun-shy for about three months before I made my second dating mistake in a row. Stupidly enough, I had not cared to read my class notes on dating from York College, nor listened to simple common sense, the much I had it so far in the area of American-style dating. I was back in Lisa's net before I knew it. Not Lisa PerSe, but her sister. It was not all my fault. But I was stupid enough to think I could make a clean switch from Lisa to her younger sister without skin pain. Over the period of my friendship with Lisa, I became acquainted with her sister (I don't remember her very uncommon "designer" name) who started calling me when she was sure that I had broken up with her sister for good. She seemed quite a well-behaved girl although a few years younger than her sister. I was fooled into believing her claim of simple unalloyed concern for me and my well being.

One bright Sunday afternoon, she talked me into going out with her to the Space Center, there in Huntsville, Alabama, and that's when she told me many more "secrets" about her sister, Lisa, in an effort to win me for herself. After a few more outings and visits to my house, Lisa's sister told me that Lisa was actually married, and her husband was known to be a very violent man. She told me that Lisa's husband owned many guns, and that Lisa had asked her to tell me that she, Lisa, would give her husband my address and phone number unless I paid her fifty dollars by the end of the following week.

I knew immediately that that was it for Huntsville, Alabama, and me. Earlier, I had secured admission to transfer to the University of Houston School of Architecture for the 1978 fall semester but had wanted to work through the summer in Huntsville before relocating to Houston, Texas. However, summer job or no, it was paramount for me to react quickly and stay very far away from any man with a gun. Coincidentally at that time, a collection agent for the Huntsville hospital to which I was admitted after my car accident had just started calling me everyday to make me pay the enormous medical bill. And so were many other business affiliates to the hospital sending me unexpected bills for a number of other medical services related to the accident.

As if the bill collectors' harassing phone calls were not enough, I had also been stopped by a policeman on an early Sunday morning, a few days earlier, for alleged overspeeding. The unmarked police car had followed me as I drove off from a nightclub and headed home happily after a good night-out dancing in a long while. Through many traffic lights, he trailed me and changed lanes as I did so to let him pass by. When we entered a long stretch of road without lights, I picked up speed as he followed me too closely as if he were tailgating my car, but he also increased speed to maintain the same uncomfortable distance. Finally, I became nervous and speeded up to lose him as fast as I could. After what amounted to a little chase behind me, the officer turned on his lights and flashed me to a stop. As we came to a final stop, he jumped out of his police car and walked up to my car, shining a flash light straight into my face. "Get out now, nigger boy! Where do you think you are?   You shouldn't be driving around in my town in your flashy car at this time of the night. This is Dixie country, boy!" At this time, I knew I was at a crossroads and had to go by what I learned in driver's education class not too long ago when I applied for a driving license. I simply obeyed him to the letter and stepped out of my car, hands-spread and head first. He then stepped close and said a lot of things, literally in my face, with a strange accent. I did not comprehend what he said one bit but I managed to stay calm. Then, he briskly stepped on my shoes, once on each foot, and asked me from where I got the shoes. It was only then I said my first word to respond.

"From home, Sir!"

"And where is your damn home, boy?" he queried, as if I had said something very wrong.

"Nigeria," I responded.

"And what brings you here to drive in my town this time of the night? What do you do here in Dixie country?"

Again, I answered both questions.

"I went out to the club, Sir, and I am a student at Alabama A&M."

"Good! Mighty good, boy! Now, I'm gonna give you a ticket, and after that, you should turn your monkey tail and run like hell. I will follow you home, boy!"

And he did, driving off as I turned into our driveway.

When I looked at the traffic ticket the next day, it stated that I was doing 72 miles an hour in a 35 m.p.h. speed zone, both of which were not true. He further stated that I was rude and appeared drunk, both of which were preposterous.

But none of those bothered me more than the fact that my name was now "in the computer." We foreigners, at that time, had this phobia about computers, and believed that once someone's name is coded into it, the government could and did in fact follow every step of one's daily life, twenty-four hours a day. More so, we believed that only the names of criminals get entered in the computer, and that both the Immigration and Naturalization Service and the Internal Revenue Service use the information for the respective purposes of work-related deportations and tax evasion prosecutions. My name in the computer was very bad news, especially in Dixie country, I thought and felt. I was scared pink! The next week did not meet me in Huntsville, Alabama, because I packed my few belongings and drove off to Houston, Texas, via Oklahoma City, Oklahoma. It was quite a hard way to leave town, but leave I did.

I arrived in Houston with bright lights in my head, very much ready to engage in the more civilized and responsible aspects of my young adult life in the United tates—an urban city life very unlike what I had known so far in my prior engagements in York, Nebraska, and Huntsville, Alabama.

But Houston, once again, proved to be a big city with even bigger surprises. Peers and cohorts abound in Houston. I quickly got myself going in the general scheme of things. The zeal and necessity to work hard was there, so I promptly secured two summer jobs — one daytime valet parking job, and a nighttime security job guarding office buildings. With these two full-time jobs, my school fees, living expenses, and a pleasurable social life were guaranteed.

At that time in Houston, among my peers, nightclubs "were it" for social outings. We went out in packs to disco and reggae clubs, mostly to the Third Ward and Southwest areas of town, always looking to get lucky with a date or so. Nothing serious, just social dancing and occasional visitations. There seemed to be, and, in fact, there was a special kind of happiness after a night's successful outing, which served to strike a balance between work, school, and good life.

One certain unscheduled Saturday night-off from my security job, I ventured out alone to a nightclub on Griggs Road. It was a different club from the ones we normally visited. There, I literally struck gold. Or so I thought. The general atmosphere in that club was very laid-back, with a much more mature adult audience than usual. I stood by the bar for a while and looked around. Then I zeroed in on a beautiful lady sitting by herself in a corner near the dance stage. A couple of dance songs later, I summoned the courage to walk up to her and ask her for a dance. She immediately obliged and continued to dance with me for the next three songs in a row, after which I proudly walked her back to her seat and retired to my bar-side observatory. I was proud of my guts in asking her to dance with me.

She didn't have any problem at all making eye contact with me when a few dance songs later, she turned towards me and made a one-finger invitation for me to come and get her. I was quick to her side, and we proceeded, once again, to the dance floor. This time we danced more furiously together, with her taking the lead and in many ways, the control. I was beginning to like her and to count my blessings in anticipation of much more after the club hour. While we were dancing, she made the first move and asked for my name and phone number. She also wanted to know what I did for a living. My mind was racing with all kinds of possibilities, but I was reluctant to engage her in a conversation for the fear that she could hear my accent and decide to have nothing to do with a strange-talking foreigner. I managed to keep my cool and concentrated on the dancing part where I knew I was good and wanted to stay while I was still ahead.

I never noticed anything unusual about my dance partner until she saw me leaving, followed me outside, and asked if I would take her home. Of course, I said Yes. Knowing that "take her home" could mean anything —her home or mine, depending on my luck and her need at the time. It was really looking like I might have struck gold for a meaningful relationship.

But just as I safely loaded the girl in the front passenger seat of my car, closed the door, and walked majestically around to the driver's side, a young man quickly walked up to me from the front of the club house and motioned me to himself, slightly away from the car. I went to this man reluctantly, determined to keep it short with him. The man leaned forward and said to me in a low but emphatic tone: "Homeboy, she is a he." In shock, I jerked my upper body backwards and looked at the man thinking, "What the hell could you mean?" I immediately wanted to get on with my business, regardless, but the man grabbed the tip of my jacket and pulled it slightly to stop my motion. Then, he said to me a little louder: "I know you don't understand, but that person you've been dancing with in the club is really a man, not a girl that you think he is." Pausing to let me absorb the shock, he continued: "He is all trouble, don't go anywhere with him...."

The man was still speaking when I turned around and saw my passenger dash out from the car towards us in a rage, demanding to know what the man was talking to me about. They both engaged themselves in a shouting argument, with the "girl" insisting it was not the man's business to interfere in "her" business. "After all, 'she' argued, he is grown enough to know what he likes and to like what he saw." 'She' was furiously charging this man with a barrage of vulgar rebuttals to everything the man said as he retreated towards the club entrance door, when I recovered myself and took the opportunity to quickly jump into my car and drive off in a hurry.

It was when I stopped to close my passenger-side door, which was thrown ajar as I took off, that I saw the "girl's" purse lying on the car seat. I grabbed the purse, took two quick steps towards the clubhouse, and flung it as far as I could towards the "girl" who had started to run towards the car shouting at me for "her" purse. I was too afraid to let 'her' come any closer to me, seeing what "she" had done to that man. Ultimately, my so-called lucky strike of gold was a dangerous close encounter with the strange world of punks and transsexuals.

Unusual places beget unusual experiences! But in looking and counting backwards—Houston, Huntsville, York, Boston—I ask myself, Is the problem America or is it me? The answer ought to be clear. Whatever the answer may be, each unusual experience taught me valuable lessons about the milestones to my manhood in America. One such valuable lesson was that, America or not, I must steer close to my people and not fall too far away from the apple tree of our young women. I married a home-girl some six years later.

4

꧁꧂

FOUNDATIONS OF FAITH

*F*ate is the mysterious applications of the laws of the world. We must accept Fate as much as we are compelled to affirm liberty — the significance of the individual, the grandeur of duty, the power of character.... Fate is ore and quarry as evil is good in the making; as limitation is power that shall be; and as calamities, oppositions, and weights are wings and means. Ralph Waldo Emerson.][13]

The Hindus say that "Fate is nothing but the deeds committed in a prior state of existence. In the history of the individual is always an account of his/her condition and he/she knows him/herself to be a party to his/her present estate." Realistically, however, fate is a matter of life inheritance, power, and circumstance.

The circumstance is nature. In it abide unique limitations, and also therein lies the freedom of the individual. It follows, therefore, that if one believes in fate to his/her peril, one must also believe it, at the least, for his/her own good. Thus, in the omnipresence of natural laws, we can deduce that what is, must be, and ought to be, or is the best. However, a text of heroism, a name, and an anecdote of courage are not mere arguments but sallies of freedom. A double-quote by Hafiz, a Fourteenth-century Persian poet, helps drive home the point: "'T is written on the gate of Heaven, 'Woe unto him who suffers himself to be betrayed by Fate.'"

Faith contains fate and imposes spiritual control over nature. I submit that in life, natural odds notwithstanding, we can and should become masters of our own fate.

Church For Sale

What is the Church? Why is the Church?

The Institution of the Church, at first mention, may not seem to be a mystery. But when we ask: Why do churches exist? How did the Church, as an institution, come into being? What is the reason or purpose for its existence? Does it make any difference whether or to which church one belongs? then, indeed, it becomes a mystery, and the average person has no answer. If you ask people in the non-Christian world where other religions are accepted, they would probably have no answer because they know little about the church. Those in the more modernist and liberal areas of traditional Christianity would probably say the church exists merely as an emotional lift, having a psychological influence on those who have not embraced the evolutionary theory as accepted in modern higher education. If you ask those who follow one of the evangelical Christian denominations, they would probably say that the church is God's instrument in His effort to save the world from eternal hellfire. Those people assume that the church is a sort of soul-saving station to get people "saved." Nonetheless, the facts of the church's origin and its purpose are contained in the Bible.

The term "church" is applicable only to the Christian religion. Other religions may have mosques, synagogues, and temples.

Most people think of the Church as a building with a sharply sloping roof, a steeple pointing heavenward, and a cross on its face. Indeed Webster defines the word "church" as a building.

The modern Western world takes the fact of the existence of churches for granted, seeing it only as part of the world's civilized life. In the Western world today, there are many different churches: Catholic, Protestant, Independents. And within them, many denominations, sects, and divisions or congregations, each with its different beliefs, teachings, rituals and programs. But is the church a building?

In 1978, I experienced my first jolt of reality and the early dawn of my American experience while driving down a street in Huntsville, Alabama. Looking around the neighborhood in casual observation of my new environment (me being a transfer student not quite two months old in town), I saw a sign in a flash: "CHURCH FOR SALE, INQUIRE WITHIN."

Church for what? I thought loudly to myself. I pulled to the side of the narrow road, backed up, and read the bizarre sign a second and a third time. Something felt very strange. Something was very wrong; Why would anybody want to sell a church? I asked myself again and again for days and weeks. Discussing it with my peers didn't curb my anxiety one bit. Then, suddenly, it dawned on me: In America, a church is just another business!

Coincidentally, at that time, one Reverend Iyke regularly came on the radio telling people just that: "Invest in my business," he preached, "Send me your seed money, and you'll become rich through my prayers for you." Presumably, the amount of prayer said was in direct proportion to the amount of one's contribution to the entrepreneuring Reverend Iyke, who was at the time residing somewhere in California. We listened to his radio broadcast on Sunday mornings, definitely for the false hopes we entertained as young men looking to make it in our new culture, America. Of course, we didn't have the seed money to send Mr. Iyke, so he never prayed for us. Fair enough!

In that moderate to low-income Huntsville neighborhood where there was a church on every other city block, it's survival of the fittest in every business sense of the phrase. There, and in many other places in our modern society, the biggest motivator in church ministry is the checkbook. A church has less and less to do with the purpose and will of God than with revenue: Make money or lose your business! The gospel of goodwill opens up to those who have the checkbook. Our modern soul is for sale!

No doubt, that "For Sale" sign I saw on that church in Huntsville, Alabama, left an indelible mark on me from then on, with respect to my view of religion as practiced by our modern civilization. It caused me to take a second, hindsight look at some of the activities of religious leaders I remember from the past. One such remarkable event happened in my hometown church during the Nigeria/Biafra war.

The incident was the public tearing-up of a Biafran currency note by one Reverend Chukwuka, the resident pastor of our hometown church, St. John's Church, Okoh. This pastor was upset because someone made an offering with "dirty" Biafran currency which, according to him, could not be spent by the church in the open market. During his sermon, he raised the note up to the plain view of the entire congregation and tore up the currency as a stern warning to future "sinful givers", as he put it. There was absolute silence in the church as people were shocked in disbelief of what they saw and heard: the arrogance, the hypocrisy! Everybody in church that day had risked his or her life to be in church, not knowing when and where the Nigerian fighter-bomber warplanes would strike. The young men, especially, had risked the chance of being caught and conscripted into the Biafran army. Everybody's only persuasion was the need for prayers at that point of our people's lives and history. We all went home that day dejected, hopeless, and angry.

Pastor Chukwuka was not realistic. He also was known for other rude behaviors, such as spitefully ordering away the masses of hungry folks that came to the church premises to beg for food from the church-controlled relief items donated by the World Council of Churches and other war-time relief organizations. His children were known for bragging and being pompous and for bartering relief food items for sex and other material rewards.

Two of those Chukwuka boys were my schoolmates at Boys Grammar School Agulu. Raluchukwu Chukwuka was my classmate. We were fairly good friends until the war sent us home from school and eventually put us into two different camps of haves and have-nots. To my former classmate, I had become a 'nobody' as he wallowed in prosperity: he being the rich son of a pastor in my very hometown church. The entire Chukwuka family was eventually driven out of my town almost by covert mob action. It was an ugly sight, but nonetheless a desirable end to an urgly experience.

After the war, as my people pondered and wondered about the place of faith in the destiny of the Nigerian Igbo, there were voids in my people's souls and religious minds. The Igbo people needed hope and, possibly, some spiritual healing of sorts.

One of the many evangelical missionaries that besieged my people in the early 1970s was the Oral Roberts' organization. They held rallies in big city stadiums and football fields that attracted people in the hundreds of thousands. They promised new life in Jesus Christ and condemned quests for material possessions along with other "sins".

One such "sin" that hit home to our youthful generation was ballroom dancing with girls, and other 'material world' social pursuits. Of course sex was the ultimate sin, which was sure to condemn one to eternal hell. No joke! these evangelists became the legendary pied pipers that piped away all the girls and made social life intolerable in colleges and universities. It was not long 'till the men followed suit, most in their desperate effort to stay close to the women, however possible.

Our world in the early seventies was therefore polarized into SU (Scripture Union) members and non-SU (non-Scripture Union) members: Believers and non-Believers. Quite unfortunately, some families were split along these lines. I belonged to the latter and we were a sorry minority. We lost friends in droves.

When I came to America in 1977, I was amazed to find out that the Oral Roberts Evangelistic organization is a profit-minded corporation that owns a profit-making university and a large medical service complex. Then, also, came the PTL (Praise The

Lord or People That Love) hotel resort story and the Jim Baker sex scandal. And, of course, the flamboyant bastardization of Christian ethics by Jimmy Swaggart, who also had major dealings with prostitutes and thrived on income tax scams and shady real estate deals. In all, I thought, "What organized hypocrisy! What a universal deceit!"

I have since put other things in perspective and made some crucial decisions in my life. In doing so, I considered the proliferation of churches in American cities, especially in lower income communities, the increasing siting of new churches in strip shopping centers, the disproportionate economic well-being of religious leaders as compared to their followers, and the emphasis on the importance of monetary giving as a precursor to spiritual salvation by most religious preachers in church pulpits. I have come to the conclusion that a church is truly a business, and, I have reached the resolution that my spiritual relationship to God cannot be trusted upon the doctrines of any one church nor the preaching of any one religious preacher. Come what may, my soul is not for sale!

I never attended a church service in the nine months I stayed in Huntsville, Alabama, following my 'Church For Sale' ordeal. More so, I have become skeptical about churches and religious preachers. I have increasing difficulties relating to the God I know, mainly because of certain overt attitudes and actions of some religious institutions, and certain moral conduct of some popular religious leaders. I've always found myself second-guessing the fundamental interests of the churches I worship in, even when I consciously try to separate the message from the messenger. I know this is not good if I must maintain my faith. But what's the message?

I believe that almost anyone who is seriously involved in any church will recognize that churchgoing is not synonymous with personal spirituality. There are some church-goers who get so busy in church-going that they become insensitive to the more pressing human needs that surround them, thereby contradicting the very precepts they profess to believe deeply. There are yet others who rarely attend church, but whose attitudes and behavior reflect the basic Judeo-Christian ethic.

Having been brought up in the church and having participated in organized church activities throughout my life, I have found that a church-centered life can become hypocritical and can undermine personal security and intrinsic worth. Because the formal church is an organization made up of policies, practices, and organizational goals, it cannot by itself define the path for a successful life for a person. Living the purer principles thought up even by the cheat could do this, but the organization alone cannot. The fact that most religious organizations in the United States—churches in particular— are still segregated with respect to color has not helped me either. Granted, a church is a business; why would any business continue to discriminate as to who becomes its customer? Is the colored man any less valuable than the white man spiritually, or materially, as the case has become? Could the social forces at work here have been the same at work during the time in history when white missionaries exported their religion and colonialism to Africa? What really was their original intentions—salvation, dominion, or business? Will this ever change?

On the good side, however, religion teaches reverence to and belief in a superhuman Being who is capable of shaping one's destiny through fate. It also teaches responsibility and positive action on one's part, as a demonstration of faith in this superior Being. I exercise my faith responsibly in God by subscribing to the common adage that "Heaven helps those who help themselves. No coward soul is mine, no trembler in the world's storm-troubled sphere." [Emily Bronte].

Second Chances

I am not up there yet with the cat and its enviable "nine lives" or nine second chances at one life. But I've had my lucky strikes, if you will. First, a second chance at school after the Nigeria/Biafra war meant a second chance at life for me. It was a brand new era and a chance to put into practice the artificial maturity into manhood I had attained by virtue of the three years of shrewd activities inherent in a war of basic survival of the fittest. The result was a negation of the common computer language acronym, "garbage in garbage out", or GIGA — as this computer wisdom is generally espoused and universally accepted. The fact is that we went into the war young and innocent, but we came out in less than three years, weathered and determined. The Igbo person is a resilient creature!

'Eze Goes To School'

School was the popular thing on the minds of most our young adults in January of 1970. But, immediately after the war, there was no money, very few schools, and often no parents or guardians. There were no means of transportation, no amenities in the few school that existed, no confidence in the powers that be and, certainly, no robust vision of the distant future for us, the young adults. But we went back to school!

As for me and my cousin, Henry, we fixed up two old bicycles in the family and, five days a week, we biked the twelve miles of rugged one-way distance to my alma matter, Agulu Boys High School, through the hilly, mostly unpaved, public road from my town, through a few more towns, to the war-torn school. Everybody came from home, except for the very privileged few who could afford to set up camp in the few habitable dormitories and provide their own amenities, including food. Every Igbo person (or Igbo family) was broke after the war, and every little thing amounted to luxury.

My cousin, Henry, moved into one of these dormitories after the first term or semester. Thence the road to and from school grew longer and lonelier for me. But I had more than one reason to continue biking the distance every school-day: I had a small farm at home to attend, I had joined my mother as partners in her palm oil production business, and I had also started a small retail business to earn money for school fees and supplies. The thoughts of these occupied my mind and provided me some relief from loneliness during the tiring rides home (mostly walks because of the steep hills on the return) from school. Also on big market days (*Eke Ogbu* market), I enjoyed the company of women returning from the market through the more lonely and often scary segment of the roadway, some six miles from school to the paved highway.

On Fridays, I skipped the last class periods and hurried back home because, on Fridays, I had to travel to Awka (the nearest township of any sort at the time and, presently, the capital of my home state, Anambra State) on public transportation, to buy stock for my small retail business. I attended to my farm in late evenings and on weekends when I was not helping my father on his farm. In all, I did quite well for myself and in helping to provide "second chances" for my family.

We took the West African School Certificate (WASC) exam in 1970, but the result for East Central State, the Igbo State, was cancelled. The reason given was that the exam questions leaked out to students before the examination date. I never saw the questions and, to the best of my knowledge, nobody in my school did. But the West African Examination Council (WAEC) cancelled the result and dubbed us the EXPO set, "EXPO '70." It was almost a tragedy for me given all I had gone through to take that examination. Many students did not return to school to retake the examination in 1971. They were too heartbroken and too poor. But I did!

This time, I could afford to live in the dormitory and, moreover, I was too mentally drained to garner the energy and determination I needed to bike-ride it again from home. The experience of living together and studying with other boys was fulfilling, notwithstanding the frustrating circumstances. We burned gasoline lamps into the late nights and early mornings during the short time we had to gear up spirits again and face a special examination for Igbo students of East Central state, the "defeated" ex-soldiers of the Biafran war. We could not claim ignorance of what's coming to us.

With a not-so-distant spirit of survival, we went into battle for our academic lives. Sure enough, the questions were much tougher than the first time, but we were also more determined to succeed. The boys of EXPO '70, the special exam class of 1971, proudly maintained the motto of my Alma Matter, Distinction! We registered a one-hundred-percent pass record to continue the trend of excellence for the school. We did not fail our school nor did we fail ourselves. Once again, the Igbos in general, managed to send the strong message to WAEC and the Nigerian government that we would not be vanquished. For me, personally, it became the backbone of my mental readiness to shoot for the skies.

A straight course university education was a long shot for me for financial and other reasons. Therefore, I went in for a crash program in teacher training. For two years, I was a primary school teacher. Although I went in with a heavy heart knowing that I possessed the brains to be at the university with my peers, it proved to be the most rewarding experience of my young adult life. It provided me tremendous emotional growth, maturity, and wisdom. Teaching challenged all aspects of my being: mental, physical, and emotional. It gave me the opportunity to view my future through a window in my present. It allowed me to become a child again in the company of the first innocent generation of real children after the war, who in their innocence could resurrect the child in me and excite the natural world around us all. We played, joked, worked, and learned together with infectious camaraderie. I taught them, and they soothed me.

As a young teacher, I was schooled in adult wisdom and challenged with official responsibility to the very limits of my capabilities. Like all other teachers in my school, I taught all subjects from arithmetic to writing, to physical education, or whatever else appeared in the school curriculum. I was solely in charge of my 30 to 45-student class (a class was as full as there were seating spaces in the classroom) and reported only to the school headmaster. I could fit seamlessly into the world of my students because I was not much older than, nor different from them. In fact, some of my students were bigger than I was. But there was discipline and respect for the teacher, a common element of school life in Nigeria. Moreover, it was not difficult to know who the teacher was because, by provision of the school uniform code, I could wear trousers (or pants), but they could not. I could address them by their first names, but they could only address me as, Sir. Very important!

Later, the opportunity came, and I went to further my education in the teaching profession at the College of Education, Owerri, where I majored in mathematics and physics. Still, by another stroke of luck, I took advantage of the benevolence of a generous, future-thinking native of my town, Dr. Alex Ekwueme, who offered me and many more others the opportunity of further studies abroad. Dr. Ekwueme was a successful architect who had received help from the community in his school years and knew enough to give back to the same community and beyond. He did so very willingly and generously. This marvelous philanthropist knew enough to invest in young minds. Dr. Ekwueme later became the first civilian Vice President under the only civilian government of Nigeria since the civil war.

I arrived in the United States in January of 1977 to study architecture, obviously after the footsteps of my wonderful sponsor and mentor, His Excellency, Dr. Alex Ekwueme. I literally forced my way into architecture as a professional choice. No doubt I was more equipped to study engineering or any of the sciences, including medicine. But the star I saw in Dr. Ekwueme was too bright not to follow, and follow I did. I wanted and still strive to live, think, and act like this icon of a human being whose example is definitely a rare gift from above to any community of fellows anywhere on earth.

The study and practice of architecture gave me more than a profession. It brought me vividly into the real world of God, man and nature; and it gave me the senses to visualize and apply the three in a wonderful symphony of life. The study and practice of architecture catered to the total being of my human self. Architecture is a social science, or art, that invites us to "design with nature," and to always consider all the sensuous elements not quite obvious to the naked eye, or naked mind— the ethos, the pathos, and the logos. The study and practice of architecture would broaden anybody's horizon as it did mine. One masters degree in urban planning (1986) and three years of part-time law school (1991-1994) later, I've had the benefit of education and experience in three very rewarding areas of professional knowledge. It is in this broad perspective of enabling vision that I operate and assess my performance in the fated experience of life. In these academic achievements, my second chances at imbibing human knowledge— a chain of second chances at academic life—have been nothing but very rewarding.

Miracles Happen!

There were many "second chances" at life for every Igbo person who stayed on the active side of the defunct Biafra during the Nigeria/Biafra war. Every place in Biafra was a war front and daily survivals were, in effect, second chances at life and more. Nevertheless, one miraculous second chance at life for me I must document in this book is my near-death experience in Huntsville, Alabama in the summer of 1977. I was presumed "dead-on-arrival" in a Huntsville hospital, but I lived to tell my own story, the little bit of which I was conscious enough to remember.

I arrived in Huntsville, Alabama in the early summer of 1977 from York, Nebraska. I had few friends attending school at Alabama A&M University, and I needed to transfer away from a small Christian college, York College, which was my school of entry into the United States and where I had attended school with the other students from Nigeria under the sponsorship of Dr. Alex Ekwueme. Life was literally cold but quite good in York, Nebraska. There were about thirty of us. We lived in the dormitory and bonded together in that rather strange environment. Every one of the foreign students ("Ekwueme students" as we were referred to) came to York College one semester before my arrival. A strange delay in my securing a passport in Nigeria had separated me from the group and delayed my travel by one semester. But I took a remedial examination upon my arrival and was able to assemble enough credit hours to catch up with the best of the group.

At the end of the spring of 1977, almost all the students in our group made arrangements to transfer to other schools more fitting for careers in fields other than religion. Nobody wanted to spend the two years necessary for graduation in the Christian College. I opted to go to Alabama where a few of the previous group of "Ekwueme students" were attending school at Alabama A&M University.

We lived together in a rented two-bedroom house, two boys to a room, with more than occasional squatters in the living room. The standing rule was that in the rare instance of a visit by a female date, the lucky person with the date got the right to a room for the duration. He was agreeably the king of the hill and deserving of it. We didn't have much, but we were very happy. All that mattered was school and school-related undertakings, one of which was maintaining at least one regular full-time job during regular school months and more hours during the summer months. It was the only proper thing to do, and everyone was drawing energy and example from another.

I quickly secured two full-time dishwashing jobs at two restaurants in opposite ends of town. I had listened to the many advice from the other boys, which they gave freely starting from the time they picked me up from the Trailways bus station. "Summer is it!" they told me and that I needed to make enough money to pay for at least sixteen credit hours of course work, cover my living expenses, and possibly purchase a used car for transportation. Meanwhile, one boy, Michael Ekwueme, already owned a car, and for few dollars a week, we fueled it and shared rides amongst ourselves and a handful of friends. The rent was divvied up to about twenty-five dollars a piece, but with school fees and a dollar-fifty minimum wage, twenty-five dollars was big money. Our address, 207 Richmond Avenue, was a popular address. Many students visited from the dorm for a rare taste of home cooked food, different from the staple rations of hot dogs, burgers, and fries normally served in the school cafeteria. Most of us foreigners were not that crazy about American food at the time. Other entertainment flowed freely and generously if the visitor came with some girls.

Not long into the summer, one more boy, Noel Okeke, bought another car, a yellow two-door Chevy Vega. It was in this car that I "died but rose again from the dead." Two dollars in hand, one Saturday mid-morning, I had grabbed the keys to the Vega and proudly headed to the gas station through the back road. I was going to fuel the car in preparation for Noel giving me a ride to work later in the evening. I had taken the back road to avoid being seen by our regular mechanic, James, while I bought gasoline from a competing station across the road which had gas prices posted at one cent cheaper than James was selling in his station. James didn't see me fuel the car, but he was reportedly the first on the scene when I was smashed into oblivion by another vehicle as I crossed the street to his gas station, for a minor checkup. All I remembered was seeing the green light for me to proceed through the intersection. The rest of the story is hearsay or active dream at best. The yellow Vega was crushed beyond repair, and nobody ever saw it again. The story was that my car was hit on the driver's door, flipped two or three times and hit again. By the time the paramedics came and yanked my unconscious body out of the rubble that was the Chevy Vega, everybody around was quite sure I was "dead".

James immediately called the house, and told everybody what he believed he saw — that I was dead. He told them that my body had been taken to the hospital in an ambulance. In utmost panic, the boys got on the phone and called all parts of the country where our folks lived to convey the sad news, as they knew it. A death of one of us at that time would have been the first and much beyond their capacity to handle. They would have called Nigeria if it were possible. We had a standing rule against making long distance calls for fear of the cost, but that was a special situation.

I woke up in the hospital about midnight and requested from one of the many doctors and nurses surrounding my hospital bed that I called home. One of the doctors offered to do the calling for me, but I insisted on doing it myself. He handed me the phone, and I dialed home. On the first ring, somebody picked up the phone: "Hello! he answered with a drowning voice. I recognized the voice anyway and said: "Mike, I am in the hospital, come and get me." "Who is this?" he inquired in a heightened tone. "This is Benneth, my friend, come and get me!" Then he kept quiet for a while (probably to recollect himself) and said to me, "Hold on!" As I held on for Mike, I looked up at the people surrounding my bed (more staff had joined in than when I first asked to use the phone, and they were paying attention to my phone call). I started to say something, but Mike came back on the phone: "Are you sure this is Benneth?" he asked assertively. I could now hear a crowd's noise at his end of the line and wondered what was going on. "Mike!" I called out in anger, "What's the matter with you? I am in the hospital, come and get me!" And I hung up the phone with an angry bang.

Immediately, one of the doctors motioned away the rest of the hospital staff who had gathered around me and leaned forward to talk to me. He told me I could not go home because I was in a very serious accident and had suffered serious injuries — broken jaw, lost tooth, broken knees, and possible head injury. Still confused and angry about Michael's attitude on the phone, I shot back at the doctor that I've never slept in a hospital before and that was not going to be my first time. Then, he toned down even more and asked me if I had insurance. Strange it may sound, but I didn't know what insurance was at that time. So, I answered No. But, in fact, I had comprehensive medical insurance coverage with Mutual of Omaha as part of my foreign student package at York College. My coverage was still good until the end of the year 1977. I carried the identification card with me but didn't know what it was. Insurance or not, the doctor told me bluntly that I could not leave the hospital care under my condition. But I was equally adamant in my demand.

Unknown to me, he motioned for help and got me restricted to the bed. However, upon my persistence and upon his further assessment of my condition, he called my home boys and released me to them with the condition that they should bring me back first thing in the morning the next day. It was when I got to the house that I learned the extent to which the news of my "death" had spread in and outside Huntsville, Alabama. It was also the next day, during my return visit to the hospital, that I learned the magnitude of the miracle they believed had occurred by virtue of my complete recovery against concurrent prognosis by all the emergency doctors on staff. Everybody came to see me to believe. They told a story of "the strange African" who nobody thought would survive but surprised them all. The strangest part was that all through my unconsciousness they had listened to me engage a fictitious second-person(s) in a prolonged dialogue in a "strange language." They had actually recorded portions of the dialogue (or monologue because the only audible voice was mine) out of curiosity, for further analysis as to content and language. So, they played back the tape for me but would not release it to me.

On the tape, I was having a discussion with a second person, or persons, in my native language, Igbo. In that discussion, I was arguing a point and explaining why I must stay. There were long pauses on the tape between my responses, indicating preceding statements from the second person, or persons, which I could not recollect upon my regaining consciousness. It could not have been an active dream.

I was back at my two jobs the following day after a recommended visit to an orthodontist. I was aching all over and limping around, but my spirit was up and determined not to fail my people or myself. For the sake of my family at home, I could not afford to have died at that time. And my God agreed!

I became a proud owner of a red-and-white 1974 Chevy Nova, 2-door Sport Coupe, by the end of summer 1977. Today, I'm still totally convinced that it is not my fate that I should die by vehicle accident, here or anywhere else. My philosophy in life has also changed dramatically for good.

A Third Second Chance to Boot

"They were not thieves; they were robbers!" Before I could wonder aloud to myself what the difference was, His Excellency, Dr. Alex Ekwueme quickly explained that thieves and robbers differ immensely in their motivations and actions in criminally taking what belongs to others – life and/or property. While thieves mostly steal out of want or greed and would rather do so unnoticed under cover of darkness, robbers take brazenly, by brute force, and with naked impunity. While thieves recognize and somehow respect a victim's right to personal space and dignity, robbers choose to trash both first off.

I had called Dr. Ekwueme in London, as arranged, to continue a discussion we started on the political situation in Nigeria at the wake of his unsuccessful bid for his party's nomination as their presidential candidate at the 1999 Primaries. He happened to be home for a short time during my one-month visit to our hometown, and I had seized the opportunity to confer with him. We could not finish our discussion before he traveled, so he asked me to call him in London as soon as I arrived back in the United States. I obliged.

However, I skirted the pre-arranged political discussion and went straight to a personal ordeal I had gone through at the tail end of my stay at home which had quickly overtaken all political issues in priority: I was violently robbed, in my father's compound, by five heavily armed men, about eight o'clock on a bright Tuesday morning. They knew me by name, and told me they were sent to kill me. I had wrongly referred to them as thieves as I narrated my ordeal to Dr. Ekwueme and talked to him about security in our hometown, particularly my section of our village.

There were at least twenty people on hand and around my compound that fateful Tuesday morning, when my working trip home almost became my literally returning my body home for an impromptu traditional burial alongside my father's grave. Tuesday, the twenty-second of March, 1999! That was the one last day in my village before my scheduled travel to Lagos on my way back to the United States. The last working day for me on the family house I had come home to begin construction, after many years of postponements due to unforeseen circumstances— the death of my father in 1992, and many other financial handicaps in the way of progress many years in a row. It was the final payday, by me, for the local construction crew who had labored hard, though happily, to see the big house take shape in foundation and blockwork up to lintel level. They were already two hours into our regular workday, which lasted from six in the morning to seven in the evening, Monday through Saturday. I had gone to the bank the previous day to withdraw money, in preparation for my meeting my obligation to them, and for leaving them on a good note the next day.

It had rained the night before, leaving a pool of needed water on the concrete foundation slab where the workers were mixing concrete for the day's work, casting the lintel beams. Some of the workers were on the ground, and some on wooden ladders receiving and pouring the concrete as it became properly mixed and ready. My younger brother, Chika, was helping to assure good work.

In front by the entrance gate, I had just finished paying some of the tipper drivers who had brought in sand and gravel late the previous night and had either brought in some more that morning or stopped by to collect their money before proceeding for more trips. One driver, a relation of mine who brought in gravel that morning refused payment, noting that I should know better than worry about him before I made sure I had paid the other drivers. "Mine can always wait," he said. "I am just happy to be a useful part of this effort to elevate the image of our kindred in our town." As I pocketed the left-over bundle of currency notes, I jokingly told Eugene that he should better take his money while I still had it, *maka ada ama-ama* (because you never know). We both laughed, and he took off.

I was still grinning at the pleasure of my relation's words as I walked to the back house to talk to my brother about going out to a neighboring family to represent our family in the community task of digging up a grave for the burial of a deceased relative. It was required of us to do so, since we happened to be home at the material time.

Chika started off after I talked to him, while I stood by and was directing the young man mixing concrete on how best to prevent excess water from washing away the cement. I did not see that two men had walked past Chika and made their way towards me. A little tap on the back, I turned around only to see a young man grab my right wrist. "Come on lets go!" he said.

A bit confused, I asked, "What's going on?" "Who are you?"

But he furiously slapped my face and pushed me. "Come on go! Go towards your car!" This time he had kicked and punched me at the same time. It was when I looked down in dismay and saw a pistol that it dawned on me that I was in for armed robbery. I immediately kicked in my number six senses and resolved that I must concentrate all my wits on finding a way to stay alive through the ordeal. The family yellow Mercedes was parked in the neighboring compound across the street from ours, away from traffic and construction activities in our compound. My captor was directing me to the car.

Upon instinct, Chika had turned around to see what kind of

strangers would walk past him into our backyard without caring to speak to him or anybody else. But immediately noticing the resemblance between us as brothers, my captor ordered the second robber to hold him. This second robber pulled out an automatic rifle from under his flowing, oversized shirt and apprehended my junior brother, ordering him to walk slowly in front towards the car. Unknown to us, there were three other robbers in a red Mercedes parked on the main road in front of our entrance gate. The first two robbers had gained access to our backyard through a secondary entrance created to facilitate delivery of materials for the construction project.

But suddenly, as God would have it, my younger brother saw an opportunity. He quickly ducked to the edge of the fence wall and bolted away to safety. The three men in the car dashed out from both sides with three more automatic rifles, but were just short of ample time to stop the escape.

I was alone but quite relieved. My brother is a hot-tempered young man. Any little temper would have been lethal for us under the circumstances. I was then doubly sure that, with God, I was going to calmly deal with the situation and come out of it alive. The crowd in my compound, workers and all, had scrambled away in a frightened rush to safety. But my older sister ran towards me instead of away from obvious danger. It was this amazing demonstration of sibling love and sacrifice that helped save my neck from these men who had at that time converged on me, and were popping me from all sides with fists and rifle butts.

As they demanded the keys to my car, which I did not have on my person, I asked my sister to run into the house and search for the keys, while hoping that my brother had not run away with it. He had moved and parked the car earlier in the morning and could easily have put the keys in his pocket. My sister ran for the keys. Meanwhile, the robbers were getting restless and increasingly violent. I was constantly talking to them and telling them that there was no need for violence, since I was willing to cooperate fully with them. It was then that one of them, my first captor, bluntly told me that they were sent by somebody to come and kill me.

At this time, I looked up straight to his face and managed a smile: "Did the person who sent you tell you what bad thing I have done to him or her? And, for you who is going to do the killing, what joy will you derive?"

My response took him rather unawares and actually touched off certain 'humanness' in him. He looked down and remained still for a moment. I continued to talk to him and started walking slowly away from the car. I did not want my sister to come with the keys while we were still around the car, because they would probably order me into the car and hold me hostage to assure themselves a safe escape, or worse. It worked! The robbers followed me and suddenly became a little less violent at the urging of their leader, my first captor. He then began to ask for money, immediately reaching in and taking the bundle I had in my pocket. We were headed for the house for more money, as they had demanded. They snatched my neck chain and wristwatch as we went. My sister ran up with the car keys and handed it to one of them.

"Is this the key?" She asked the robber.

He looked and nodded, yes; and quickly put the key in his pocket. We then continued towards the house to "get the money". They were still hitting me to maintain authority and control. But this time my sister took on the role of wedging in and taking most of the punches herself. She did not think I possessed such strong jaws to continue to take all the pounding. She was pleading, howling, and crying. I was calmly talking to the robbers to gain psychological control. Miraculously, I had more courage than panic and fear, literally displaying grace under fire.

Once in the compound, the robbers cut off the overhead power supply cable with a barrage of gun shots. They pushed me into the house and to the bedroom. My sister followed in.

My mother was right there at the entrance door, too shocked to move— all seventy-something years of age, one hundred and twenty pounds of her. But as more gunshots rang out from inside my bedroom, she had sprung into action and held the robber standing guard outside my living room door, insisting that they, the robbers, would not leave unless they killed her too. She really thought they had killed me inside. Poor her! The young man flung her away to the concrete wall, and she fell almost unconscious.

Inside my bedroom, the robbers took shots at any boxed item on sight. They shot open the boxes, closets and cabinets. They took money and clothing and demanded to have my gun, insisting that the person who sent them told them I owned one. Of course, I truthfully denied ownership of any gun, calmly explaining that if I had one, they would have found it since everything in the room was now in plain view. As one of them punched me, knocking off my eyeglasses, something remarkable happened. The lead robber, my first captor, leaped forward, picked up the eyeglasses, handed them back to me and said, "Sorry Sir!" He had been motioning to the more aggressive robbers to cool it, and was shouting to them: "It is enough! We've got the money! Let's go!" At that time, they could hear the specific beating of the big community wooden gong (Ikoro) by certain member of the village security council, frantically alerting the community to the occurring event of armed robbery.

The robbers hurried out of the room – money, clothes, and boxes in hand.

Once outside, they fired several gun shots in the air and then in the general direction of a sea of people down the street who had been alerted to the event and were now looking and shouting from a safe distance. They could do no more. They had neither the guns nor the police presence to confront the heavily armed, trigger-happy robbers, who then jumped into the two cars and took off in the direction of the bordering town of Nanka.

I came out of my room and went immediately for my mother. I had to assure her that I was still alive. I scooped her up, kissed, and shook her, telling her to touch me and see that I am Ok. She finally heard me, touched, and believed. But I had to scramble away through the backyard to avoid the mob that was quickly congregating in my compound. I needed a quiet place to reflect and try to get my head back. Out of sight in the woods, I took a deep breath and cried deeply for a short while.

The police arrived some thirty minutes after the robbers besieged us, and ten minutes after they had left. In the beginning, one carpenter had jumped down from where he was nailing the wood casing for casting the lintel beams and ran the one-and-a half miles to the nearest police station. They came in a wagon of six officers, the carpenter in tow, and went after the robbers.

The next day, we drove to other police headquarters in surrounding towns and made reports. The day after, I took public transportation to Lagos on my way out of the country. A message came to us two days later, in Lagos, that the police had recovered my car. There were no further details. My nephew called me one week later in Houston and told me that all six robbers were killed in a gun battle with the police during yet another robbery operation, two days after our ordeal. They had apparently picked up one more colleague after they terrorized us. Good news! But I hated it. Because even robbers have souls!

"A mind is a terrible thing to waste," theirs or mine! Six young Igbo minds! Six lives that could have been much different. Six sad testimonials to the most unfortunate demise of the legendary Igbo culture of hard work, non-violence, mutual love, and high personal and community moral integrity. Things have really fallen apart when young, full-blooded Igbo men lose hope and make a career out of armed robbery. Unfortunately, because of what we have for police protection at home in Nigeria today, the armed robbery "business" is booming. In my mind, I wished I had thirty more talking minutes with that lead robber. I sincerely believe that I could have touched his soul in a redeeming manner. I could feel his remorse even as he beat and robbed me because, I believe, he had to. But now they are gone to meet our Maker. They are dead, and I am alive! Yet, one more second chance at life for me with sobering lessons.

I penned a letter to my family to emphasize the true value of our ordeal in divine lessons:

"... As a family, we must take time to thank God for the lessons learned through the event of our temptation— that being mutual love and sacrifice. And, in so doing, sincerely pray to the almighty God that He may grant eternal grace to the souls of those hopeless young men.... We now know that we have a good God, and that He is indeed on our side.... I love you too!"

Does it always take a near death experience to achieve a

higher order of living? That I cannot answer! However, I now experience an expanded sense of being and appreciate more deeply the chance at my purpose and value to society.

I Believe I Can Fly

The ambivalence of the 'true' definition of success suggests a subtle truth: At any point in time, the meaning of "success" is not the same for all of us. Life does not require us to be the same things at the same time. Therefore, "success" depends upon the gifts we have been given; the call we have received by fate.

We each progress and achieve at our own pace. At any stage, one may seem a success to some, or a failure to others. But only the fulfillment of life reveals our ultimate fate in "success" or "failure".

Faith contains fate and imposes spiritual control over nature. When it comes to my calling in life, I believe I can fly! Be it what it may, it is real and ideal to me, so long as I cannot try the accuracy of my senses. Wherefore, premises considered, I can then sing along the lyrics of musician R. Kelly in his appropriately titled song, "I Believe I Can Fly":

I believe I can fly
I believe I can soar the sky
I think about it every night and day
Just spread my wings and fly away
I believe I can fly....

I read a little poem in my secondary school years as a young boy. Although this poem may sound contradictory to the theme "I believe I can Fly," it is actually complimentary because it recommends the ground zero as the natural basis for any successful flight take-off. The poem is a song by one young boy of about the same age as myself at the time, who was pictured sitting on a rock by a fishing pond in the quiet solitude of a tree's shade, fishing-pole in hand. I don't remember the name of the author of this poem but its words and the picture of the young boy have remained with me ever since. Two simple but powerful verses of a young boy's song worthy of a reprint below:

He that is down needs fear no fall
He that is low no pride
He that is humble ever shall
Have God to be his guide.
I am content with what I have
Little be it or not
But God's contentment still I crave
Because He savest all.

Moreover, in conjunction, while commenting on the power of positive thinking, Walt Disney, the mega-famous California fairy tale entertainer, once stated:

Somehow I can't believe there are many heights that can't be scaled by one who knows the secret of making dreams come true. This special secret can be summarized in four C's. They are Curiosity, Confidence, Courage and Constancy; and the greatest of these is Confidence. [14]

Wherefore, it is said that "sorrow looks back, worry looks around, but faith looks up in confidence." Spiritual confidence begets physical courage, as curiosity begets constancy. These are human operational tools, sharpened duly by superhuman fate as it may. He that is down needs fear no fall! Therefore, when I dare to be powerful and confident, to use my strength in the service of my vision, then it becomes less important whether or not I am down, afraid, or capable. I believe I can fly!

Fast-forward And Stop

It is conventional wisdom that most things people want to achieve in life come out of their personal envy for other people's achievements around them. It follows, therefore, that for all the enthusiasm and positive energy involved in the human striving for success, envy is not always a bad word. If I was ambitious when I first came to the United States as a student, I have no apologies. If I was naive, no regrets. I was very envious of the achievements of people that came to America before me, and very thirsty for matching or surpassing their known and registered successes. My world was full of possibilities, and I embraced it foolhardily with zeal. I wanted all I could get in the least possible time, be it at school, work, or play.

The typical foreign student's scheme of events in our time was to graduate from college in less than four years, make the most earned income possible during and immediately after studies, and hurry back home to help manage the affairs of his/her folk. We had honest intentions; very ambitious goals! The pace was inherently fast and furious with high hopes. Envy and competition abounded; the only apparent obstacles were time and self. Most of us overcame both, graduating in record time and poised for our individual piece of the action in the workforce. But alas! it was hurry up and wait, whether orchestrated by circumstance or manipulated by design.

Within the first five years of my stay in the United States, I came to the cumulative knowledge of what it meant and still means to be black and foreign in the United States. The language, culture, character, and history of the colonial state are innately, if not consciously, adamant in the commitment to social subjugation, economic frustration, and political marginalization of the African person. The 1960's rhetoric of Black affirmation as human beings, culminating with the academic integration of the cultures with all the promises of equality of participation in the dream that was America, had proved to be nothing but a mere chasing of the wind. Both Whites and Blacks mostly believe in this dream that was America—a dedication to equality of and for all. However, as time went by, some of the falsehoods of this assertion became evident. Now, we know that democracy does not and cannot cure all that ails America, that having the same or better education does not equalize the color scale for all, and having a vote does not readily change social, economic and political systems. So at middle age, while being temporarily shut out of the affairs of our mother country, Nigeria, by circumstance, unfortunately; we sit and wait in limbo in America, by design, unfortunately. That's two strikes of "unfortunately" and one strike to go. A third and final strike-out will come when we give up the ghost and die prematurely, by fate, unfortunately.

Celebrating Diversity:

Waiting To Unwind

The testing of one's faith produces patience. (James 1:13.) I have managed to remain faithful and patient. But for how long and for what ultimate purpose? After more than twenty years of living in America, to date, my total experience continues to be pestered with many culture shocks from numerous aspects of the American social, economic, and judicial systems. When simplicity of character and the desire to be good are broken up by the prevalence of secondary desires: the desire for freedom, for power, for pleasure, for justice—the power over nature as an interpreter of the will is to a degree lost. I've become perplexed by a displacement of order, and by the recurring thoughts of what could have been but is not. Can anyone of my type get justice in America? At best, it's a constant struggle!

America is a world of differences—different people, different cultures, different colors; a country of strangers. Americans come in many shapes, sizes, and colors, and it is a real challenge to sum up who they (we) are. The ethnic diversity myth is that large numbers of international immigrants to the U.S. foster the perception that the nation is becoming truly diverse. Yet, an analysis of the latest population estimates from the Census Bureau shows that truly multiethnic cities and counties are few and far between. Recently, in Steven Spielberg's Amistad: The Movie, the world bows down and drools in awe at a Supreme Court of the United States' argument over the issue of property ownership of human souls. Imagine an early 19th century reality, play-acted in the eve of the 21st century with no historical surprises. And, more than one-and-a-half centuries removed from this episode of American history, it is still hard to imagine how, if at all, scars could ever form over such a wound in man's vivid imagination of past human behavior. Can time readily heal all wounds?

I came to America wired to spark, wired for success: an active brain, two busy hands, and a heart to run. But I've been "sitting in limbo", waiting to unwind! I had faith in the American system, in the common creed that education, diligence, and hardwork literally guarantees one the American dream of a comfortable place in the social order. But literally, at school, I have educated my lecturers where they were too ignorant to deduce that the system of universal knowledge is no respecter of persons; at work, I have trained my eventual supervisors where the work culture dictates that I remain the led rather than the leader; and at play, I try to chisel into the heads of the few folks within my circle of influence the very fact that this world does not begin and end in the United States of America, drunken patriotism not withstanding.

Human experiences, in general, differ in culture — the complex interweaving of attitude, concerns and views; and in history— the record of social and personal behavior. I am a product of nature, fate, history, and culture. The religious person in me tends to show a concern for character, morals and values, and to seek appropriate actions to embody these. The story of my life is history, very different from biography where acts can be deemed individual and responsible. There will be nothing scientific about my history. There's no scientific liberty of eliminating all but a very few aspects or components of the story so as to ascertain, precisely, the nature and amount of a given effect. It's all in the pot for me!

5

᚛ ᚛

THE DAWN OF EXPERIENCE

I have known trials before—accidents, problems, and war. Grief and weariness are no strangers to me. Now, I look back and see that the circumstances from which I initially cringed prove to hold the richest and sweetest lessons of life. The trials that beset me have become a benediction in disguise. It is said that adversity tests our ability to survive and prosperity our integrity. I have developed strength by testing, and attained my character and integrity by overcoming in the valley. I have weathered many storms by subscribing to the reading of Psalm 112 in the Living Bible:

> For all that fear God and trust in him are blessed beyond expression. Yes, happy is the man who delights in doing his commandments.... He himself will be wealthy and his good deeds will never be forgotten. When darkness overtakes him, light will come bursting in.... Such a man will not be overthrown by evil circumstances.... He does not fear bad news nor live in dread of what may happen. For he is settled in his mind that Jehovah will

take care of him. That is why he is not afraid but can calmly face his foes.... He shall have influence and honor.

I believe the difficulties and testings in our lives are sent by God to strengthen us in faith and to make us grow in grace. Otherwise, why would there be grace unless it is needed? Why strength unless it is required? And why would there be power unless there's victory to be won?

The Fighter in Me

"Virtue is bold and goodness never fearful." [William Shakespeare]. A person needs his/her faith to build on when going through crises, and I've got it. Much of it!

For five years I squared off against the City of Houston, the fourth largest city in the United States and growing. I faced the wrath from fighting City Hall: financial strain, desertion by friends and cohorts, closed doors. This was a fight that would leave an indelible mark on my psyche, and many mouth-fulls of bad taste of America. Nonetheless, a fight worth fighting, which has equipped me with a wealth of experience and much spiritual maturity to reprogram my priorities, philosophies and paradigms in and of life. It was a fight against blatant organized discrimination in the workplace, the effect and understanding of which can only be adequately portrayed in legalese language, since invidious discrimination is a hydra-headed monster that defies description in ordinary layman's term. See Appendix A. One can only but feel and almost touch it by delving into the courtroom drama that tends to paint its picture. It demands much patience and personal discipline to survive it. Such patience and discipline the reader must exercise to read through this chapter (with its Appendix A), which is, incidentally, a major thrust of this book.

All I ever asked of the City of Houston Department of Planning and Development is to do the right thing and level the playing field for all its employees to compete equally for promotions in their respective àreas of employment. I never asked for special treatment. I was very qualified in my field, competent, proven, and enthusiastic. But all that changed in the summer of 1989, in the barely two years of my employment as a planner with the city. I was passed over for promotion in the most blatant manner, and I was bold enough to complain. It was obvious that the Department professed one policy but acted another. The color of employees' skin mattered very much in the selection of candidates for promotion. The stage was set and I was destined to learn that lesson in the most traumatic manner.

I played by the internal grievance complaint rules and followed all the available steps of that process. At the Step II level, I tasted the first dose of reality when the then-Acting Director of the Department of Planning and Development, Mr. J. Hal Caton, in his letter responding to my Step II complaint, and under the advice of the City Legal Department, maliciously attacked my credentials instead of responding to the relevant issue of my complaint. In that Step II complaint, I had only asked to be told the reason for my non-selection, since I was much more qualified than the white employee who got the promotion.

With a heavy heart of disappointment at the judgment of Mr. Caton, I wrote him the following response and proceeded to the next step, Step III, of the process:

Dear Mr. Caton:

I reject your response to Step II of my grievance because, like the response to Step I, it failed to provide me with the specifics of the criteria used in the job evaluation for the promotion of Mr. Kramer. It did not state the specific recommendation that you claimed was tendered by Ms. Sukup and Ms. Gafrick. Conclusions and recommendations of your response were not based on actual evaluation of my job performance, but rather, on innate and non-factual presumption of need by reason of my place of origin. The comparison of my education and experience with that of Mr. Kramer is non-parallel and arbitrary. Your response is inadequate, unobjective and biased. Your attack on my memo is unreasonable and malicious. It is the first time anybody has raised the slightest doubt about my writing ability. No average educated person should have any problem understanding my memo, in the context of its purpose and audience. Records will always indicate that I am very well rounded in education, with outstanding ability in written English. In 1978 when the University of Houston required a score of 450 in TOEFL (Test of English as a Foreign Language) for its admission of foreign students, I scored 610. Ask any of my past professors at the University of Houston School of Architecture and Texas Southern University graduate school of planning, you will receive a profile of one of their most outstanding students of all time. Moreover, a close look at the Sector 2, Draft Sector Plan for Sharpstown, Fondren/Southwest will show that it was not written by a person who "lacks communication and organizational skills". There are also written comments about me by certain people I have worked with. I remain proud of my records.

The offer and, subsequently, the recommendation for me to take courses in oral and written communication is a good gesture but for the wrong reason. As much as I always strive for professional excellence through continued education, I don't see the need and relationship of taking those courses to the facts of my grievance. In fact, Mr. Settle did not find any need for me to take the courses because he never responded to my application for funds to take a similar course, on my own time, few months earlier. It is quite obvious that the issues of organizational and written communication skills is an afterthought, as Mr. Settle struggled to find an excuse for his biased and erroneous decision to promote Mr. Kramer over me. These issues never came up during the job interview, and surely, Mr. Kramer was not evaluated for them.

Mr. Settle should admit total reliance on the opinions he received about me from Ms. Sukup. He had admitted lack of adequate personal knowledge about me. He had not consulted the people I have worked with, and had failed to consider evidence of my written report and past job performance review (JPR). Since Mr. Settle's appointment as Manager of Long Range Planning division, there have not been much structured planning activity by the division. This brings to question not only the basis he claims for his management decisions, but also the total planning experience of Mr. Kramer, since Mr. Kramer's only planning experience is the eight months, to date, he has been employed in the division.

Ms. Marina Sukup has personal vendetta against me. She had promised me that: "This is not going to work!" Now I see what she meant!

The statement in quotation was used when I rearranged the partitions in our offices because, as ordered by Ms. Sukup, the set-up posed a firetrap and was an example of bad space planning. I also suggested that people should not be treated as pieces of office furniture but rather, should be consulted on matters that affect their safety and welfare. I recommended that the only way to proceed with effective comprehensive planning should be by group effort, rather than separatism and dictatorship.

During the time of acting directorship of Mr. Mike Marcotte, I championed a group appeal to Mr. Marcotte by planners in the Comprehensive Planning division. The issue was salary inequalities within the Department. We got a positive result from Mr. Marcotte and Ms. Sukup didn't like that.

On certain occasion, I had stated to Ms. Patti Knudson, former Director of the Department of Planning and Development, that the deliberate dismantling of the Comprehensive Planning Division was a mistake and a show of ignorance. I had also pointed out to her that City guidelines were not being followed in filling the open positions in the department.

The latter was in the event of the importation of Ms. Margaret Wallace by Ms. Sukup into a Planner III position in the Long Range Planning Division of the Department of Planning and Development without due process of posting and interviewing other interested candidates for that position. Ms. Wallace was an Administrative Assistant in the Department of Housing and Community Development. She is now a Senior Planner in the Long-Range Planning Division. To the best of my knowledge, Ms. Wallace had no previous experience in Comprehensive Planning.

Ms. Sukup stated that the only reason for changing the name of Comprehensive Planning Division to Long-Range Planning Division was to "remove themselves from the failures of the past group of Planners in the division." A group of five (5) minority Planners. The only five people who stayed through the economic bad times in the Department, against many odds. However, the Department continues to take credit for the marvelous achievements of the same group who produced four (4) Draft Sector Plans, notwithstanding the limited resources available to us during the process. Evidence of such credit can be found in Department's fiscal year 1990 budget.

Of the two of us who have resolved and are determined to remain in the division, Carlos Zapata has been constructively demoted and passed over for promotion; I have been ostracized and denied promotional opportunities. No doubt we both possessed what Ms. Sukup wanted for other people of her favorite.

Yes, I have not been timid in expressing my opinions. I am also not afraid to challenge the statusquo, in the most civilized manner, if it needs changing to accommodate the interests of the common people.

Frankly, I can begin to understand why Ms. Sukup would do what she has done to me, nonetheless, but I cannot figure out what is in it for Mr. Settle. If and when we must continue with the function of developing a long-range plan for the City of Houston, Mr. Settle will definitely need the experience and dedication of both Mr. Zapata and myself. I can assure him of my unconditional cooperation. However, I will continue to demand fairness and justice. I will continue to pursue my full rights under the constitution of the United States of America of which I am a bonafide citizen.

It is my sincere hope that somebody would care enough about the reputation of the Department of Planning and Development—in due consideration of the public interest of the citizens of Houston—and decide to honestly address real issues and seek real solutions. Continuing to play games with human mind is very sinful and very unprofessional.

Sincerely,

Benneth E. Okpala

As mentioned in my above letter, prior to my special problems, it had become necessary for some of us, the minority professionals in the planning department, to get together and brainstorm on how to begin to address our collective plight in the department.

In March 1991, as leadership of the department changed once again, we got together and wrote to the new Director, Donna H. Kristaponnis, to welcome her and to express our concern up front. The text of that inter-office memo is reprinted below:

To: Donna M. Kristaponis, Director
Planning and Development
From: Concerned staff members

Date: March 8, 1991
Subject: Staff Concerns

We would like to take this opportunity to extend our heart felt welcome to you. Collectively and individually, we look forward to working under your direction and leadership.

With this in mind, we feel it is imperative to bring to your attention some of our collective concerns:

1. In the past, we have often felt disenfranchised and deliberately disallowed the opportunity to be an active and productive part of this Department. However, as professionals, we are not only interested in contributing to the planning effort, but are also very eager for the opportunity to continue to grow and develop professionally, and thereby enhance our contributions.

2. Despite our continued efforts to be an active and productive part of this Department, we have both collectively and individually been too often ignored and underutilized. We only ask to be given the opportunity to be a legitimate part of the decision-making process; and for our professional efforts to be duly acknowledged and compensated.

3. At numerous times we have been victims of, and witnesses to, inappropriate and unfair practices in regards to salaries and promotions. We only ask that the "equal opportunity" clause of the City's employment policy be adhered to in the future.

We collectively represent more than seventy-five years of professional planning experience; more than sixty-five years of service to the City of Houston. We take pride in our loyalty to this Department. Our past difficulties not withstanding, we would like to turn a new leaf with your administration and join all well meaning employees of this Department in planning for a bright future for our City and all its people.

At your convenience, we would welcome the opportunity to meet with you to further discuss these and any other issues you may have. Again, welcome to the City of Houston.

Your ardent subordinates,

Charles Mock
Carlos Zapata
Mohdudul Huq
Kevin Calfee
Christopher Fisher
Naeem Husain
Benneth Okpala
Robert Chatmon

After all the internal mechanisms of the City of Houston had failed, I turned to outside entities to seek redress for my employment problems. On June 24, 1992, I filed the first lawsuit against the City of Houston and the perpetrators of employment discrimination in the Department of Planning and Development. See Appendix A for text of my Second Amended Complaint and portions of the Pretrial Motion.

Our first test of battle was in the fighting that ensued to remove one Judge Ewing Werlein Jr. from the case for perceived conflict of interest. The said Judge was a former partner in a law firm that did extensive business with the city at the time of his partnership in that law firm. Our concern for this issue was triggered when the said Judge expressed personal concern at my filing a lawsuit against the City of Houston. He openly wondered "whether the City of Houston will ever get a break from lawsuits." He was not concerned at all about the issues of the lawsuit at the time.

Finally, Judge Werlein recused himself from the case, after much resistance, and the case was reassigned to Judge Venessa Gilmore on June 20, 1994.

After one hundred and fourteen (114) Docket entries of Complaints, Amendments to Complaints, Motions, Supplemental motions, Answers, Responses, Objections, and other related legal correspondence (see Appendix C), the Court denied Defendants' motion for Summary Judgment on Defendant's contested propositions of law and case # 92-CV-1867 proceeded to trial by judge and jury on April 19, 1995.

At jury selection or Voir Dire, I assisted my attorney in the evaluation and eventual selection of the twelve men and women who served as jurors. The City brought in a team of jury selection experts on their part.

We were a little apprehensive that the pool of prospective jurors from which the twelve jurors (seven men, five women) were selected was all white. I was particularly apprehensive of one man, out of nothing but mere unexplainable instincts. My attorney had the same gut-feeling about this man, who eventually became the Jury Foreman, but he explained to me that we had a strong case and that he believed that with good presentation of our overwhelming evidence, any person can be trusted to do justice under the system. Nonetheless, we did our best at *voir dire* and proceeded with the trial. The twelve white men and women were seated by Judge Venessa Gilmore and instructed as follows:

1. Do not mingle with nor talk to the lawyers, the witnesses, the parties, or any other person who might be connected to or affiliated with or interested in this case, except for casual greetings. All are governed under the same instructions. Therefore, you can expect that only casual greetings will be reciprocated.

2. Do not accept from nor give to any of those persons any favors, however slight, such as rides, food or refreshment.

3. Do not discuss anything about this case or even mention it to anyone whomsoever, including your spouse, nor permit anyone to mention it in your hearing until you are discharged as jurors or excused from this case. If anyone attempts to discuss the case, report such incident to me immediately.

4. Do not even discuss this case amongst yourselves until after you have heard all of the evidence, the Court's charge, the attorney's arguments, until you have been sent to the jury room to consider your verdict.

5. Do not make any investigation about the facts of this case. Occasionally, a juror will privately seek out information relative to a case on trial. Such investigation is

improper. All evidence must be presented in open court so that each side may question the witnesses and make proper objections. This avoids a trial based upon secret evidence. These rules apply to jurors the same as they apply to the parties and to me. If you know of or learn anything about this case, except from the evidence admitted during the course of this trial, you should report such information to me immediately. You have just taken an oath that you will render a verdict on the evidence submitted to you under my rulings.

6. Please do not make personal inspections, observations, investigations; nor experiments or personally view premises, scenes or articles not produced in Court. Do not allow or solicit anyone else to do these things for you.

7. Please do not tell other jurors about your own personal experiences, nor those of other persons. Do not relate any special information in regards to this case.

8. A juror may have special knowledge of matters such as business, technical, or professional matters, or he may have expert knowledge or opinion, or he may be knowledgeable of the facts of this or some other lawsuit. Please do not get involved in any such opinions and/or experiments and/or investigations. To relay to the other jurors any of this information is a violation of these instructions.

9. Do not consider, discuss nor speculate as to whether or not any party is or is not protected in whole or in part by insurance of any kind.

10. Do not seek information contained in law books, dictionaries, articles, public or private records or elsewhere, which is not admitted into evidence.

Special Issues

Upon the conclusion of all evidence, I may submit to you a written charge asking you some specific questions about the case. You will not be asked, and you should not consider, whether one party or the other party should win. Since you will need to consider all of the evidence admitted by me, it is important that you pay close attention to the evidence as it is presented. You may keep these instructions and review them as the case proceeds. A violation of these instructions should be reported to me immediately.

I testified on my own behalf for the first four days of the trial. It was not a pleasant experience at all, to say the least. At certain points during my testimony, I was overwhelmed with painful emotion and bloody tears flowed out of my person in open court. I could not have wished my ordeal at the time on my worst enemy.

Everybody on our side performed extremely well in presenting a clear case of employment discrimination and an organizational effort to cover up its tracks. We had seven (7) days of brute effort by my two Nigerian lawyers, Bartholomew Okonkwo and D. A. Chris Ekoh. They worked very hard at presenting my case and at keeping an eye on the City of Houston's lead attorney, Danita Roy Wiltz, who was caught several times trying to improperly direct and influence the testimonies of defense witnesses as they testified under cross examination. It was bizarre! So bizarre that at some point I had to position myself squarely opposite to make constant direct eye contact with this cheating attorney in order to curtail her actions. Attorney Danita Roy Wiltz was really going beyond the call of duty to WIN a discrimination case for the City of Houston. Ironically, she was the only black attorney on the City's defense team of many.

My case went to the jury in the morning of April 28, 1995. Jury deliberation was interrupted by an emergency evacuation of the Federal Courthouse in Houston by the bomb squad, for a bomb sweep following a false alarm. The tragic incident of a terrorist bombing of a similar federal building in Oklahoma City, a few days earlier, was still fresh on America's mind. The jury reassembled a few hours later and handed out a verdict that surprised everybody, including the judge and city attorneys. They had found no discrimination!

Judge Venessa Gilmore openly expressed her surprise at the jury's verdict when it was first handed over to her. As for my attorney, and me, we were beginning to lose faith in the American system of justice.

Understandably, we were not alone in our feeling of immense disappointment at the failure of the judicial system in redressing the cause of the common man. God willing, at least one of the jurors had a prick of conscience and wrote us as follows:

NANCY HAVEY
10334 Cook Road
Houston, TX 77099

May 2, 1 995

Mr. B. Okonkwo
2646 South Loop West, Suite 215
Houston, TX 77054

Dear Mr. Okonkwo:
    Last week, I was juror 5 in Mr. Okpala's suit against the City of Houston. I did want to talk with you afterwards, but I did not want to have another group discussion of the case with the other jurors.
    Please know that we had to answer the questionnaire the way we did. The questions were worded in such a way that we could not answer in favor of Mr. Okpala. And believe me, I tried every interpretation and comparison I could think of to turn the meaning of the questions around.
    It was apparent that Mr. Okpala was not treated fairly by his employers. The testimony and evidence showed this department has double standards, an abstract and unwritten communications policy, unpublished conditions and exemptions to policies; showed favoritism, and went out of their way to cover up ... probably more than we know. And yes, there was discrimination in regards to the Planner of the Day program. Unfortunately, it was not linked with the questions on the questionnaire.

I personally do not feel that justice was served. After listening to the witnesses and reviewing the testimony, I was shocked by the questionnaire. The logical side of me knows we had to answer the questions the way we did, but the rest of me felt railroaded into answering a certain way. I have spoken with an attorney who assured me that in these situations, the questionnaire wording is decided upon and accepted by both sides prior to the end of the hearing. Therefore, the situation is out of my control. If you or Mr. Okpala would like to discuss particulars of the testimony from my Juror # 5 point of view, I would be happy to visit with you. My office number is 530-6671 (the voice mail will answer, if I do not). I wish you and Mr. Okpala the best of luck in this cause and wonder if it is time to change some laws in order to protect our citizens who speak English as a second language. Being bilingual should be a benefit not a burden.

Sincerely.
(*Original signed by Nancy Harvey*)

At trial we had the City of Houston beaten, cornered and scared. But the all-white jury tripped us to a knockdown. Not long after, thank God, we were up and fighting again and were determined to fight them to a finish. We made one last attempt to persuade the presiding judge to use her good office to salvage justice. On May 12, 1995, we filed the following motion for new trial, vacation of judgment, and making of new findings and conclusions of law:

IN THE UNITED STATE DISTRICT COURT FOR
THE SOUTHERN DISTRICT OF TEXAS
HOUSTON DIVISION

BENNETH E. OKPALA §
Plaintiff, §
§ CA NO. B-92-1867

vs.   §

THE CITY   OF HOUSTON, et al.
        Defendants.   §

PLAINTIFF'S AMENDED MOTION FOR NEW TRIAL, VA-
CATION OF JUDGMENT, AND MAKING OF NEW
FINDINGS AND CONCLUSIONS OF LAW

COMES NOW BENNETH E. OKPALA, hereinafter referred to as "Plaintiff" and for cause files this motion for
a new trial, vacation of judgment, and making of new
findings and conclusions of law. Plaintiff moves this honorable Court to grant him new trial under Rule 59 and
60 of the Federal Rules of Civil Procedure.

I
BACKGROUND
A new trial may be granted to all or any of the parties
and on all or part of the issues (1) in an action in which
there has been a trial by jury, for any of the reasons for
which new trial have heretofore been granted in action at
law in the Courts of the United States; and (2) in an action tried without a jury, for any of the reasons for which
rehearing have heretofore been granted in suits in equity
in the Courts of United States. On a motion for a new
trial in an action tried without a jury, the Court may open
the Judgment if one has been entered, take additional
testimony, amend findings of fact and conclusions of law
or make new findings and conclusions, and direct the
entry of a new Judgment. Fed. R. Civ. Pro. 59
On motion and upon such terms as are just, the Court
may relieve a party or a party's legal representative from
a final judgment, order, or proceeding for the following
reasons: (1) Mistake, inadvertence, surprise, or excusable
neglect; (2) newly discovered evidence which, by due diligence, could not have been discovered in time to move
for a new trial under Rule 59(6); (3) fraud (whether here-

tofore denominated intrinsic or extrinsic) and misrepresentation. Fed. R. Civ. Pro. 60

On or about April 19, 1995, the above-styled and numbered cause was called to trial and concluded with the return of jury verdict on or about April 28, 1995. The jury answered in the negative to all the issues concerning whether or not the Plaintiff was discriminated against for promotion to Planner III positions, Senior Planner and Planner Leader positions. The jury also answered in the negative to the issue of whether or not the City of Houston retaliated against Plaintiff for filing EEOC complaints against the City of Houston. On May 3, 1995, the Court entered a final judgment on this case. New trial must be requested within ten (10) days of the entry of final judgment.

Plaintiff moves for new trial on seven major grounds:

(1) Certain jurors had bias, prejudice, and preconceptions about employment discrimination and employment hiring policies, which could not be set aside in deciding this case. These jurors failed to disclose such conflict by either withholding information or providing false information to the Court or Plaintiff during the voir dire;

(2) The jury applied an improper higher standard of burden of proof in deciding this case. This misapplication and/or misunderstanding of the law was a result of jury confusion and/or biases and prejudices;

(3) Misapplication/ and or misunderstanding of the jury instruction caused by confusion and/or biases or prejudices;

(4) Certain juror failed to disclose (during the voir dire) prior acquired experiences of knowledge of the City of Houston's manner of operations that she wrongly imported into the making of the decisions in this case;

(5) The Court was wrong to have accepted the jury's advise on the issue of Planner III positions;

(6) The judgment reached by the jury was not supported by the great weight of evidence offered, admitted

and adduced at the trial of this case; and

(7) Justice demands it.

II.
JUROR'S FAILURE TO DISCLOSE (DURING VOIR DIRE) BIAS AND PREJUDICE AGAINST EMPLOYMENT DISCRIMINATION ACTIONS

Immediately following the Court's dismissal of all parties and while we were still within the Court premises, Defense attorney, Danita Roy Wiltz engaged the jury foreman in a conversation, with hopes of learning why the jury found for her clients, the Defendants. Plaintiff attorney, Bartholomew C. Okonkwo, requested to be allowed to join the conversation, which was granted. Plaintiff, Mr. Okpala, also immediately joined the conversation unopposed. Attorney Bartholomew C. Okonkwo requested to know from the jury foreman, what other further proofs that Plaintiff failed to provide to the jury, which if he had, would have caused the jury to find for Plaintiff. The jury foreman answered and said: "We were looking for pattern of discrimination and Benneth's willingness to change." This answer prompted Mr. Okpala to ask him if "pattern of discrimination and willingness to change" was part of their jury charge, to which he did not answer.

Even more disturbing was the foreman's admission, after the fact, that he is prejudiced. He made the above statement before all the above-identified persons. He stated, "You are prejudiced" (pointing to Plaintiff's attorney, Bartholomew C. Okonkwo); "You are prejudiced" (pointing to Defense attorney, Ms. Danita Wiltz); "I am prejudiced" (pointing to himself); and "Benneth, don't tell me that you are not prejudiced!" (pointing to Plaintiff).

This clearly shows that this particular juror either withheld or provided false information during the voire dire. The Court in this case specifically asked all the potential jurors whether any of them had any prejudice against the parties involved; whether any of them had any prejudice against discrimination cases; or whether any of them had any prejudices that might affect their ability to decide this case in a fair and impartial manner. In an employment discrimination case, a juror's views on prejudice are obviously material. In fact, several potential jurors admitted to having certain prejudices and biases that would have rendered them unfit to sit as jurors in this case. The jury foreman, despite his views, failed to reveal to the court his dispositions on this highly material matter. Had this juror revealed his prejudices during the voire dire when he was asked questions related to possible bias and prejudice by this Court and the attorneys, the juror's response that he was in fact prejudiced would have provided a valid basis for a challenge for cause. See McDonugh Power Equipment, Inc v. Greenwood. 464 U.S. 548, 556; 104 S.Ct. 845, 850 (1984). The fact that this juror did not reveal such pertinent information that would have provided a valid basis for a challenge for cause prevented Plaintiff from having his case heard by a fair and impartial jury.

III.
JUROR'S FAILURE TO DISCLOSE
(DURING VOIREDIRE)
PRIOR-EXPERIENCES AND KNOWLEDGE ABOUT
DEFENDANT'S EMPLOYMENT PRACTICES

The problem of jurors withholding material information during the voire dire can be further seen by examining another juror in this case, Mrs. Nancy Havey. This juror was so concerned about the unjust decision reached in this case that she contacted this Court and requested information on how to contact Plaintiff and his attorney, which was provided to her. She was able to contact Plaintiff's attorney, Bartholomew C. Okonkwo, and expressed the feelings of having been railroaded in this case. A copy of such letter is hereby attached as

"Plaintiff's Exhibit N.T. I."

More importantly, Plaintiff's counsel, Bartholomew Okonkwo, has had the opportunity to speak with the concerned juror, Mrs. Nancy Havey. Aside from what was contained in her letter, she also informed Mr. Okonkwo that she should have disqualified herself from sitting in the jury because of her prior experiences or knowledge gained about how the City of Houston conducted its business with respect to employees. She shared the fact that she had been aware of the fact that the City of Houston plays favoritism with respect to hiring and promotional opportunities, and therefore, was inherently predisposed to believing that Mr. Okpala was a victim of favoritism, as opposed to race or national origin discrimination, and was unable to set aside such knowledge and focus on the evidence in this case. She stated that she regretted not disclosing this information, and not disqualifying herself during the voire dire of this case, especially in light of the unjust result she thought was reached in this case.

This clearly shows that this particular juror withheld information during the voire dire. In an employment discrimination case, a juror's pre-trial views or experiences with regards to the Defendant's hiring policies are obviously material. Had the juror revealed her views and experiences during the voire dire when she was asked questions related to experiences and knowledge about the Defendants employment practices by this Court, and the attorneys, this juror's response would have provided a valid basis for a challenge for cause. See McDonough Power Equipment, Inc v. Greenwood. 464 U.S. 548, 556, 104 S.Ct. 845, 850 (1984). The fact that this juror did not reveal such pertinent information that would have provided a valid basis for a challenge for cause prevented Plaintiff from having his case heard by a fair and impartial jury.

It was also interesting to learn from this juror that the jury unanimously agreed about the following points:

(a) That most of the City's witnesses were coached and not speaking the truth while on the witness stand respectively;

(b) That most of the City's witnesses were perceived as not telling the truth. In fact, she went as far as stating that some of the City's witnesses "lied" on the stand;

(c) That the City did not impress any of the jurors;

(d) That most of the City's witnesses appeared to be covering up their deeds, and that the cover up might be deeper than anyone knows;

(e) That she thought Plaintiff more than met his burden of proof.

(f) She also revealed that she was not the only juror concerned about the unjust outcome of this case.

Given the proceedings of the trial, it is Plaintiff's contention that there were various instances of confusing events and instructions that led to the type of jury confusion, which created the potential for injustice. Specifically, it is Plaintiff's contention that the jury confusion in this particular case was caused by the instructions and interrogatories to the jury; as well as the inability of some of the jurors to understand Plaintiff and his attorney during the trial proceeding and their failure to reveal this inability to the Court or the attorneys.

The juror, Nancy Havey, revealed to attorney, Bartholomew C. Okonkwo, after the trial that she had been confused about how the Planner of the Day Program related to the other evidence provided during the trial, and how she was expected to apply it in reaching a final verdict. She stated that she and some of the other jurors looked for specific instructions and questions in the jury charge on the issue of exclusion of planners with Nigerian origin from the Planner of the Day Program.

Mrs. Nancy Havey revealed to Plaintiff's attorney that the juror sitting besides her complained to her about her inability to comprehend Plaintiff and Plaintiff's attorney during the trial proceedings. In fact, this juror had to constantly ask Mrs. Havey about what was being said during the trial. Had this information been revealed to Plaintiff's attorney during the trial, as it should have been, steps could have been taken to ensure that this particular juror was in fact able to comprehend everything that was said during the trial. Instead, what we ended up with was a confused juror that was unable to fully follow one side of the proceedings (the Plaintiff's side), and therefore in almost all likelihood misunderstood the law and the facts of the case.

IV.

The existence of extensive jury confusion can further be evidenced by the revelations made by some jury members at the end of the trial.

First, the jury foreman revealed that the jury was looking for a pattern of discrimination by the Defendants, a standard that is not appropriate for a non-class action employment discrimination case. This clearly shows that at least one of the jurors failed to understand the instructions provided in the jury charge and, therefore imported his own standards and burden of proof to decide the case. Based on the revelations of the foreman after the case, it became apparent that the jury decided this case on the basis of whether all Nigerians have continually suffered discrimination by the City of Houston.

Another issue that the jurors, especially the jury foreman, focused on was Plaintiff's willingness to change. This is not a proper standard for deciding whether or not Plaintiff was discriminated against. Such consideration is only proper if the jury had found discrimination in favor of Plaintiff and was considering the issue of damages. It can be logically speculated that the jury was referring to the evidence at trial which showed that Plaintiff rejected the City of Houston's offer to take two (2) free classes as remedy for the discrimination he suffered. However, evidence was also provided that Plaintiff enrolled in a one (1)-year program with ToastMasters at his own expense.

Also, Defense witness Mr. Madan Mangal, testified that both comments contained in Plaintiff's Trial Exhibit #19 and 20 relating to the need for improvement stated in Plaintiff's job performance review, was the same exact comments made for all the planners in their job performance reviews.

The witness further testified that the comments were not intended to suggest that Plaintiff was not organized or could not communicate with the public. But instead they were made with the intent to bring about improvement. Mr. Mangal, who was a Defense witness, and had, in fact, been Plaintiff's manager for three (3) years, stated that Plaintiff was extremely qualified in every respect.

The statements made by the jury foreman that everyone is prejudiced (see above), goes to show that an improper and unattainable standard was applied to reach a decision in this case. The law does not deprive an individual the right to prevail on a suit brought under Title VII, Section 1981 and Section 1986, if it can be found that everyone of the face of this earth may, in fact, be prejudiced. The law assumes that a lot of people are prejudiced and, therefore, seeks to forbid certain types of prejudices that have the effect of denying a certain person or a class of persons the opportunity to be promoted or hired for employment purposes. The effect of using the standard—that "everyone is prejudiced"— simply means that with this jury, the Plaintiff never had a chance to use Title VII to seek the justice he deserves.

V.
CONCLUSION

All these clearly show that the jurors misunderstood and/or misapplied the law. The combination of preexisting bias, prejudices that were not revealed by the jurors during the voire dire, and confusing events and instructions created an atmosphere that caused the terrible injustice to be placed upon the Plaintiff. Given this, Plaintiff requests this court to use its subpoena powers to subpoena the jurors to determine the validity of Plaintiff's above stated allegations and contentions, and thereafter vacate the jury's decision and grant a new trial.

This Court also has a duty to reverse its part of the decision related to whether or not Plaintiff was discriminated against on the basis of race and national origin with respect to promotion to Planner III.

This Court, through the trial, witnessed the fact that Plaintiff did prove his case, met and exceeded the burden of proof required of him under the law. However, less than half way through Plaintiff's case in chief, the Court announced its decision to submit to the jury, in an advisory capacity only, the issue of whether or not Mr. Okpala was discriminated against and refused promotions with respect to Planner III positions on the basis of his race and national origin. This decision was within the exclusive jurisdiction of the Court alone, however the Court wanted and sought the advice of the jury with respect to those issues. Unfortunately, given the biases, prejudices, and/or preconceptions of the jury (none of which was revealed during the voire dire), and the confusing nature of the Court's instructions to the jury, the result was a misapplication and/or misunderstanding of the law.

If the Court allows this decision to stand, the Court will only be permitting itself to be used as an instrument of furthering injustice. The jury foreman's private standard and prejudice cannot be legalized as the law and the standard upon which Mr. Okpala's case should be decided. Also, Plaintiff refuses to believe that this Court will allow individual jurors bias and prejudices to control the outcome of any case, particularly, where such hidden prejudices, biases, and/or preconceptions have been uncovered.

Plaintiff also request the Court to reverse its decision on Planner III positions and find for Plaintiff as the evidence adduced at the trial demands. Also, the Court has an obligation to justice to grant a new trial on the Senior Planner and Lead Planner positions already tried before it. The Court has the power to do both under both Federal Rule of Procedure, Rule 59 and 60 respectively.

WHEREFORE PREMISES CONSIDERED, Plaintiff, Mr. Benneth Okpala prays this honorable court to vacate the jury's decision and grant him a new trial; also for the Court to reverse its own decision on Planner III positions and enter a finding in favor of Mr. Okpala.

Respectfully submitted,
BARTHOLOMEW & ASSOCIATES

Judge Venessa Gilmore denied our motion for new trial without explanation.

At this point we were out of steam and out of money. My attorney could not continue the fight, so I proceeded into the appeals process as a ProSe plaintiff/appellant. However, I needed to obtain the court transcripts to be able to file the appeal.

Not having close to the five thousand dollars ($5,000) quoted as the cost of purchasing the more than one thousand pages of trial transcripts, I motioned the court, requesting transcript at government expense, on the basis of indigence. That request was also denied. I scouted the Nigerian community for the money but to no avail. Finally, on November 16, 1995, I submitted an unopposed motion to dismiss the appeal because of my inability to obtain trial transcripts. The Court so ordered the appeal dismissed, thereby bringing a sad end to the first phase of my one-man fight against the giant City of Houston.

It was not easy, but I made a conscious decision to stay in my employment with the City of Houston. In my mind, I took stock of the price I've had to pay compared to the huge sacrifices made by the many heroes of the American civil rights movement, and mine didn't measure up. Moreover, through the four (4) years, to date, of my legal war against the city, there had been noticeable changes in promotional practices of the Department of Planning and Development. It has not been all in vain! Many Nigerians and other professionals belonging to minority groups had been hired and/or promoted, in an effort by the Department to cover its tracks and possibly mitigate damages in the event of a Court finding against the city. I had to continue the pressure somehow, even though it meant my being blacklisted and blackmailed. I prayed, accepted my fate, and dug in in my little office cubicle tucked away at the remotest rear section of the comprehensive planning division of the Department of Planning and Development.

As expected, beginning almost immediately after the Final Judgment Order was issued, management intensified its strangle hold on my neck, literally. There were several unwarranted reprimands and professional abuse of my person continuing from the time I filed my first lawsuit. These included open criticism and hostile statements by one Charles Fredericksen, Administration Manager, and unrealistic workload assignments by the same. There was unwarranted written counseling by Patricia Rincon Kallman, Assistant Director; and several denials of promotional opportunities by Ms Kallman, and by Mr. Miguel Garcia, Assistant Director, Neighborhood Services division— all orchestrated and/ or supported by Robert Litke, Director, Department of Planning and Development. Through all these, I continued to complain and fight off other attacks through memos, and by filing several complaints with the City's Internal Grievance Administration, the City Affirmative Action office, and the federal Equal Employment Opportunity Commission (EEOC) office. But once again, when every internal effort had failed, I was forced to file a second lawsuit, ProSe, in December of 1995. The complaint was later amended to include later incidences of denial of promotions, and job harassment. At the same time, I hired an attorney, Patrick J. Gilpin, who substituted as my attorney of record.

Mr. Gilpin's duty started with a major effort to fight off City's motion to the court for summary judgment. In the wake of Republicans' massive attack on Affirmative Action laws and programs, new rulings in courts all around the country have made it little short of automatic for new-wave Republican judges to grant summary judgment to defendants of affirmative action employment discrimination cases like the City of Houston. We filed a timely opposition to Defendant's motion for summary judgment as fully published here in Appendix B. On March 19, 1997, Judge Lee H. Rosenthal signed an Order granting Summary Judgment to the City of Houston. Yet another closed door, another justice denied. My only resort has then become to seek help from certain members of the Houston City Council who have shown personal sympathy and interest in my ordeal. Meanwhile, regardless of my superior qualifications, and at the time of this writing, I have practically remained in the same position after nine (9) years of professional employment with the City of Houston.

In The Eyes of The Judge and Jury

America has never stopped telling those who cared to listen how fair its justice system is. But one thing it has not told the world is that the system is fair to all but its black citizens and foreigners. The U.S. justice system, to put it mildly, is full of contradictions.

Black activists and community leaders have attributed the failure of the American justice system to a number of factors. Prominent among them are: the stereotyped media reports, prejudicial policing, mandatory sentencing and, not mutually exclusive, racism on the judicial benches and jury rooms.

April 19, 1995, marked American history with the worst act of terrorism in the bombing of a federal building in Oklahoma City which killed 168 people, mostly children. That act was purported to have been committed by the perpetrator(s) in retaliation for the bombing of a cult group in Waco Texas by the U.S government on the same date in 1993, which killed 87 people. April 28, 1995, was the day I experienced the wrath of the American justice system, first hand, as a foreigner.

Some say the militias are coming. Some say that they are

sleeping in their sacks. On April 19, and 28, 1995, the founding fathers of this nation of immigrants, and myself, a black immigrant from Nigeria, felt the excruciating pain of a proverbial sharp knife in the back. The wrath of an all-white jury with a deep-seated hatred of the intrusion of foreigners into their lives and social system, came down on me strongly.

The jurors in my first lawsuit had every chance to do justice but didn't. There is no doubt about the dubious interest of one man—the jury foreman—influenced or, in the words of juror #5, "railroaded" at least that one juror #5 into joining in a decision that she knew was wrong. There is also no doubt that the personal interest of one judge in keeping her politically-appointed position blinded her to the fact that a wrong message was being sent to the City of Houston that it should continue to do what it has been doing—defending the agents of persecution—which is very wrong, and needed to be corrected to accommodate the interest of the common people. This Judge even swallowed her own words and abdicated her duty to rule separately on the first part of the case, which was placed outside the reach of the jury decision by language of law. This judge managed to live with herself in failing to be persuaded to give due consideration to the exposed facts of jury error and severe prejudice and grant our motion for a new trial.

In thinking it over, anyone will have cause to wonder why the American judicial system works so well in allowing a few ill-intended people to do so much damage to other innocent people's lives. I have also pondered why it should take so much to get a governmental entity like the City of Houston to make it difficult for some unscrupulous elements of its legal and administrative staff to utilize their positions of office for inflicting irreparable damages on certain employees' emotions and quality of life. I will ever ponder why a judge and a jury of twelve could not suffer themselves to do the right thing when given the rare opportunity to do so.

That jury was blind and intentionally oblivious to a fault. The members of the jury could not see the far-reaching implications of their decision to overlook the weight of evidence and render a verdict to suit the limited interest of a racist jury foreman. They could not see beyond the urge to erroneously protect a governmental entity in all its obvious policy of disparate treatment of its employees with respect to race and national origin. They limited their collective vision to what the City of Houston, through her attorneys, wanted them to do. Through the prodding of the jury foreman, they went out of their way to create an improper, biased judgmental standard and to tailor their decision to suit this jury foreman and the City of Houston; but to the unfortunate detriment of the American judicial system they had a duty to uphold.

Attorney Bartholomew Okonkwo took it very hard. His faith in the judicial system was dashed, despite the usual professional practice of attorneys emotionally removing themselves from their clients' cases. Poor him! At *voir dire* he had enthusiastically instructed and admonished the prospective jurors as follows:

The case that is now on trial is BENNETH OKPALA V. MAYOR BOB LANIER, CITY OF HOUSTON, DEPARTMENT OF PLANNING AND DEVELOPMENT, MARINA SUKUP, CHARLES SETTLE, MARLENE GAFRICK, J. HAL CATON, DONNA H. KRISTAPONIS, BOB LITKE, PATRICIA RINCON-KALLMAN, and CHRISTINE BALLARD

This is a civil action, which will be tried before a jury. Your duty as jurors will be to decide the disputed facts. It is the duty of the judge to see that the case is tried in accordance with the rules of law.

In this case, as in all cases, the action of the judge, parties, witnesses, attorneys and jurors must be according to law. Federal law permits proof of any violation of the rules of proper jury conduct. By this, I mean that jurors and others may be called upon to testify in open court about acts of jury misconduct. I instruct you, therefore, to follow carefully all instructions you will receive while this case is on trial. If you do not obey the instructions, it may become necessary for another jury to re-try this case with all of the attendant waste of your time here, and the expense to the litigants and the taxpayers of this country for another trial.

In his later address to the Nigerian community in Houston, Mr. Okonkwo painfully lamented: "I was naive. I thought white men and women can do justice...."

There is a different kind of juror/judge myopic vision in my second lawsuit. This time it is the very professionally-manicured, biased report of Carmen Petzold, Ph.D., a psychologist hired by the City of Houston to evaluate my person. My attorney in this case had cautioned me that if I must read her report, I should do so knowing that she operates as a hired gun—a mercenary or professional prostitute—who would say anything for money under the shield of a licensed expert. I found him to be very right, considering some of the excerpts from Ms. Fetzold's report to Danita Roy Wiltz, the Assistant City Attorney.

The report started quite objectively as Ms. Petzold stated indisputable basic information about me and the profile of my credentials. In this area she could not twist the truth nor attempt to negate published information and indisputable facts. Therefore, that portion of her report reads as follows:

CARMEN PETZOLD & ASSOCIATES
Carmen Petzold, Ph.D.
Psychologist
820 Gessner, Suite 1680
Houston. Texas 77024

713-1984-9842

January 29, 1997

Danita Roy Wiltz
Assistant City Attorney
City Of Houston
Legal Department
P.O. Box 1562
Houston, Texas 77251-1562

Re: Benneth Okpala v. City of Houston, C.A. No. H-5249

Dear Mrs. Wiltz,

As was requested, a psychological evaluation was completed on the above-named individual. In addition to the five-and-a-half hours of clinical interviews completed on December 13, 1996, and on December 18, 1996. The following evaluation techniques were utilized: The Shipley Institute of Living Scale, the Minnesota Multi-Phasic Personality Inventory-II, the Sixteen Personality Factor Inventory, the FIRO-8, the Incomplete Sentences Blank, the Mooney Problem Checklist, the Diagnostic Problem Checklist, and the Biographical Data form. The following ancillary materials were also reviewed: psychological report. dated July 16, 1996 on this individual by Dr. Robert Bell; complete records of Dr. Robert Bell; complete records of Dr. Walter McCoy, the plaintiff's First Amended Original Complaint, the deposition of Mr. Okpala, dated January 6, 1997, various memorandums between the plaintiff and City of Houston personnel, a copy of a sworn affidavit from Susan Norman, dated January 22, 1997, relating to the career ladder for planner, job descriptions from the City of Houston for Planner Leader, and the work records regarding Mr. Okpala. It is my understanding that this individual has filed a lawsuit alleging discrimination, retaliation for having filed charges of discrimination, and mental anguish subsequent to those actions alleged in this civil action. The purpose of this evaluation is to provide information regarding his current mental functioning, especially as it relates to the allegations of discrimination and retaliation.

A review of Mr. Okpala's First Amended Original Complaint was accomplished. The first allegation listed is one of retaliation for the five previous EEOC charges made by Mr. Okpala and due to the previously filed lawsuit against the City Of Houston. Mr. Okpala's petition claimed that he had been denied promotion for any of ten different positions, between March, 1994 and June, 1996, including one Senior Planner position, five principal planner positions, and four administrative manager positions. Mr. Okpala also alleged that Ms. Patricia Rincon-Kallman had issued him an "... unwarranted general reprimand...(on 911/94) for alleged 'unacceptable conduct.' Mr. Okpala stated that he had suffered emotional pain, sleep loss, and mental anguish.

Mr. Okpala also complained that Ms. Rincon-Kallman treated him unfairly for his conduct at that meeting about which the reprimand was written. He also alleged that he had been unfairly assigned duties on a project on which he did not care to work when two other employees left the department. There was also an allegation of sexual harassment brought against Mr. Okpala by another employee, Ms. Cox, which Mr. Okpala characterized as both untrue and another retaliatory effort on the part of Ms. Cox's supervisor, Mrs. Rincon-Kallman.

The examiner reviewed copies of memos originating from Mr. Okpala regarding these events, and corresponding memos in response to these allegations from Ms. Rincon-Kallman, Ms. Cox, Ms. Kristanponis, and from Mr. Charles Fredericksen. City Attorney Danita Roy Wiltz provided these copies.

But then, Ms Petzold remembered that she must find something to deliver for her money. So she added these subjective statements:

> The language that Mr. Okpala utilized in his memos at times appears to be hostile, insubordinate, and even evidences paranoid thinking. For example, from his memo to Ms. Rincon-Kallman dated September 2, 1994, he states, "It does not surprise me that you would jump on any apparent excuse to build a file on me. However, I think you should first build a better mousetrap and wait until I've actually done something wrong. Believe me Patsy, I am HUMAN."
>
> It was also clearly apparent that Mr. Okpala did not recognize the authority of his superiors to decide how the

workload for the division should be distributed. In his memo to Mr. Fredericksen, Mr. Okpala stated that he did not choose to work on the project to which he had been assigned. In his response to Mr. Okpala, Mr. Fredericksen stated that he had to make these decisions regarding the manner in which the work would be distributed, that Mr. Okpala had experience in the area, that his project on utilities was less demanding, and that in comparing his workload to that of all the other planners in the department Mr. Okpala had the lightest load. Additionally, Ms. Kristaponis, Director of the Planning and Development Department in a memorandum dated August 15, 1994, detailed how each planner spent the average week during the first twenty-one weeks of 1994. Mr. Okpala worked the fewest number of hours weekly, with 7 to 12 hours spent in meetings, continuing education, or miscellaneous endeavors. The time sheets also indicated that Mr. Okpala and one other planner had worked the fewest number of weeks of overtime during the period of time in question, with one planner having worked five times as many weeks of overtime. It appears that no one had a lighter workload than Mr. Okpala did at the time in question. The memorandum also stated that Mr. Okpala had recently completed his assignment of working on the Utilities profile.

Ms Fetzold's report continued with actual observations and material interview statements, with occasional interjections of rather irrelevant, less-than-professional "expert" opinions:

A review of Mr. Okpala's January 6, 1997 deposition was completed. He appeared to be unaware of the career ladder requirements that applicants must have supervisory experience for the positions that he had applied to fill. He stated that he believed that he was being retaliated against because he had not been chosen for these positions. In response to the question regarding what evidence he had to support his claim of retaliation he made the following statement. "I have a superior education than everybody—most people that filled those positions. I have superior experience. I have a work product that has been used as a model in the whole department. I am a certified planner. I'm better qualified for those positions, I cannot see any other reason why I shouldn't get them." Mr. Okpala acknowledged that Mr. Young, Mr. Martinez, Mr. Imoisi, Mr. Barker and Ms. Goode had held senior planner positions prior to their promotions. However, he stated that he was more qualified than these individuals because he had a superior education, more years of experience, that he had managerial skills; and that from his observations of their work, his work product was better.

Mr. Okpala also testified that he believed that the verbal and subsequent written reprimand which he received from Ms. Rincon-Kallman was evidence that he was being retaliated against for his having filed five or six EEOC charges and a prior lawsuit against the City of Houston. He further testified that he believed that the reprimand was retaliatory because Ms. Rincon-Kallman "...made no effort to verify the facts." However, Mr. Okpala also stated that he had arrived twenty-eight minutes late for the scheduled meeting, and gave no explanations to anyone regarding his late arrival, nor did he remain at the end of the meeting to help clean up. Mr. Okpala also stated that he was claiming that Mr. Fredericksen had harassed him by assigning him work in which he was not interested, and by talking to other employees about his legal action against the City of Houston. Mr. Okpala stated that he accepted the assignment under duress.

Estimates of intellectual functioning place this individual in the above average range of intelligence (Wais-R equivalent = 115). At this level he should be able to take in new information and apply it to the world around him more readily than the average individual. However, given this individual's combined Associate degree in

Mathematics and Physics, Bachelors' degree in Architecture, his Master's degree in Planning, and his two years of law school, it is likely that this current assessment is an underestimate of his innate intellectual abilities. Individuals who are bilingual, as Mr. Okpala often tend to score slightly lower on standardized tests. It is also possible that the presence of some negative internal emotional state, such as depression or anxiety, artificially depressed this individual's performance. This finding could indicate that he may have experienced lower grades in all of his academic endeavors. It is quite probable that the more demanding the academic work is, the more advanced he became in his graduate studies, the more pronounced these difficulties with test-taking would become. These problems with test-taking could easily have become overwhelming in law school, as it is generally considered to be quite demanding, difficult, and challenging for those individuals who speak English as their first language to advance. This factor alone could have been depressing, stress producing, and anxiety provoking.

Objective tests designed to assess an individual's current mental status were also administered. The results were considered to be valid. It appears that this individual approached the test in a straightforward fashion, neither minimizing nor exaggerating any symptomology. The responses appear to be realistically truthful, and are likely to reflect his current mental status. Additionally, emotional maturity, and positive self-image are often seen in individuals who score in a like manner.

Mr. Okpala wrote that he had additional problems, to those noted, including withdrawal, needing to reach inside for strength and consolation. He also noted that he felt angry " ..., that I have to live out of character and many people walk away with wrong impression of myself." He noted that he had lost faith in the system and his profession, had acquired disrespect for persons in authority, especially female; that he felt inadequate and defeated, and had unending "Why me?" questions. Mr.

Okpala also wrote that he was "...afraid of my acquired ability to hate and see things in Black and White; constantly fighting the thing I have become." When asked to write a brief summary of what he considered to be his chief problem, he responded as follows: "Total obsession with the determination to make a change, and the attendant frustration at the slow pace of justice. Feeling of anger."

This individual was also given the opportunity to complete a second problem checklist. He endorsed items consistent with those endorsed by individuals suffering from depression, and anxiety. The last section of this checklist was specifically designed for those individuals who would have experienced a significant trauma, abuse, or had been the victim of a crime. The instructions for this section were as follows, "If you have experienced a trauma, abuse, or been the victim of a crime, do you have any of the following symptoms?" Mr. Okpala specifically stated that the symptoms, which he endorsed, were not due to his war experiences, despite these instructions. He stated that these symptoms were due to his experiences with his current employment, and his pending litigation. These symptoms specifically included intrusive symptoms, (distressing recollections, dreams, and flashbacks, feeling as if the event were reoccurring, intense psychological distress at exposure to events that resemble the traumatic event) avoidance or numbing symptoms, (efforts to avoid thought/feelings, detachment, no sense of future) and increased arousal symptoms (outbursts of anger, and hyper-vigilance). Although these symptoms are typically associated with post traumatic stress disorder, the primary features of such a disorder were not present in this individual's descriptions of his experiences at the City of Houston. The criterion for Posttraumatic Stress Disorder are as follows, an individual must have been exposed to a traumatic event of an extreme nature (i.e. life-threatening), in which both the following were present: the person experienced, witnessed, or was confronted with an event that involved actual or threatened death or serious injury, or a threat to the physical integrity of self or others, and the person's response involved intense fear, helplessness or horror. According to the criteria, despite the endorsement of the other symptoms, Mr. Okpala does not meet the criterion for a Posttraumatic Stress Disorder. The more appropriate diagnosis would be an Adjustment disorder wherein that pattern of symptoms occurs in response to a situation that is not life-threatening.

Responses by this individual to a projective assessment technique underscored statements which he had made during the clinical interviews regarding his disappointment in his circumstance was also apparent from some of his responses that he had always perceived of himself, and thought that other people perceived of him, as outstanding. Some examples of his sentence completion items are as follows. "In school... *I was always among the best.*" Also, at home ... *I am acknowledged and respected.*" "When I was a child..., *I was the envy of the town...*" "*I am at my best when challenged....*" There are reflections of this individual's self-determination and desire to make a difference in the world: "The best.... *thing in life is self-actualization..*" "The future.... *is what we make it....*" What pains me .. *is that very few people choose to show concern*" This place ...*can be made better for all.* These statements are contrasted with others which inculcate that he suffers internally most of the time, that he sometimes feels overwhelmed by his thoughts; that he needs all the help that he can get, and that he is annoyed by people taking him for granted. He also responded, "I feel... *trapped in the system.*" Two other responses were noteworthy. "My greatest fear ... *is dying without offspring.*" My greatest worry is ... *for my people back home.*

In summarizing her report, Ms Petzold took more than five pages to render what amounts to a legal argument on behalf of her employer, the City of Houston. She completely forgot that she was only hired to render a professional psychologist's opinion on a subject individual, not a closing argument to a jury or judge. She opted to become the psychologist, lawyer, jury, and judge for the money. So she addresses me strictly as "the Plaintiff" and wrote as her SUMMARY:

It appears that this forty-four-year old Black man of Nigerian descent and, at least, above average intelligence is suffering from a significant degree of emotional disturbance, including both depressive and anxious features. Both the test results and the clinical interview suggest that Mr. Okpala suffers a much wider range of symptoms, including paranoia, cognitive difficulties, relationship difficulties, sleep disturbance, and hypomanic episodes. However, the majority of his psychological symptoms would be consistent with a diagnosis of Posttraumatic Stress disorder, with the exception of the alleged stressor, failure to be promoted, retaliation, and harassment, which would not be considered life-threatening. As has been previously stated, the diagnosis of Posttraumatic Stress Disorder is only made when the individual is exposed to an extreme, usually life-threatening event. This raises the question of the etiology of these symptoms due to such a stressful event, and whether it was a premorbid event or if the symptoms resulted from a predisposition towards the development of these symptoms due to personality structure or life experiences.

In reviewing all the materials provided in this case, it appears that misperception by the Plaintiff (emphasis added) is a critical element. He appears to expect to have others treat him as special, and to expect that he does not have to follow the same rules and guidelines as others, regardless of ethnicity, or national origin. This finding is apparent in the test results. In Mr. Okpala's statements about himself, in his memos, and in his deposition. He perceives of himself, as he stated, as being better educated, qualified, and having a superior work product to that of the other individuals chosen for promotion. He fails to even ask what he could do to improve his chances of advancement, including even applying for any new positions. Therefore, his failure to be promoted must be, in his mind, due to unfair treatment. One of the difficulties for Mr. Okpala is that he is not out of touch with reality to assume that he is an exceptional individual. Very few individuals world-wide have overcome the obstacles which confronted him not just to survive, but also to achieve his educational status. He is admittedly the only one in his large family to have done so. Even beyond his educational achievements, compared to his beginnings as the son of a farmer, his achievements as the executive president of two large Nigerian cultural organizations are noteworthy. Additionally, his success in having a professor removed from the Architecture department and the University of Houston, while he was an undergraduate student, made him, as he said, a celebrity at graduation. It is also important to note that although the end result of that process seemed to validate Mr. Okpala's claims, the process commenced because he failed to follow the rules required of the Architecture Department. The Plaintiff (emphasis added) perceives that he was validated in being able to break the rules. More than that, he failed to see why he should be "punished for challenging myself?" He did report that the fact that he was helping those other foreign students who were not being given adequate opportunities to advance due to alleged problems with communication. This event appears to be both pivotal and characteristic for Mr. Okpala. He definitely perceives of himself as a type of Don Quixote, a champion of "those spirits who will come after me." This event also seems to have solidified for him the perception that the rules are not for him to have to obey. This individual's history of studying while working at his position as security guard is another example of breaking rules.

There is another component of Mr. Okpala's difficulties with perception related to feeling that he has suffered harassment, discrimination, and retaliation. In another sense, his assertion that he only needed four hours of sleep nightly, is also "breaking the rules." It also suggests another explanation for Mr. Okpala's misperceptions that he suffers from hypomanic episodes. The symptoms consistent with this diagnosis are include a distinct period of persistent irritable mood, lasting at least four days, inflated self-esteem, or grandiosity, a decreased need for sleep, a subjective experience of thoughts racing, increased sociability, and distractibility. This change in functioning should be observable to others, which Mr. Okpala has stated is true, and it has not been severe enough to cause marked impairment in social/occupational functioning. Although it could be argued that the level of impairment has interfered with the plaintiff's work performance, this criterion is used to distinguish hypomanic episodes from manic episodes. These symptoms are not consistent with Posttraumatic Stress Disorder. This Mr. Okpala's stated history would suggest these hypomanic episodes have been in existence for him at least since he was an undergraduate student. There are numerous examples of his inflated self-esteem, despite his very real assets. His listing his virtues on his resume, his stated superiority, his comparing himself to Martin Luther King, and his obsession with bringing about change would be consistent with this diagnosis. Also consistent with this diagnosis is his being a full-time employee, while attending graduate school. It should be noted that frequently individuals who suffer from hypomanic episodes are able to be quite productive. However, even for a highly intelligent individual who is suffering from hypomanic episodes, being a graduate student, a full-time employee, and the executive of two large cultural organizations outside of work would seem overwhelming in time demands alone, not to mention energy and focus. Yet, Mr. Okpala maintains that he was involved in all of these endeavors simultaneously, at least until he quit law school, sometime in 1994.

Mr. Okpala does acknowledge other external causes for his emotional distress, such as his inability to "control" his family difficulties. However, he ultimately projects the blame for these other life difficulties on his reactions to the alleged unfair treatment by the City of Houston. The perception of discrimination alone could lead to emotional distress if no discrimination occurred. It is also interesting to note the parallel between the way he describes what happened to him when he returned to Nigeria, and what he perceives that is happening now. Northern, non-Igbos were given jobs whether or not they were qualified, and he believes that he is being passed over for promotion even though he believes himself to be more qualified. This perception of discrimination is maintained despite others' attempts to inform him that he must have more experience as per the career ladder to advance.

There are other stresses related to cultural factors that may affect this individual which need to be addressed or reviewed. Although Mr. Okpala is now an American citizen, fluent in English both in writing and speech, he maintains very strong cultural ties to his Nigerian homeland. It is possible that he experiences some of the stress, which often appears for those individuals who live in "both worlds." It is also possible that, despite Mr. Okpala's fluency in English and his having worked in the United States for the past twenty years, there are still slight variations in terminology which both he and the examiner assume is equivalent. For example, he reported hallucination, yet does not appear to be out of touch with reality.

Mr. Okpala perceives his emotional distress to be due to the discrimination, harassment, and retaliation, which he alleges that he has suffered. However, in this examiner's opinion, Mr. Okpala suffers from two preexisting conditions, chronic Posttraumatic Stress Disorder, and

Hypomanic episodes, which have led to a tendency for him to misperceive of the activities of others. His expectation that he is being mistreated because he has not been promoted, and has to follow the rules of the organization, has probably also contributed to his feelings of depression and anxiety. External factors, such as feeling unable to ever really live in his homeland again, stress due to trying to manage two large organizations, and feeling as though he has failed for the first time by dropping out of law school, all appear to be significant sources of stress which contribute to his emotional difficulties.

Sincerely,
Carmen Petzold, Ph.D., Psychologist

Ms Petzold reminds me of the mercenary soldiers who came to fight for Nigeria during her civil war against the now defunct Republic of Biafra. They were always of the white race and from places very far removed from Nigeria; and always without the slightest interest in the issues fundamental to the war. They flew Nigerian warplanes, and dropped bombs indiscriminately on the Biafran civilian population in markets, churches, and other public places in remote areas far away from the war fronts. They prostituted their military expertise for money and didn't care whom they killed in the process. They were "good" at what they did for a living!

If Carmen Petzold owns an ethics book in her professional practice, it definitely does not show in the text and language of her conclusions about me. It is definitely obvious, though, that she earned her wings with the City of Houston's legal department and will be returning for more mercenary work in similar cases in the future. After all, Ms Petzold is "good" in what she does for a living; and she has a very willing ally in the Assistant City Attorney, Danita Roy Wiltz. It is interesting to note that in all of Ms Petzold's lengthy "expert" opinion and conclusions about what's wrong with me in regards to recognition of authority and obedience to civil rules and regulations, she conveniently faled to mention that in my more than twenty (20) years of stay in this country I have zero record of any run in with the laws of the land. Instead, she chose to dwell on and refer to affidavits sworn to by the likes of Susan Norman and Donna Kristaponis to the effect of fictitious, non-existent rules, policies, and other tools of discrimination employed by the same people in blatantly violating the rights of minorities within the constitution of the United States, under color of their authority as agents of the City of Houston.

To reiterate, all I ever asked the City of Houston is for it to live up to its creed and act in accordance with its professed Affirmative Action policy of Equal Employment Opportunity for all its employees, irrespective of color, race, or national origin, the same policy information the city widely publishes on the notice boards of its many departments' walls. "It is beyond question that discrimination (in employment) on the basis of sex, race or national origin, or any of the other classifications protected by Title VII of the United States Constitution is an invidious practice that causes grave harm to its victims." Griggs vs Duke Power Co.; 401 US 424.

To date, it has been difficult to see administrative action, or get substantive response, from the new administration of the City of Houston. On or about October 1998, I wrote the mayor the following letter, to keep him aware of the deteriorating situation in the planning department:

Benneth E Okpala, A.I.C.P
8227 Wednesbury lane
Houston, Texas 77074

October 15, 1998

The Honorable Mayor
City of Houston
City Hall, Houston Texas
Dear Mayor Lee P. Brown:

On August 20, 1994, I appeared before the City Council to ask a poignant question on behalf of myself and my community — the Nigerian community in Houston. Councilman Michael Yarbrough responded with great emotion; Mayor Bob Lanier promised action.

Prior to, and after that appearance, I have complained repeatedly through the City Affirmative Action office, and I have gone to court twice to seek redress for tons of disparate treatment against me in the matter of denial of promotions at my place of employment with the City of Houston. The last time I checked, I had spent well over fifty thousand dollars ($50,000) of personal and borrowed money in fighting the City of Houston, which in turn, I believe, had spent at the least ten (10) times that amount defending acts of blatant discrimination by her managers, in total negation of the city's professed Affirmative Action policies.

Subsequently, I have talked to Mayor pro tem, Councilman Jew Don Boney Jr., on the continuing saga of my being blacklisted in the Department of Planning and Development with respect to promotions, and he too promised action. Meanwhile, I had to go to law school just to be able to respond to series of unwarranted attacks on my person in order to keep my near entry level position I have had for nine years.

Mr. Mayor, all is not well in the Department of Planning and Development under the directorship of Robert Litke.

Not quite one year ago, we had a recorded suicide by one of the employees, Phil Bergeron. Two weeks ago, another employee broke down in serious distress and was rushed to the emergency room in an ambulance. She too expressed the desire to die. Personally, I am barely managing to maintain sanity and have become the unofficial counselor for so many others at the brink of insanity in the planning department.

I can only do so much! I have neither the zeal nor the resources to continue to fight for my right and that of too many other minority employees like me in the planning department. Together, we wonder how much more money and effort would the City continue to invest in keeping some good people down?

Mr. Mayor, if Robert Litke, Director, and Patricia Rincon-Kallman, Assistant Director, have a godfather in City Hall that allows them to continue to do the injustices they have been doing, I would like to know. I would also like to know the content of Mr. Litke's 'blackbook' (or "shit list" as one of his assistant directors had called it), which I am sure has my name and such others as Christopher Fisher and Mohdudul Huq, to guess a few. I am inclined to say to you, Mr. Mayor, that enough is enough!

Over the years, eleven years to be exact, I have been passed over for promotion in many categories of open positions in the planning department at least forty (40) times. As I write this letter, Patricia Rincon-Kallman is filling four (4) positions of Principal Planner in the Long Range Planning division. She has just informed me, after more than six months of stalling the positions, that she intends to bypass me yet again for promotion into any of these positions. Ms. Kallman is hiring applicants from outside whom I am sure will prove to be no more qualified than myself, not to mention my hands-on experience in the very duties they will be performing in the division.

Soon, I will be forced to go to court again against the City of Houston. Very soon, I will be taking unpaid time off to appear before the City Council to ask the powers there are, one more time:

1. What is it exactly does the City of Houston claim to celebrate in cultural diversity when well-educated, hardworking foreign citizens like myself cannot secure decent jobs, or are denied the right to fair competition for promotion in their places of employment even by the city itself?

2. What is it in the Nigerians' speaking voice and/or native accent that renders us almost unilaterally unemployable, and/or unpromotable, usually for purported *"lack of organization and communication skill"*?

3. What will it REALLY take for the Nigerian commu-

nity in Houston to belong in this City's social, economic and political mainstream?

Mr. Mayor, all I ever asked and still ask the City of Houston Department of Planning and Development to do is level the playing field for all its employees to compete equally for promotions in their respective areas of employment. I have never asked, and will never ask, for special treatment. I am superbly qualified in my field, competent, proven and enthusiastic.

I urgently request a meeting with you on this very serious matter. I can be reached at work (713) 837-7834.

Sincerely,

Benneth E. Okpala

cc:
Councilmember Jew Don Boney, Jr.
Councilmember Michael Yarbrough

I have since gone back to address a session of Houston city council under Mayor Brown, the first African American mayor of the city since its founding in 1836. I implored these city managers to conduct a reality check and find that there is a new tool for on-the-job discrimination—the denial of opportunity for promotion and career advancement against foreigners—within the city of Houston employment service system. Further, I implored them to note the following about this "new kid on the block:"

What it is —
• Purported "Lack of Organization and Communication Skill";

What it means —
• Discrimination on the basis of foreign accent;

What it creates —
• Frontier area of malicious acts of invidious discrimination in the workplace;
• A blank check for people in authority to act as they please against foreigners in city employment;

- Disenfranchised and dismayed underclass population of employed foreign individuals;

What it takes to engage a solution —

- Understanding the total situation and official administrative willingness to confront the oppressors;

What can be achieved —

- A level playing ground for <u>ALL</u> Houstonians;
- A win/win celebration of <u>TRUE DIVERSITY</u> as a virtue for city-building and society growth;
- Genuine hope! The belief in self and the American Dream.

Now, let's digress a little.

Back in 1978/79 while I was in my second/third year in the school of architecture at the University of Houston, something happened that made me very apprehensive of the phrase, 'lack of communication skill.' There was obvious railroading of minority (black and foreign) students by certain professors away from their pursuit of full professional degree in architecture, and I questioned that practice. It so happened that I had gone to the Dean of the School of Architecture to address an issue, whereby my second year design professor, Mr. Allan Hirshfield, was chastising me for allegedly violating certain unwritten rules of study in the School of Architecture. This professor was angry at me for taking a new design course in the summer; for skipping class order and taking a higher design course (third year design II) before third year design I; for taking two design courses (third year design I and fourth year design I) in the same semester; and, in total, for negating his plan for me to be in his special design class in the fall semester following the summer session at issue. He had promised me that he would make sure I did not graduate from the School of Architecture.

Mr. Hirshfield was a friend and a very good professor. He had plans for me, in his own words, "to become the best architect you can be." He had wanted me to take a study trip to Italy with the rest of his "special design class" that summer, but I could not afford it. He really meant well for me but he failed to consider my opinion and priorities in the general scheme of my education in the United States—the inherent cultural urge to finish quickly and go back home for good. Things got a little nasty when Mr. Hirshfield, upon his finding out rather late into the fall semester that I was then in fourth year design class, instead of his special third year class, approached my fourth year design professor and requested that he flunked me out of the class. I was lucky. Because the class had just finished a preliminary design review by some visiting architects, and the architects had ruled my project the best in the class. Professor Vu was proud of me and did not hesitate to communicate that to professor Hirshfield as he rejected his request. Professor Vu also informed me of Mr. Hirshfield's approach to him and urged me to work even harder. Like me, he did not see why I should be punished for pushing the limits and challenging myself to achieve more.

The situation with my third year design-I class was different. Mr. Hirshfield was the coordinating professor for all third year design classes. I had registered for third year design-I the same time I was taking fourth year design-I, allegedly in violation of an unwritten rule. Back during the summer, while Mr. Hirshfield was in Italy, I had registered for, taken and passed third year design-II with a grade of A-minus, which was a major score in any architectural design class. But he simply asked my third year design-I professor to ignore me in class and not grade my work in the end.

Architectural design evaluation is subjective. The design student must rely on constant and progressive critiquing of his/her work by the instructor to successfully complete a design course or project. The absence of this vital student/instructor working relationship only means that the student is doomed at the end of the semester when the instructor would simply rule his/her project "not satisfactory" without further explanation. A failing grade in third year design meant that a student could not proceed to fourth year architectural study, and, therefore, must settle for a Bachelor of Science degree in architecture, instead of the desired Bachelor of Architecture degree that qualifies the individual to register and practice as a professional architect. It so happened that too many minority students were falling victim to this glass ceiling effect in the school of architecture, and until my situation developed, I had wondered why many Nigerian students before me did not 'choose' to pursue full professional degrees in architecture.

I took my case to the Dean of the School of Architecture who advised me in writing, upon my insistence that it be in writing, that any grade I made in my fourth year design-I class would be applied to the third year design-I class. It was a good deal enough to satisfy me, because I was doing very well in my fourth year design class and was almost sure to make an "A" grade.

But I had also developed this concern about the apparent railroading of foreign and minority architecture students out of professional degree program. I had followed through and collected some two dozen signatures from such students attesting to the existence of the alleged railroading practice amounting to discrimination. So, I put the question to the Dean asking why it was that many minority/foreign students didn't make it through third year, and his answer startled me. The Dean had responded that "most foreign students don't make it through third year design because they lack communication skill;" and upon my further questioning, he had admitted that by 'lack of communication skill' he meant lack of ability to communicate effectively in English language. I was shocked into immediate action.

I immediately challenged the Dean that he should set an English language test. I would invite every Nigerian student in the school of architecture to take the test, along with himself and me. I bet him that if he should beat me in the test, or any of the invited Nigerian students, I would drop out of the school of architecture forthwith. Of course, the Dean didn't take me up on my challenge but he got the message. Communication is a two-way process and both sides must be willing to engage in the act of communicating. The problem of the Nigerian students was not that they lacked the skill to communicate with the instructors, but rather, the problem was that the instructors lacked the willingness to communicate with the foreign students, whether by design or by default. Mr. Hirshfield lost his job with the University of Houston School of architecture over this matter. Sad but good, because beginning that fall semester of 1979, many foreign and minority students started to make it through third year design classes and to graduate with professional degrees in architecture.

Oppression doesn't destroy people, but acceptance of oppression destroys any person. I refuse to brand myself a "victim" and rest at that, because that would mean a willingness to die a spiritual death on my part, and a declaration of ultimate victory on the part of the City of Houston et al. God forbid!

6

ANATOMY OF MY TEARS

sk the animals, and they will teach you; the birds of the air, and they will tell you. The animals, the birds, and all life declare the goodness and value of all creation and nature's good intention to sustain them all. Yet it is predicted that by the year 2030, one quarter of all known species on earth will be extinct. As a culture, we seem no longer to see or value what lies beyond our immediate concerns. We seem to have stopped caring. We are dying. Our opaque windows of civilization and self-serving interests have put our generation at risk of spiritual extinction.

When Men Cry

They say real men don't cry. And it's also said that real men don't eat quiche — a [French] dish consisting of unsweetened custard baked in a pastry shell, often with other ingredients, such as vegetables and seafood. I've cried some cries: some good, some bad. I enjoy a dish of quiche; and I am a real man — mind, body, and soul!

Real men cry from the heart. In that depth, tears are drier than they are wet: dry, mournful tears of loss and apparent defeat; wet, joyful tears of hope and achievement. The good news is that in most human relational contexts, dry tears have therapeutic value in their cleansing of painful emotions. In such contexts and emotional depths flow deep dry tears of human resolve to effect a lasting change in the underlying conditions. Such a resolve that would make a man to say, "never again!"

First, my wet tears. You and I cried one such tear at birth to announce our manly (or womanly) entry into this living world of human experiences. It didn't matter what you and I felt or thought at that time, it was nonetheless a joyful event of hope and achievement for all the interested actors in our respective human families. With such tears we signed, on the dotted line, a contract with culture and with fate. And, therewith these tearful signatures, promising and offering ourselves up to manly or womanly roles in the dutiful propagation of our kind. It was my first tear I didn't have to understand or remember, but a manly tear nonetheless.

There are few other wet tears that dot the memory lanes of my manhood experiences. I cried some wet tears of joy, along with many other men, that fateful day in January of 1970 when we popped out of our foxholes in the ground, assured that the Nigeria/Biafra war was over and that we had actually survived it. It could be debated, but everybody who cried the same tears as I did would have agreed it was a joyful event of hope and achievement, a celebration of life, whatever it meant to us under the circumstances.

My next wet tear came as I bid my emotional good-byes to friends and family on another January morning in 1977 as I jetted off to America for further studies. Then again, we had some mixed feelings, but we all knew it was for the better. Some four years later, I cried some over my mother's sick bed, having returned home upon my hearing the news of my mother's near-death illness and her promise to hang on until she had seen me once again. This time, it was undoubtedly a joyful tear when my mother assured me she was determined not to leave me unless I bid her otherwise. I cried knowing that my mother was not going anywhere because I wouldn't let her. She made a miraculous full recovery from that illness in the three weeks I visited home in December 1981.

I have not enough fingers and toes to count all the many instances I have cried some dry tears. But, of course, I don't need to count them to remember some of the more traumatic circumstances of my deep emotional tears. All it takes is a step or two back into the suppressed private chambers of my aching soul, on the darker side of my memories of painful manly experiences. The mystery of death, though not plainly bad because it is a necessary part of the natural cycle of life, has always been a cause of my many dry tears.

But in considering the mystery of death, why is it, sadly, that when much intercourse with a friend or mentor has supplied us with a standard of excellence, and has increased our respect for the resources of God, who thus sent that real person to out-go our ideal; when that person has, moreover, become an object of thought and while his or her character retains all its unconscious effect on us; when he or she is converted in the mind into solid and sweet wisdom, it is often a sign to us that the office of this person is closing, and he/she is commonly withdrawn from our sight in a short time? The feeling of loss is always automatic and overbearing, leaving no room in the immediate for a more spiritual probe into the meaning and continuing mystery of this divine undertaking. It is a feeling not unlike that of a drowning person lost in the odd and incredulity in the silent wondering that "this is actually happening to me?"

I was deeply bonded, as a young boy, with my first cousin, Appolos Nwankwo Okpala, who provided me with "big brother" protection during my elementary school years. He took the fall for me even when he didn't have to and kept a protective vigilance over me as I ventured out into the violent world of boys. I always trusted and looked up to my strong and very versatile cousin for courage and protection.

During the Nigeria/Biafra war, while my cousin served as an army engineer, I wrote him to complain about an ordeal I had gone through at the hands of a relation of ours who was a policeman at the time. This trusted relation had lured me to the police station and tried to force me to sign a false statement which he had intended to use against my father. I was locked up for hours in a holding cell for refusing to sign the prepared statement. The bizarre event stirred up quite a scandal in our town and caused my family and me a lot of pain. My cousin, Appolos, wrote me back and promised me that "everything will be okay" when he comes back from the war. "Don't worry my brother," he wrote, "I will deal with that man when I come home, soon." But he never did! Appolos died with his officer when they inadvertently stepped on a mine. His body never came home because there was no 'body' to return. We had a symbolic burial for Appolos in 1970, immediately after the war. He was only about twenty- one years old. I had lost my mentor, my strong "big brother", and my protection.

My big uncle, Jonathan Enemibe Okpala, died in mid 1979, a little more than two years after I had left home for further studies in the United States. I was a grown man at the time, much wiser and surely mature enough to handle personal tragedies like everyone else. But my deep pain came from the fact that nobody in the family told me about my uncle's death. Instead, I was surprised to find out in late 1981 when I visited home and had hurried over to his house to pay him due homage. It was most painful to learn of my uncle's death in that manner. He was my pride and the pride of the entire Okpala family. I wept deeply and instructed my father and the rest of the Okpala family that "never again should I be kept in the dark about any future deaths in the family." In all, five deaths had occurred in the extended Okpala family at that time within a one-year period and all were kept from me. I was beginning to seriously regret my being so far away in America, so far away from the emotions of my people. My dry tears have never really stopped flowing for my great uncle.

This regrettable situation was again reinforced when I graduated from school with a bachelor of architecture degree from the University of Houston, Texas. I had done everything within my limited resources to expedite my studies, and finished my course-work within a record time of less than five years, as opposed to the recommended six years of normal course-work. In 1983, I gathered all my belongings, shipped them home, and went home for good to the envy of most of my cohorts. But it was the most painful thing that, after a proud one year of Youth Service Corp in northern Nigeria, and after the overthrow of the Nigerian civilian government once again by the Army, I had to make a very painful but rational decision to move back to the United States.

Once again, therefore, at a chilly midnight family meeting in March of 1984, I tearfully explained the situation to my family and received my marching orders. They all understood that in my position as the first son of my father, I had and still have full responsibility for the welfare of the family, and that I could not do much to meet this responsibility under the precarious political and economic circumstances in Nigeria. We all cried our dry tears—some drier than others. I had, once more, been doomed by fate to remain in emotional exile in the United States of America. Shame again to my country that this should be!

I stole two quick weeks from my 'busy' work life to go bury my father in 1992. Two weeks! I had no time to cry. Or did I? There were too many things to cry over, for an old man who wished me good-bye on my "second missionary journey" far away from home, knowing fully well that he might not have a chance to pass over the mantle of family leadership to his first son in his lifetime and, more especially, the privilege of doing so on his deathbed. There was too much to cry over lost years of father/son adult bonding; too much to "cry over spilled milk." So I sucked this cry in, for the tears ever to remain in the most private chambers of my aching adult soul. Even my dead father seems to understand!

Many more of my dry tears dot the bizarre memory landscape of my rather shocking experience of real life in America. They include those personal experiences elaborately narrated in the preceding chapter, Chapter V (with appendix), and in many more chapters of this book: the disappointments of expected results, the curse of diversity (it being the dichotomy of the black and white worlds of America), the regrets of what could have been but isn't, the many fights for the control of my soul and my destiny, and all the emotional pains that shouldn't have been— the many "Why me?" questions that have remained, and will ever remain unanswered in the sublime, most unfortunately!

Where We Live

When a community's integrity is called into question, as is the Nigerian community's integrity in America, the future of that community's culture is at stake. When our concern for integrity is rooted in the survival of the shrewdest rather than the benefit of truth and honest effort to improve everyone and society, we have become endangered. When two or more people in marriage, business, or similar interpersonal relationships are more concerned about getting the proverbial golden eggs (the personal benefits) than they are in preserving the relationship that makes them possible, they often become insensitive and inconsiderate, neglecting the little duties, kindness and courtesies so important to deep human relationship. They begin to use control levers to manipulate each other, to focus only on their own needs, to justify their own position, and constantly look for evidence to show the wrongness of the other person. The love, the trust, the richness, the softness and spontaneity begin to deteriorate. Ultimately, the goose that lays the golden eggs gets sicker day by day. Not surprisingly, most Nigerian-Americans when faced with a new politico-social equation and a new socio-economic reality, want to live it both ways. They want a sort of no-fault survivorship— to keep enjoying the far greater personal freedoms, choices, and entitlements of their dual citizenship to Nigeria and the United States, with the vastly improved American lifestyles and greater professional possibilities, while their cohorts are to revert to the more disciplined life of community service and social activism. We are, in effect, a great free people, anxious for everyone to start making sacrifices except, of course, ourselves. We have become judgmental, with hearts that loathe, detest, and despise others. We get carried away by our own importance and, instead of helping, we inflict much injury on our already wounded community of our fellows, and we seldom leave something to build on along the way.

Once upon a writing, the vice president of the Igbo People's Congress, Sir Festus Okere, put it brutally frank to the Igbo community in Houston, Texas, in his article titled *"Mind Search."* Sir Okere urged the Igbo community to conduct a mind search and find for themselves that:

> Rather than contending over who is "His Royal Highness" for the Houston Igbo community, we might do better to return to the Iron Workshop, to conceivably and honestly (honest:- upright, just, equitable, sincere, candid, unreserved, unadulterated, genuine, ...) refine and reshape (in the shadows of ancient wisdom with *ofo-na-ogu*) our understanding of the problems we face as Ndigbo, and collectively do our best in solving them.

If YOU want to destroy the Igbo People's Congress (IPC) or your smaller local organization, do the following:

- Stay away from regular meetings; or
- If you come, find fault and forget about the purpose of the organization;
- Promote your own selfish interests;
- Criticize the officers and forget that they were elected or appointed to their positions;
- Decline any nomination to office or appointment to a committee, but
- Get angry if you are not nominated or appointed, or
- After you are named to a committee, do not attend the meetings, or
- If you do come to the meetings, do not speak until after it is done, then
- Philosophize on how things should have been done;

- Do not do any organizational work if you can avoid it, but
- When the old reliables pitch in to get the work done, accuse them of being a clique;
- Oppose all new programs or ideas as being a waste of members' money, but
- When nothing new happens, complain that the officers lack imagination;
- Read your IPC newsletter only now and then; and
- Don't call IPC Hot Line number nor seek out community information, but then
- Complain that you don't know what's going on.

Sir Okere cited *The van guardian courtesy of the rotary club* and quoted Charles Kingsley to note that: "There are always two freedoms: (1) the false where a man is free to do what he likes; and (2) the true where a man is free to do what he ought." To these I concur with a quote from Ella Wheeler Wilcox: "There are always two types of people in our world — those who lift; and those who lean." The point is that we are all to search our minds to determine for ourselves in which of the two camps we choose to belong.

The Nigerian community's culture is, at best, in total shock in America, with a potential to self-destruct. In its larger context, the social attitudinal pulse rate can be taken from some of the more dramatic headlines in the few Nigerian-owned "local" newspapers in Houston. The very unfortunate among these headlines resurrect and re-emphasize ugly tribal differences imported from home which feed on dirty politics of spite, exclusion, and hate of one segment of Nigerians by the others. Such questionable headlines as *"Igboman Cannot Rule Nigeria Now"* (Houston Punch, January 1996), and *"Meet the Queen of 'Igbo' Hemp"* (Houston Punch, October 1996) strike a familiar chord in the hearts of experienced Nigerians. They open up old wounds of past experiences of marginalization of the Igbo people in the Nigerian polity, and often beg for bitter responses from the offended group.

One such response by the Igbo Peoples Congress (IPC)— the

resident umbrella organization for more than fifty (50) local Igbo organizations in the Houston area— finally led to a wise decision by the publishers of the Houston Punch newspaper to tender a due apology to the Igbo people in their *"Open Letter to IPC"* (Houston Punch, January 1997), as reprinted in full below:

For the common good, Houston Punch Management and Editorial Board members hereby apologize to the Igbo People's Congress (IPC) on the ongoing issue between the two organizations.

We concede that a Newspaper with a mission like the Houston Punch should avoid detractions in whatever way or manner.

We shall like to restate here that the Houston Punch will, among other things, remain a friend of the Igbos, and will refrain in future from using the word 'Igbo' for marijuana as a courtesy to all our friends and supporters who are from Igboland.

We also like to state that the Houston Punch shall remain a non-partisan, non-tribal and unbiased information medium to all Nigerians in particular, and Africa in general.

We shall continue to strive towards excellence with full realization that we are neither perfect nor infallible.

We concede that we can make mistakes like any other human being or human organization, but we shall want to make it clear that whatever mistakes are made, they are not deliberate nor directed against a particular group or sector of our community.

We sincerely hope that this kind gesture will be enough to end all kind of hostilities between the two 'brother" organizations.

Long live the Igbo People's Congress.

Sincerely,
Jubril Adelagun
Publisher

Accepting Mr. Adelegun's apology as the Executive president of IPC, I acknowledged that the present Nigeria has image problems with drugs, crime and conduct, but also emphasized that Nigeria's image problems are neither tribal nor parochial. I further recommended that we, Nigerians all over the world, must own up to our responsibility and start dealing with our problems collectively. Prior in a related article, *"Gone are the Days of the Jackal"* (Houston Punch, November 1996), the same publisher had rightly, though sarcastically, opined that:

> .... For those still living in the prehistoric years of the politics of hate, tribalism and nepotism, I say come on board to a new world of harmonious co-existence and cooperation; of team spirit and of unity in diversity. I say it is time for all Nigerians to rise above ethnicity, tribalism and nepotism. It is time for us to downplay the politics of division and rancor. It is time to condemn the enemy of merit.
>
> For those among us that have risen above the ills of tribalism, ethnicity and petty jealousies, I say a big congratulations!. You are the chosen ones, the leaders of tomorrow, the Moses of our time, the captains of our ship to the Promised Land.
>
> Gone are the days of the jackal.

I ignored the apparent sacarstic intentions of the Punch publisher and said, "Amen!" to his well-meaning proposal.

Nonetheless, the politics of hate is not at all prehistoric in Nigeria. As late as 1992, two former Nigerian Heads of State — General Yakubu Gowon and General Obasanjo (now an elected civilian president of Nigeria) — turned an occasion of the launching of an august book chronicling the 129 years of the Nigerian Army into a harbinger of ferocious insult and assault to the living and dead heroes of the Nigerian struggle who are of the Igbo extraction. *"Gowon Hates Nzeogwu/Ojukwu"* was the caption of a special article published in the CITY NEWS, July 24, 1992. Regrettably in this article, the two former Heads of state who are of Hausa (Gowon) and Yoruba (Obasanjo) extraction respectively, and both major players in the history-making Nigeria/Biafra war, took it upon themselves to decide who deserves honor in the Nigerian history and who does not. According to this article, General Gowon did not hide his feelings and told the august gathering bluntly that:

Historically, we do acknowledge their (Nzeogwu and Ojukwu) role in our history. But they should not be given a pride of place as was given to them in the book written by the army.... My contention is that we went to war to keep Nigeria one, and to us, there never was a Biafra and, therefore, we cannot talk of the leader of the rebellion as Head of State of Biafra (1967 - 1970). I will be very angry if such people are given prominence in future.

But an analyst who spoke to CITY NEWS reminded the ranting generals that the history of Nigeria can never be complete without devoting a considerable space to the crises of 1966, the secession of Eastern Nigeria, and the resultant civil war. To this, another major player in the civil war, Brigadier Benjamin Adekunle, added:

I have said it before and I will repeat it. They (Gowon and Obasanjo) addressed personalities rather than issues. Biafra existed, that was why we fought the war to re-unite Nigeria. I think we have to discuss issues and not personalities. After all, the war was not between Gowon and Ojukwu, but Nigeria and Biafra.

CITY NEWS had commented that the high point of the raving controversy were Obasanjo's aspersions on Nzeogwu, the same man he (Obasanjo) described in his book, "Nzeogwu", as follows:

Chukwuma was a kind-hearted, open and generous man, who believed that there should be no dividing line on any basis between Nigerians in one part of the country and those in other parts. His birth and up bringing in

Kaduna— a town that was a microcosm of Nigeria in the thirties, forties and fifties— had principally conditioned his broad and detribalized Nigerian outlook. Chukwuma was politically aware but he was not what I would call a political activist. He was both a Nigerian and a Pan-Africanist.

Chukwuma had a dream of a great Nigeria that is a force to reckon with in the world; not through ineffective political rhetoric but through purposeful and effective actions. He had a dream of an orderly nation through a disciplined society. He also dreamt of a country where national interests override self, sectional or tribal interests. He wanted a country where a person's ability, output, merit and productivity would determine his social and economic progress, rather than political and ethnic considerations.

He had a dream of a country free of graft and greed. He believed in virtues and values other than mere acquisition, glorification and adulation of material wealth. He dreamt of a nation where social justice and the economic interest of its citizens will not be subjugated to foreign control and manipulation. He believed in the ability of the Blackman.

He had a dream of a country where everybody is everybody else's keeper, irrespective of language, tribe, or religion. He lived for thirty years, the last two of which he spent trying to achieve his dream for the country of his birth and the country he loved. He failed in the realization of this dream and became a victim of the dream. But he left a permanent imprint on the country, as well as lessons for all Nigerian citizens.

It is reported that soon after the book was launched, it elicited criticism in the north. Copies of the book were publicly burnt at Ahmadu Bello University, Zaria, in protest of the praise accorded to Lieutenant Colonel Chukwuma Nzeogwu, a revolutionist whose January 1966 putsch led to the assassination of the Sarduana of Sokoto, Sir, Ahmadu Bello. The primary motives of both Chukwuma Nzeogwu and Chukwuemeka Odumegwu Ojukwu were generally to rid Nigeria of the corrupt politicians and the feudalistic incubus represented by the Sarduana of Sokoto. CITY NEWS observed that the controversy generated by the book launch reawakened sentiments among the many ethnic groups in Nigeria. The Igbos whose kinsmen were mainly the target of attack now question the Nigerian government's "administration" of the nation's history. The Igbos would want to understand why succeeding governments pay tribute to late General Murtala Mohammed, annually, while late Major General Aguiyi-Ironsi who saved the nation from total collapse in 1966, before he was cut down by northern mutineers led by Gowon himself, has never been equally immortalized.

Nigeria seems to conveniently design its history through a policy of selective amnesia. An historical occasion of a combined political visit of the then chairmen of four Nigerian political parties to Houston in January 1997 presented a situation that underscored the point of a "Nigerian history by design". People say the mere assembly of the chairmen of four competing Nigerian national political parties made history on January 10, 1997. At the time, they gathered under the common theme of inclusive determination of Nigeria's future. I agree!

History is a matter of unplanned accumulation of records of remarkable experiences, successes and tribulations alike. History is made when, whether by design or default, a remarkable event is registered indelibly in human lives in the context of human culture and/or human social organization. It is very difficult to influence history and quite impossible to erase it. This is so, simply because the depository of the registered experiences of human life lie in the bedrock of human soul and human spirit which live in perpetuity. The Biafran experience is no different in the context of Nigerian history.

Remarkably, the response by one of the visiting political party chairmen to a policy-issue question about the so-called 'kwashiorkor children' (children afflicted with severe protein deficiency disease caused by malnutrition) of the Nigeria/Biafra war raised some more concern about the effort of Nigeria to artificially design her own history. Wherefore to the question: ... *If you win, what will be your government's policy on the matter of the thousands of Kwashiorkor children shipped away to Gabon and Ivory Coast at the tail end of the Nigerian civil war?*... the responding chairman of the Democratic Party of Nigeria (DPN) preached a sermon characterizing my above question as "divisive", "retrogressive", and all the rest of his very negative connotations.

But the call and thrust of my question to our august guests was really to put the five competing Nigerian political parties at the time on notice, that whichever one or a combination of them that constitutes the next civilian government of Nigeria should remember and never forget that the memories of the conveniently-forgotten kwashiorkor children of the Nigerian civil war are still fresh in the depths of the wondering minds of their relations, presently through limited efforts of the Houston Igbo People's Congress (IPC) and the World Igbo Congress (WIC). The standing request is that the next civilian democratic government of Nigeria should conduct a search-and-recover diplomatic mission into the countries concerned, for the sake of those Nigerians living in unplanned, undeserved exile.

This party chairman preached with impunity that "It has been too long a time ago, and Nigeria must forget the events and lingering outcomes of the Nigeria/Biafra war and move forward." This "loyal Nigerian" forgot that time has no effect on history, but is only a part of it. That it is not, and cannot be, acceptable for the great country of Nigeria to pick and choose which part of its history it must forget in order to "move forward." He forgot that a government policy of selective amnesia does not augur well for any country, including Nigeria. History cannot be swept under the carpet! The unfortunate statements of the DPN party chairman are laden with naked ironies. For a group of four political leaders preaching a common gospel of inclusiveness, sacrifice, and continuity, the dismissal of this important policy-question about the lost Nigerian children (now young adults) of war as divisive and backward-looking, is ironic at best. Divisive? Can Nigeria draw a parallel in history and tell the Jews that any question about the victims of Jewish Holocaust is divisive? Or, say that to the American people about the dead bones of the MIAs in South Korea.

A greater irony, of course, is that we are not talking dead bones here, but rather, living adult souls and wandering spirits of the most innocent victims of Nigerian history. Suffice it to say, generally, that it is a common mission of the IPC/WIC organization, on behalf of Igbos of Eastern Nigeria; the ODUDUWA organization, on behalf of the Yorubas of Western Nigeria; and the ZUMUTA organization, on behalf of the Hausas and Fulanis of Northern Nigeria, to strive and persuade the present government or any future government, of Nigeria to hearken to the voice of reason and world opinion.

IPC's mission derives from and coincides with WIC's vision for Ndi-Igbo. The mission is to create future scenarios and facilitate a community-wide process to seek consensus on matters of self-actualization and cultural posterity. The Nigerian Igbos in the Diaspora have all come of age and are laden with nostalgia. We understand not to dwell in the past to the extent that we tarnish the present and ignore the future. We want to be able to identify our collective interests, articulate and express our opinions and concerns, and direct or influence actions towards the achievement of our collective goals and objectives. We earnestly seek every bit of knowledge, every crumb of truth, that will lead us to wise actions. We seek those actions that can be leavened with wisdom of the ages and lessons of history, as well as the events of our time, such that they may rise to the fullness of our complex and perplexing needs. We are not ashamed, and must not hesitate, to ask questions, even if it embarrasses the present or any future government of Nigeria. We truly believe that honest answers to legitimate questions, and positive actions towards legitimate concerns, will benefit Nigeria rather than divide it.

The common hope of all Nigerians, home and abroad, is that any government of Nigeria would choose to act in the best interest of all Nigerians, and labor to bring Nigeria up to par with the common-sense pursuits of the 21st century world. Also, in whatever language we happen to state the foregoing purpose, respectively, and by whatever means we organize to achieve it, reality demands that, in this modern age, both the governors and the governed of Nigeria must come to grips with the complex issues of the Nigerian polity, in all its existing and emerging national and global contexts.

The fact is that Houston has become to Nigerian-Americans what the city of New York and the state of California are to Americans. Most innovative ideas of business and social organization for America's Nigerian community originate in Houston. Ideally, public forums like the one made possible on January 10, 1997, by the Houston Nigerian Foundation are desirable. So also is the opportunity thereby provided for Nigerians in the Diaspora to be part of a necessary political process. That political forum was a great opportunity made even greater by virtue of our being here in the United States of America, where both the right to freedom of speech and the rules of public conduct are written in plain English language and widely published for all to be informed. There should be no more excuses!

But then, again, in the matter of politics and history, why is the plight of Igbos in Nigeria so deplorable? Why is such a large group of people who have contributed so much to the political, social, cultural, economic, intellectual and technological development of Nigeria and its unity so hated by other ethnic groups of Nigeria?

I can only elaborate on the above questions by citing pertinent excerpts from a paper presented by Professor Mkpa, Deputy Vice Chancellor of the University of Abia State, Nigeria, at the 1997 World Igbo Conference in New York, narrating, briefly, the fundamental qualities of the Igbo person and commenting on the present plight of the Igbo in the Nigeria's politico-social agenda:

- Not long in the past, the Igbo occupied a pre-eminent position within the socio-political set-up in Nigeria. They were prominent in education, civil service, the Armed Forces; and maintained a relatively strong hold on the economy. They possessed such enviable attributes as hardwork, dynamism, courage, endurance, resourcefulness, reliability and sacredness of life, prudence and thrift. They occupied enviable positions in the decision-making process and could hardly be discounted in the socio-political equation of the country.

• The philosophy of the Igbo had been the inexorable fact that they must take their destiny into their own hands. To this end, both man and woman worked tirelessly in any venture they engaged in. In these endeavors, no challenges were considered insurmountable; no distances or linguistic barriers as obstacles in their quest for economic self-actualization. The dignity of labor was ingrained in the psyche of all and sundry with the result that no job or economic activity was perceived as demeaning, provided it quarantined the expected returns. Unlike the other ethnic groups in Nigeria, the Igbo were found in every part of the country where they carried on their legitimate businesses, and so, helped in no small measure to develop these areas where they lived.

• In the practical execution of their self-assigned economic tasks of guaranteeing for themselves improved economic fortunes, as well as developing their immediate environment, the Igbo often adopted the principle of healthy competition, which engendered the urge among peers to excel against all odds. Amidst the tempting effects of competition, the Igbo had brandished the rare but indispensable attributes of unity and solidarity among their trading or business partners, as a result of which they were known to have mastered, and productively exploited, the economic landscape of their host communities, and often with incredible rapidity and amazing precision.

• Until recently, education was not only the major industry, it was, in fact, the only viable industry that manufactured excessive amount and varieties of high, medium, and low-level manpower from various school levels. Education was the singular pride of the average Igbo family, as parents and communities would literally skin their teeth to raise funds for their children's education. All economic activities of families were targeted at providing educational opportunities for their children no matter the cost. This underlying rationale was the incontrovertible fact of the indispensability of education in economic and political empowerment of the Igbo.

• In the past, the Igbo people were a formidable power-bloc in the political calculations of the country. Not only did the Igbo evolve potent, viable, political associations, among them were found crops of highly enlightened, brilliant, and astute statesmen and politicians who made ground-breaking contributions to the development of Nigeria. They had a target, which was to do the best they could to improve the overall quality of life of the Nigerian nation through honest application of their enormous capabilities. Early European anthropologists and administrators had often remarked that the Igbo-speaking people constituted, perhaps, the largest cohesive and republican group of all sub-national groups in Nigeria.

• Regrettably, the Igbos have become an object of wide-spread hatred by the other ethnic groups of Nigeria. From the 1960s it has become clear that the admiration which the other ethnic groups had for the hardwork and dynamism of the Igbo was tinted with envy. The unfortunate civil war and its aftermath made matters worse, leading to a systematic undoing and marginalization of the Igbo by joint actions of the other two major ethnic groups of Nigeria — the Hausa and the Yoruba. The Igbo has become an endangered species, perceived and treated as a kind of lethal virus that stall the interests, ambitions and opportunities of those other ethnic groups and, thus, deserves either joint or separate strategies or programs for containment, curtailment and/or elimination. With the unfortunate civil war, the gains of the past were lost and the onward march to the destination of the Igbo socio-political and economic achievement in Nigeria was rudely truncated.

- Today, the Igbo must chart a new personal, social, cultural and political course in order to meet the challenges of their unique socio-political alignment in Nigeria. Today, the misconceived idea that the Igbo have no kings has been so misdirected that it has degenerated into political propaganda against the Igbo. This tends to negatively affect leadership in Igboland, generating hairsplitting divisions among Igbo leaders, which render them very vulnerable in the rough theatres of Federal politics.

How has the mighty fallen? When shall the bones rise again, if at all they rise?

Now, let's get back to our Nigerian community in the United States. Our adult population is stressed out, vicious, and in perpetual denial. Our family and interpersonal relationships suffer from the negative attitudes of all concerned. Experts warn that when we are dependent on a person with whom we are in conflict, both need and conflict are compounded. Love-hate overreactions, fight-or-flight tendencies, withdrawal, aggressiveness, bitterness, resentment and cold competition are some of the usual results. When these occur, we tend to fall even further back on background tendencies and habits in an effort to justify and defend our own behavior, and we attack the other person or persons. There is only phantom security in such relationships when all appears to be going well. Guidance is based on the emotion of the moment. Wisdom and power are lost in the counter-dependent negative interactions.

Some of us, or yet most of us, can still count our blessings in the land of opportunity that America is. We have chains of academic degrees, big cars, big houses, acquired titles, and dollar-inflated egos. But we also have children, Nigerian/Igbo-American children, who are grown or fast growing. We have duty, heavy duty owed to our children and to our ancestors for posterity. In our community's chaotic maze, the children are bewildered, confused, and sometimes plainly disappointed. Their plight can be seen in a writing by one sixteen-year old Chigoziri Okere, published in the USAfrica the Newspaper, April 1997. Master Okere wrote in part:

> Sometimes I wonder why I cannot speak in my parents' ethnic language, Igbo. I want to read and write Igbo. My parents and their friends always try to speak and communicate to me in Igbo language, expecting me to respond. Whenever I fail to do so, they tell me: "You should be speaking Igbo by now!"
>
> It is true that some of us may speak the language and therefore have no problem, but the majority of us do not even understand "Kedu?" (How are you?). Considering what has been stated, our parents and other elders must understand why we do not understand our native tongue.
>
> To begin with, the majority of us began school around 4 or 5 years of age. The elementary schools we attended were filled with young English-speaking kids that perhaps never heard about Nigeria. When we needed to communicate to those kids, we had no alternative to English, so English was used. This act continued throughout elementary and into the present day. For at least 8 hours a day and five days a week, we speak in English at school.
>
> Furthermore, we must acknowledge the fact that this preoccupation does not stop there. When school is over, we turn on the television, perhaps for entertainment or to watch the news. All we hear is in English.
>
> Then we try the radio; it is the same result. We read newspapers and magazines, everything is in English. We go to the movies, sports events, parks, and the library, but find that English is spoken 24 hours a day, 7 days a week. Most of us Nigerian youths may have to wait for mother or father to come home in order for us to hear our language.
>
> Our parents must realize that it is not our unwillingness, laziness, or an "I don't care attitude" that prohibits us from learning our native tongue. Language is not hereditary, but must be leaned as part of the environmental

influences of life. Our parents, perhaps, should not bombshell us with their disappointments at our not knowing our language. Rather, they should help to improve upon our reading, writing, and hearing our native language. We are willing to accept our part of the challenge with the hope that one day we shall prevail, so that our language will be preserved for the future generations.

Yet, in another quiet occasion of one Igbo family's dinner table conversation, a father preached to his family of seven (typical two parents and five siblings) on how important it really is and his personal wish that, upon his death, his body should be shipped home to Igboland to be buried with his ancestors. There was silence. Cold silence!

Then, one worried older sibling spoke up on behalf of the rest: "But Dad", he asked, "we live here in Houston, why must we be denied your grave site here in America?"

"Yeah!" chorused the rest, "Where do we go to place flowers on Memorial Day holidays? To Nigeria?" "That's not fair!" they all concluded.

That Igbo father of five was stunned, as any other farther would be. Could he have expected such reasoned challenge to his culture-driven, self-centered but honest last wish from a set of good-mannered, very loving children? Has he or any other Igbo fathers like him done enough to reasonably prepare our generation of Igbo/Nigerian-American children to consciously pay homage to this difficult but important aspect of a marriage of two cultures?

To build confidence and self-esteem of a child is to prepare a confident and fulfilled adult. A comment made by Abraham Lincoln many years ago fits in well here:

A child is a person who is going to carry out what you have started. He is going to sit where you are sitting, and when you are gone, attend to those things that you think are important. You may adopt all the policies you please, but how they are carried out eventually depends on him or her. He will assume control of your estate. The fate of your humanity is in his or her hands.

We would be remiss in our duties if we did not attempt to reach the full potential of our children. Somewhere out there lies the realization of our youths' most troubling hopes, but certainly not in the American social system. It obviously not in our progressively dysfunctional social attitude toward collective action. Individual family unit's effort is not enough; schools don't have it; and, scattered, "broomstick" sectional organizations lack the requisite broad-base strength and follow-through needed to deliver the required social base for our desperate immigrant community's youth.

Then again in the core domestic relationship arena, one Reverend Okey Muoneke took time to interview some Nigerian housewives and published a brutally frank report on the issues and problems affecting many Nigerian women [and men] in America. I have chosen, with the permission of the good Reverend, to present here, the entire report because it is germane to the basic issues of "where we live" in our Nigerian communities in the Diaspora, and it is socio-culturally educative to the non-Nigerian reader of this book.

Coming To America: Issues And Problems Affecting Migrant Nigerian Women In America.
(by Reverend Romanus Okey Muoneke, Ph.D.)

For several people all over the world, America is a land of great expectations, and so it is. Before the 1980's, there had been tidal movements to America by Nigerians who came mainly to acquire knowledge and technical skills and return to their country. They usually returned to take up appointment in highly paying jobs, and the temptation to stay back and work in America was not there. Recently, however, greedy politicians and criminals in uniform, plowing more intensely at the corridors of power, have plunged the country into an economic ruin. The orientation has now changed: what used to be an ebb-and flow movement has become a one-way traffic from the "dungeons of hell" to the "eldorado" of America. But, as many an immigrant will soon discover, coming to America many times proves to be nothing but an adventure into the world of Charles Dickens's *Great Expectations.*

Until the mid-80's, most Nigerians in the United States were students who had plans to return to their country at the end of their studies. The Nigerian economy was at that time strong enough to provide them decent jobs for a decent living. Later, as political instability and bad governance collapsed the economy and made life un-bearable, more and more Nigerians began to migrate and settle in America. Women, whose numbers had al-ways trailed behind that of men in the new Trans-Atlantic or middle passage, have since tripled their numbers. To-day, more and more women are coming to America as students, as professionals (nurses, pharmacists, doctors, etc.), and, in greater numbers, as wives. Since about 85% of the Nigerian women migration to America are marriage related, our discussion will focus on issues and problems of married women.

For many young women in Nigeria the prospect of marriage with a Nigerian resident in America is consid-ered a prized blessing. In the 70's and early 80's, the Nigerian naira was very strong in world market. When I left Nigeria in August 1981, for example, one thousand naira was exchanged for one thousand three hundred dollars; today, ninety-four thousand naira will trade with one thousand dollars (at the rate of one dollar to ninety-four naira). This means that if you change ten thousand dollars to naira, you will need a truck to carry it home. No wonder that many Nigerians here, in their periodic home visits, are stupendously extravagant. For the short period of time they stay in the country, they exhibit such flamboyant lifestyle that creates the false impression that America is a paradise where dreams are quickly realized.

The craving for the "American dream" makes Nigeri-ans gloss over what otherwise would be a thorough in-vestigation of a suitor in accord with traditional norms.

In traditional marriage, a detailed investigation of the suitor's background is carried out, requiring information about his character, health, family, marital status, education, religious persuasion, and so forth. When the American nouveau riche comes marching in with his mighty dollar and when his coming is perceived as a door opening to a golden future, all valuable considerations are put aside, and all that counts is the expensive and lavish traditional and Christian wedding ceremonies that the naira exchange from the dollar can procure. The enticement towards America is so intoxicating that any suggestion for caution based on reasonable doubt or foreseen danger is easily misinterpreted as an attempt to subvert the American dream. In the present political and economic crisis in Nigeria, the rush to escape from the dungeon drives lots of people to leap before they look.

Impersonation and pastiche behavior by the Nigerian American residents and suitors further enhance the illusion about America in gullible minds. The quantity of raw cash and gifts they send home creates false impressions of affluence, when in reality they are struggling to make ends meet. Some print cards claiming to be Ph.D. holders when they are yet laboring in schools or have even dropped out of school. Many are suspiciously reticent or vague about the nature of their employment in America, while some lie about it just to make an impression. I know a suitor who had informed his fiancée that he was a company manager. To a young lady just out of law school in Lagos, there was no way of knowing that what he managed was Circle K!, a tiny convenience store that also sells gas. There are several such impostors today who claim to have highly paying professional jobs even though they are taxi drivers, security guards, or teaching aspirants. I do not denigrate any of these pursuits, just that some who are caught up in them are not proud of what they have but lay claims to what they yet do not have, just to impress and deceive.

Many Nigerian women in pursuit of marriage come to America as victims of deceptions and thus find their dreams shattered from the onset. Once in America, they will no doubt notice, albeit with the eye of a newcomer, that the place is fabulous: good roads, undisturbed power supply, availability of telephone, and malls beaming with quality goods, most of them within their reach, especially during sales. But they will eventually notice that every heaven has its purgatory and that their lot belongs there in the American purgatory.

The first shock a woman might experience is that her man does not fulfill her basic expectations. To begin with, his character is different from what it was in the jamboree days in Nigeria. Magnanimity, ostentation, and squander now give way to thrift, miserliness, and sometimes cruelty. Now the dewy pretensions to wealth and scholarship disappear under the rays of everyday reality. Far from being fully established in life, her man is just beginning life, still groping in the dark trying to find a direction. And now fairy-tales give way to reality.

She herself might constitute a problem that will come round to haunt her. Her not being a professional (a nurse, a pharmacist, or an engineer) and her not having the ability or the willingness to become one might spell a disappointment. For him, marriage involves more than a love relationship; it includes financial and material benefits to be derived. In my field research, I interviewed groups of women and individuals, and the one issue they always raised was that these days many Nigerian men in America marry for treasure. As one woman attested, "They (men) count themselves lucky if they marry a nurse or a doctor. Where they don't, they expect that whoever they marry must get into a professional school, graduate, and begin to produce money for them." These women believe that they are now perceived as a commodity. Marriage therefore becomes not a union of two hearts but a profit-making venture.One woman observed that in the past women were accused of gold digging in marriage, but now, ironically, men are the real treasure hunters. I understand that a number of Nigerian marriages have broken down because of the woman's refusal to take to a profession dictated by the man. The one million-dollar question, of course, is why the man himself would not strive to become a professional: nurse, pharmacist, or doctor. The more disturbing revelation from the women is that some of the men quit their low paying jobs once their wives graduate with a professional degree. "Then," said a woman, "they stop working, stay at home, and wait for your salary."

A few weeks after her arrival in the U.S., just after the initial excitement begins to thaw, the woman is confronted with a number domestic problems. The need to contribute to the payments of household bills means that she will have to seek for a job. A few men who are well off prefer their wives to remain full-time housewives, but this arrangement often hits the rocks because soon a wife discovers that total dependence on the man for every dime, no matter how magnanimous he may be, is a refined form of slavery. In most cases however the men want their wives to be employed. Some women would have to wait for a long time to have the right immigration papers to qualify to work. Some who have the right papers for work may not have the type of education the job market demands. Degrees in history, religion, education, sociology, political science, etc. sell low in the American job market, but then one finds this out too late. There will therefore be a need to go back to school to retrain for the job market. Some who have all the qualifications for a job may still be frustrated as they discover that the job market could discriminate against people because of accent, color, or gender. Waiting to get a job or find a school can be stressful and does occasionally add to the friction between the newly married.

Most women who need to get a college education after they join their husbands face the dilemma of choice between education and child bearing, each being a full-time job. Many choose to combine the two, but the choice leaves them in the lurch. They find it frustrating going to school full-time, working, rearing children, cooking for the family, and doing all the chores without help. There is a general outcry among the women interviewed that husbands are insensitive and unappreciative of their suffering. These husbands stay away from the kitchen and do not help with the chores; worse still, they expect their over-burdened wives to serve them food on the table and treat them like ancient lords. In such situations, women become overwhelmed with a sense of nostalgia, knowing how easier it is to rear children back home where a woman is spoilt, surrounded by serving maids and by relations who are ever ready to offer their services. One bitter lesson to learn in coming to America is that, although you come from a background where it takes a village to raise a child, here you are entirely on your own. Loneliness and temptation, frustration and depression, as well as high blood pressure have made acquaintances with many a Nigerian woman in America.

Breakdown in communication between husband and wife often rubs salt into the wound. It might sound incredible, but it is a fact that many Nigerian men do not know how to make conversation their wives. The women interviewed believe that men's reticence is a form of intimidation or punishment. These men are loquacious in public and, indeed, pretend to communicate well with their wives in public, whereas it is mere window dressing, for privately they are statues.

One possible explanation of the poor communication between Nigerian couples is blamed on men's distorted perception of their role in marriage. For them, the notion of *"primus inter pares"* (first among equals) in a spousal relationship is un-African; rather, they would propose the *"patriarchal cum Medieval comitatus"* relationship of lord and thane, which totally subjugates the woman to the man. In this relationship, the man's authority is absolute; by right, wife, children and property, all belong to him. The wife therefore has no right to question, challenge, or argue with her husband. A woman disclosed that her husband would never admit to being wrong, and where he blunders having been forewarned by her, he turns round to blame her for 'bad mouthing' the issue in the first place; if only she would keep quiet the blunders would not occur.

Like this woman who learns to keep quiet, women generally maintain their silence for a long time and some interpret that as surrender. But such internalization is by no means a recapitulation but a form of rebellion. And this rebellion manifests itself in their sex life where the man's lack-love, lack-luster sexual approach is always refused. Many of those interviewed complain that the men see them as sex objects. One expressed her disgust with men's mechanistic sexuality thus: "Sex without love, it is ridiculous! You continuously abuse me verbally and psychologically and then you want to lie with me in bed as if I am a prostitute!"

Finance is another important area of disagreement among Nigerian couples in America, and women seem to feel the impact more than the men do. A key issue is the type of financial arrangement the family needs to adopt: common purse or separate accounts? Usually, at the beginning of marriage, when the man is the sole breadwinner, the common purse system is acceptable to both parties. The man manages his or, should we say, their resources the way he wants. But, as soon as the woman begins to earn money and contribute to the account, a conflict develops. The husband continues to manage affairs as he is accustomed to doing without any form of accounting. If the wife desires to have a part in the control of their money or if she protests that their hard- earned money is being mismanaged or improperly spent, a crisis flares up. Some husbands, for example, are so thrifty with their in-laws, but spend lavishly on their own parents and close relations.

Relationships with in-laws are a huge problem for

many Nigerian women in America. The root of this problem seems to be cultural, for in Nigeria, marriage is treated as a union not only of two spouses but also of their families and extended families. In a relative sense, a woman is therefore married not just to the man but also to his father, mother, uncles, aunts, brothers and cousins. These relations sometimes over-reach themselves by their claims, demands, and unrestrained interference in the affairs of the family. The worst offenders are mothers-in-law and sisters-in-law. In their attempt to control and dominate either of the spouses, they precipitate a civil war in the family. Some of the women I spoke with complained seriously about their no-win situation: "In-laws make unrealistic demands from Nigeria; they want us to solve all their financial problems. If we fail to meet their demands, they blame the woman, and if we send some help, they thank the man." This problem gets more frustrating in cases where the woman is the principal source of income in the family. It is difficult for Nigerian in-laws to understand that a woman can be the prop of the family, and, even when they come here and see for themselves, they still argue that the husband is the head of the family and hence both the wife and her money belong to the husband. It is estimated that two-thirds of Nigerian families in America are afflicted with in-law-related problems one way or another.

We have so far dwelt on general issues, which, to a large extent, are experiences shared by immigrants from other cultures, Such issues are so vast that to exhaust them, one might need to write a book of more than one volume. We shall now focus on more specific issues relating to Nigerian migrant-women in America.

The most obvious of these is what I describe as culture conflict. While Nigerian men are generally culturally conservative, their women are more liberal and adaptive to a new culture. Although the women love their traditional attire and wear them on special occasions, they are often quick to learn new ways. Celebrations like birthdays, Mothers Day, Valentines Day, etc. do not appeal to many Nigerian men, but mean a lot to the women. The women are disappointed when flowers, cards, and other gifts - symbols of love and appreciation - are not sent to them from their husbands on special feast days. Many husbands have nothing in principle against such symbolic gestures; it's just that they forget. There are others who don't want to be bothered by such "trifles." When pressured by kids, they give them money to buy gifts for their mother, but will not do it themselves. There is the case of a woman who reminded her husband that the following day was Mothers Day and he quipped, "You are not my mother." This eminent husband obviously does not know the significance of little acts of love in marriage.

Differences in social class create problems for Nigerian spouses in America. There are instances of men from poor families raised in villages and educated in rural schools who find their way to America and later marry a Nigerian from a completely opposite background. Such class differences, though very much overlooked in considerations for choosing life partners, play up later, generating all sorts of conflicts. The inferiority complex and sometimes the superiority complex consequent upon such dichotomy is difficult to handle in marriage.

Love relations between Nigerian men and African American women, sometimes considered a blessing, create problems for future Nigerian wives. It is estimated that 75% of Nigerian men have had some kind of love relationship with an African-American woman, and about 45% end up in marriage and reproduction. In time, as a result of culture conflicts, the relationship breaks down. The ex-spouse is granted custody of the children, and the Nigerian ends up paying child support. When later the man goes home to marry a fellow Nigerian woman, he often fails to inform her of the previous relationship, as well as the financial and emotional implications involved. Later, the new wife discovers the problems she has come to inherit, gets upset, but learns to cope, even though the issue continues to bite and blow within her. Even where the man has been granted custody of the child, the new wife still has her hands full as she labors to please the man and a son that has been raised in a culture totally alien to her.

Polygamy, to the Western mind, is an African scandal; serial polygamy, to an African mind, is a Western scandal. The new Nigerian— the Nigerian- American—is tempted by both. Divorce and remarriage are not strange phenomena in Nigeria, but they are rare. Traditional African marriage is so richly sacramental and communal that it precludes divorce in its dynamics. When conflicts drive couples to a point where cohabitation is virtually impossible, separation, sometimes lasting for years, becomes an ultimate solution. On the other hand, polygamy, the marriage of one man to two or more women, is accepted in Nigerian society. It used to be not only the norm but also an index to social ascent. Contact with the West and the effect of Christianity on local customs have trivialized polygamy to where it is no longer a popular practice but something merely indulged.

Nigerians in America cannot practice polygamy because law forbids it. However, recently, some Nigerians are beginning to practice it in an interesting manner. As we have suggested earlier, serial polygamy, which many of them practice in America, is easier when marriage involves African Americans. Break-up of such relationships could be blamed on a number of factors, principal of which, I think, is the lack of a cultural backing that sustains traditional marriage. When marriage involves two Nigerians, divorce is greatly resisted, and that is not to suggest that the practice is nonexistent. There is a new trend of Nigerians surreptitiously contracting a second marriage while the first is still on. Without the knowledge of the wife, the man gets himself another wife, not a mistress, but a full-fledged wife, whom he keeps in Nigeria and caters to with the resources that rightly belong to him and the legal wife. Before the first wife knows about the new marriage, the new wife is already settled with a new baby in the family home that the first wife helped to build in Nigeria. This act of villainy is not common, but the few known instances of it are very disturbing to the Nigerian community in America.

There are men who will exploit their wives to the bones and pick every piece of meat out of them with no qualms whatsoever. There is a case that I personally witnessed in 1994. I had then visited Nigeria during the summer. One day, a doctor I had just come to know brought a letter to be delivered to his dear wife in Houston. It turned out that his wife, a nurse by profession, and his two young girls live in Houston and he was expected to join them. Two years later, I ran into the wife at a party and she told me her story amid tears. The letter I mailed to her contained an urgent plea for a large amount of money he needed to complete a family house they were building at home. She had been sending him money on regular basis, and this time she sent him even more than he requested. The sad news is that their marriage finally broke down because her husband completed the house and married another woman, thus effectively abandoning her and her two daughters. Such heart-breaking stories that seem to demonize the men are heard among Nigerian communities in America.

But, spousal abandonment is not just a male issue. Nigerian women have also abandoned their husbands in a more dramatic fashion. Nigerians are very familiar with newly married women abandoning their husbands as soon as they come into the States. Usually it is the case of a young woman in Nigeria in love with a young man in America who for some reason cannot help her to fly to America. By some coincidence, another American suitor comes and wins her consent. She eventually comes on his ticket but only stays for a while before proceeding to her real destination. Stop-and-go marriages like this are as damaging as men's heartless dereliction.

There are a few other ways in which women have been part of the problem. A good number of Nigerian women in America abuse the phone by the length of time they spend on it and by the amount of gossiping and character assassination they perpetrate. One of them said that the phone is the only outlet they have for letting out steam in their "imprisoned" environment. That may be so, but certainly there are better ways of dealing with marital problems. Again, women are self-centered and care less how others are affected by their actions, especially with regard to their expensive life style and their relentless attempts to dominate their husbands. Some do not have the slightest respect for their husbands' relatives and thereby create enormous problems for their husbands as well as for themselves.

One major and final issue that must be addressed, because of its urgency to the Nigerian community as a whole and to women in particular, is the future of the Nigerian children born in America. If conditions were favorable, most Nigerians in America would prefer to live in Nigeria and visit America from time to time. As stated earlier, Nigerians never planned to settle permanently in the United States. Thousands had come to America to get education but were overtaken by the socioeconomic problems back home. Others fled their country to shelter in the States until the situation improves. Little did they know that they were being part of history—part of the new trans-Atlantic migration—nor were they aware that immigrants to America, past and present, always dream of going back to their home countries, but never do. Only recently have Nigerians begun to confront the reality of their situation as they watch their children grow from infancy to adolescence; only now have they come to understand that a huge problem sits squarely on their shoulders regarding the future of these children. Most of these children cannot speak any Nigerian language, most do not care about Nigerian food, which to them is "yokie." Some change their Nigerian names to American names and nicknames because to them Nigerian names sound funny. Some parents have themselves helped to create the problem by not speaking their language to them and by not training them to identify with Nigerian culture. Understandably, the cost of traveling to Nigeria is heavy (between $1,200 and $1,800 per person), yet the fact remains that many of these children have never been to Nigeria or have been there for only three weeks on the average. It means that these children do not know what it feels like to have a grandparent, an uncle, an aunt, or a cousin. All they know too well is that every male Nigerian who visits their house is "uncle." The point is that without some cultural roots, these children will one day find themselves in conditions that will be so alienating that they will themselves go questing for their roots, but then it will have been too late.

Parents are now coming to grips with this singular problem that makes them shudder to contemplate. Even women, who are usually less concerned about politics and "all that endless talk about the trouble with Nigeria," are now beginning to have a rude awakening in what is happening or is about to happen to their children. One shocking fact that is becoming clear to them is that their children are truly not Nigerians - they are full-blooded Americans. I once called a Nigerian home in Houston to report that their relation was admitted into the hospital. A young girl answered the phone with a pure American accent, which made me want to verify that this was the right home. So, I asked, "Are you Nigerians?" The answer came fast, "No, I'm not; my parents are." I know a Nigerian woman who instantly developed high blood pressure after her daughter brought home her fiancé, an African-American young man heavily loaded with earrings on both ears. Some women are worried that their children will abandon them in old people's homes in their old age.

Concerned about the uncertainties of the future, many would like to send their children back to Nigeria, and indeed, some have done so and have reported a measure of success. But the risk is high. There are ugly stories coming out of Nigeria about crime; there are security problems to grapple with. Indeed, there is no where to hide! The dilemma of what to do with their offspring is real and has given many a mother some bad dreams.

From the foregoing exposition, it is clear that for Nigerian women, coming to America is not so sweet as dreamed from Nigeria. There are great things to enjoy in America, which are not covered in our discussion, and there are other pains and frustrations to endure. Solutions and alternatives open to women will form the subject for a future presentation. The knowledge of a problem is half its solution. And that is the relevance of this work, which does not apologize for its attempt to examine reality from the point of view of women. It is hoped that one day someone may opt to explore the same reality from men's perspective.

(Paper will be part of a book Fr Muoneke is presently working on.)

Many Nigerian men would be inclined to dismiss the good Reverend's report merely with a general saying in Igbo that portends to asks: "What business has the vulture with a barber? Reverend Muoneke is a celibate priest who remains unmarried. But that could be his unique qualification in taking a bird's eye view at a very serious problem in our Nigerian community. Moreover, this very proud Igboman participates fully in all community affairs, especially marriage and family counseling.

I could read the report and tell, with a high degree of certainty, which part of it was contributed by my very own wife. However, I have held back my thought from her because I didn't want to start an argument about how come I think I know her that well. But the truth is that I recognize my faults (from my wife's perspective) and I have taken time to study my wife. The question then becomes,

How much is our community doing to address this marriage problem and how many couples really make efforts to know each other and, in so doing, allow their spouses room to be themselves?

Indeed, as Reverend Muoneke also mentioned in the report, we inadvertently belie our children with a fictitious 'wall of uncles'. Typically in a Nigerian (Igbo) family, the race for the phone is everyday happenstance in families with children. This time a thirteen-year-old girl (you know, a teenager) grabs it at first ring, her face beaming with youthful expectation. But just then, with an instant look of disappointment on her face, she rolls her eyes: "Mom, it's for you!" Although Mom whispers from a distance and gestures for her to first find out the identity of the caller, the frowning teenage daughter blurts out, looking the other way: "Its uncle...I don't know!" Sounds familiar? You're not alone. Coincidence? I don't think so!

'Nneka' retires to the other end of the living room couch. She pulls on her long beaded hair and contemplates in agony, impatiently waiting for Mom to get (the hell) off the phone. "Mom, Dad, why do I have so many uncles? Why?" The tone of her voice is not only that of anger, but also frustration and confusion. (Mom doesn't get it! The caller, 'Uncle Chima', has a fifteen-year-old son, 'Uche', who is "really cool.")

Nneka is not alone this time because her other siblings quickly join her in a serious chorus: "Yeah, Why?" They have also often wondered individually why everybody they know is always an uncle, aunt, or whatever chain of implied blood relationship to the family. How could they ever reconcile this unfortunate reality with the cultural rules of dating and marriage so often drilled into their thinking heads at the dinner table? In African oral literature, *Why* stories entertain with colorful explanations for why animals behave or look the way they do. West African *why* stories include tales of how a leopard got its spots; why a lion roars; and why chickens and hawks are enemies. But throw in the modern story of the birds and the bees and you'll get a confusing maze.

The challenge of our time and culture is for the typical Nigerian-Igbo parents in the Diaspora to come up with an animal story that explains to their children (of all thinking ages) why they need and have so many "uncles". Try the Igbo adage: "It takes a village to raise a child... (*Nwa bu nwa oha*)." Yeah, right! A village of uncles, cousins and all. How about the adage that "distance turns strangers into brothers while in foreign land (*Nwanne di na mba*)"? Obviously, we have great distance—all eleven thousand air miles of distance from Nigeria to America. But the required 'stranger' element in this adage is lacking, especially as it relates to our American born children. Then, of course, to these children, America is not foreign at all. Forget the legendary "Uncle Sam", that belongs to the U.S government. Well, the dictionary word 'Uncle' is a form of respectful address to an older man, especially by children. Okay! But then, again, what's the real *Why* story, if you know one?

There is this 'virtual reality' brotherhood that works so well for the cultural social life of our Nigerian-American adult population but does not augur well at all for the foreseeable social interests of our younger generation. The phenomenon may very well spell doom for our cultural posterity. This social confusion lingers on with our children during the most formative period of their social lives. It is indicative of the serious need for a social educational reverse osmosis in our Nigerian community, a broadly-based social re-education that must begin earnestly in the family, all families. Indeed, our African culture holds the family sacred and, yes, family includes aunts, uncles, cousins, grandparents and other distant relatives. The extended family system is normal and beneficial, both in its function as a corporate system in which family groups rely on each other for survival, and as an educational setting in which children learn the lessons of life through daily experiences and instruction by their elders. Courtship and marriage are very important aspects of these lessons of life. They are so important that parents start early to navigate their children towards potential spouses and in-laws through carefully orchestrated relationships and strategic activities between families. Plainly fixed marriages occur only at the conservative ends of some of these planned relationships.

Not very long ago, you and I graduated from this informal

school of social connections in all its splendid cultural setting. Most of us started in our youthful years to feel our ways and learn the ropes—from innocent hide-and-seek games to not so innocent playing house and, ultimately, to the hormone-triggered tasting of the forbidden fruit. It is at this critical stage, of course, that the ever-watchful eyes of parents, elders and society come to bear, making sure we fully understood the proverbial fundamental difference between apple and orange. Then the gods join in and, ultimately, we couple up in friendships and marriages to the proud satisfaction of the salient wishes of our parents and clan of relatives. In the need to replicate this community social benefits for our confused Nigerian-American children, time is of essence! If we start now, we can still create a social setting here in America that serves the prescribed function—a broadly-based community setting that will navigate our American-born children beyond the limiting walls and fences of fictitious uncles, cousins, nieces and nephews, and into modern soccer fields of boyfriends and girlfriends, suitors and damsels. The ultimate answer to our quiet prayers as parents may very well depend on how far and how soon we decide to act upon this important social goal. Better still, make it important social duty!

And guess what else is amiss in our community? Praise! The art thereof. The word "praise" is defined in the dictionary as "the giving of worth or value to an individual, verbally or in the form of written words." Everyone wants to feel that he or she has value and worth, and is loved and wanted. It should be remembered that a person's (child or adult) self-image can be formed with the assistance of everyone else of all ages. From time to time, we should all be reminded of the fact that everyone, especially those who serve the community, have the need to be praised and encouraged. To build the confidence of a community leader is to prepare a self-sustaining energetic community. But our see-no-good community of very well-educated Nigerians in the Diaspora seem to see no value in the universal magic of a Thank you, that simple accolade bestowed by one to another in humble gratitude and appreciation for a favor or service received. It is a social tool that works magic the world over for all social species of life on earth.

"Thank you! Thank you very much!" The legendary Elvis Presley would sign off each performance with this signature-phrase that's ultimately bigger than himself and his music. He was never too big to say those magic words to the very least of his huge listening audience who, I believe, reciprocated the appreciation with reverence and perpetual adoration of the legend himself. In many worlds, cultures, and languages — in both human and lower animal domains — the magic of 'Thank you' works at the innermost core of all meaningful social engagements and social associations. A well-placed and well-meaning "Thank you! I love you!" can melt the hardest heart and soothe the sorest soul: Thank you for coming; thank you for listening; Thank you for being a friend... Thank you!

Two magic words, one magic phrase, bigger than life itself. Entertainment's Hollywood would take a bow and blow off a kiss and a smile. Texans do it with a handshake and a tip of the hat. Mexicans belt out a gracious "Gracias, amigos! Muchas gracias." The appreciative cock or rooster dances out a "Thank you" with four, quick double-side-kicks towards a generous hen after a laborious chase and a successful mount. Man's best friend, the dog, barks off a couple of bow-wows, along with a wagging of the tail, to welcome a friend or show happiness and appreciation for a treat. Hence in all languages, man and lower animals give and receive the soothing magic of a friendly 'Thank you.'

On a higher level, however, the spiritual man would say "Thank you" with a hug. Here a "Thank you" can and does transcend into an "I love you!" The purest of little children hug anyone at every turn of the littlest pleasure one may provide them. Children enthusiastically hug an adult's head, torso, hand or foot — whichever is available and closest to them at any material time—to express love and appreciation.

Africans do it rather deeply! Male folk would expect a hug from the female in return for his being such a 'good provider'. Warriors employ it to soothe their warring egos and settle for a truce. Women hug one another to show warm friendship.

Our ancestors knew to give a hug and a plain ol' "Thank you!"

It has always yielded a good return on the investment. There is no cost. It is refreshing. No batteries are required. It's non-taxable, extremely personal and fully returnable. A simple hug and a "Thank you" (not necessarily in that order of application) relieves tension, improves blood flow, reduces stress, helps self-esteem, and generates good will.

Therefore, common sense should tell us that according a well-deserved "Thank you" to those people who labor selflessly in service of our society and mankind, will achieve all the above and more. So, why treat them otherwise? In our very many attempts at organizing for the power of numbers, many of our folks easily become the ungrateful 'wise' prophets of doom — the naysayers. Such folks would overlook simple soothing words of comfort and scan their old dictionaries, dusty law books, and encyclopedias for the harshest idioms, most hackneyed expressions, and most hurtful words of spite to use against fellow others. They would stand aloof and greet every venture with reproof. They are the ungrateful scavenger-birds of the society who would perch on the high grounds of their personal egos, or personal interests, and await any opportunity to convert public good to personal gain. In such people, our future is hopeless, our vision myopic, and our generational tree of life without tap roots.

It makes no common sense and pays no social or economic dividend that the few good men and women in our society who care enough to help, must be tested, re-tested, and guaranteed tough in order for them to be able to continue to offer themselves up in unflinching service to our community. By mere attitude, words, actions or omission, these few heroic men and women are tested to the last fabrics of their moral being and human endurance in order for them to maintain sanity and continue to listen to the better angels of their nature. In the end, the whole society loses — a lose/lose paradigm.

Rather, shouldn't we in one accord take a bow and kiss off a smile, shake hands or tip a hat, belt out a *"muchas gracias"*, bark a bow-wow or kick off quick quadruple-double side kicks to those people who so generously give themselves to the service of our community and society? And more so, why not accord it to the many servant-leaders of the numerous big and small organizations who break a bloody sweat every day, striving to carve out a niche for themselves and the Nigerian community in the Diaspora? The spiritual African man in me wants to embrace all of these folks in a soul-to-soul power-hug and say: Thank you! Thank you very much!

In Service Of My People

It takes a thick skin to survive in my community! In dealing with my people (in both private and public arenas), I've learned never to fear criticism when I'm right, and never to ignore it when I'm wrong. Are you being criticized? Are charges being made against you? Search your mind! If the accusations are true, mend your ways! If they are false, forget about them. Hear this from an expert:

Some will hate you, some will love you;
Some will flatter you, some will slight;
Cease from man and look above you,
Trust in God and do the right. [Macleod]

The stinging words hurled at you by your adversaries may be uncalled for. When a verbal attack comes, therefore, it's well to analyze it. If it isn't justified, let it roll off you like water off a duck's back. If the accusation is true, however, take the necessary steps to correct the situation. Additionally, as a matter of approach, we must emulate our ancestors. We must be ready to take risks, confront our oppressors, and begin to do tomorrow's work today. The task of rediscovery is a responsibility of the present generation of Ndigbo, and to accomplish it, we must individually:

- stop and take a deep breath,
- look in the mind's mirror for self-evaluation,
- reject vulgar individualism,

- suspend habitual judgement of others,
- operate from the highest moral base possible,
- trash the personal ego that prevents us from dealing with one another, and,
- never dish out to another that which you cannot and would not take yourself.

The most innocent of us faithfully adheres to the spiritual ways of our forefathers but our sense of duty has not yet extended to the use of all our faculties— it being the collective thinking of a well-organized social group with a vision. We still find it difficult to adjust our attitudes to the wisdom of a common adage by Nsukka people that: "He who patterns his behavior strictly to his father's ways is a fool. But he who diligently adheres to the prescribed behavior of the community of his fellows is a wise person. A wise person knows when to serve, lead, or follow."

As long as the above saying is not narrowly construed to mean a recommendation for rebellion by a generation against their predecessors, it essentially stresses the need for one to put community interest above self. It is simply a wise recipe for cultural survival. Its place is in the innermost personal convictions of the individual — in the very subconscious. There is intrinsic satisfaction and security that comes from service, from helping other people in a meaningful way. One important source is when you see yourself in a contributing and creative mode, really making a difference; another is anonymous service no one knows. In these, influence, not recognition, becomes the genuine and only motive. Victor Frankl lectured on the need for meaning and purpose in our lives — something that transcends life itself and taps the best energies within us. The late Dr. Hans Selye, in his research on stress, stated that a long and happy life is the result of making contributions. And, in the words of George Bernard Shaw (1856 – 1950),

This is the true joy in life — that being used for a purpose recognized by yourself as a mighty one. That being a force of nature, instead of a feverish, selfish little clod of ailments and grievances, complaining that the world would not devote itself to making you happy. I am of the opinion that my life is my privilege to do for it whatever I can. *I want to be thoroughly used up when I die!* (emphasis supplied) For the harder I work the more I live. [15]

Eldon Tanner adds that "Service is the rent we pay for the privilege of living on this earth." And there are so many ways to serve!

I have enjoyed the many privileges of serving my people in both fellowship and leadership positions. Good fellowship begets good leadership, I believe, and neither is easy when it comes to my people. In striving to give my best in the public service of my people, my motivation comes from within, rather than from without. I do so without material expectations of human rewards or acclamation. My service plan is scripted on my principle-based understanding of who I am and the divine reason for my being; and my personal paradigm is borrowed from the old Boy Scout pledge and promise: "On my honor, I shall do my best!" My reward shall be a personally assessed grade of "Satisfactory", at the very least, in my proactive delivery of this promise.

In the ensuing community-centered, work-centered environment, there is the tendency to define "self" by service roles in the community. The feeling of security tends to relate to how people treat and accept us in these roles. There is the tendency to make decisions based on the perceived needs of the people, and to limit the decision-making criterion to one's understanding of what's best for the community. Life perspective is, to some extent, scripted upon the roles we play; actions are limited by organizational constraints and the possible inability at some point to do the particular things one wants to do. The power to act is also limited by other societal and personal weaknesses.

Sometimes in this thankless work, one must endure tremendous hardship. At such time, it's easy to 'throw in the towel' when there seems to be no end to the needs of others and our efforts appear to make little or no difference. "Just a drop in the bucket," one might say, "what's the use? I quit!" Then again, the natural elements of human frailty would kick in, and you can feel and hear your body (be it friend, family, wife or husband) rebelling each time you set out to yet another place of public service: "Look, man, I'm tired and hurt. I've done enough. Why do you insist on such insane acts of love for these difficult people? There's no way I'm going to risk more abuse. It's time to retire. Retire!" But you must discipline your mind and say to your body (friend, family, wife or husband): "Hey partner, I know you hurt. I would like to give in to you, but for the sake of the children, I have to keep going. And I can't go without you. Come on!"

It is my fate that I should be like the Good Samaritan. The biblical Good Samaritan was not sent by a church, a denomination, or a committee. He was one man who stopped and cared. I want to be thoroughly used up when I die!

A Messenger of Hope

Hope is one thing that is gained from prolonged adversity. "There is always hope when people are on their knees." [Robert Dortch]. "Nothing worth doing is ever finished in a lifetime; therefore, we must be saved by hope." [Renhold Niebuhr]. "In the presence of hope, faith is born. In the presence of faith, love becomes a possibility. In the presence of love, miracles happen." [Robert Schuller].

In all the towering mountain of worrisome things and pressing responsibilities, I've always allowed myself to dream. That has kept me going. Dreams represent a call to the higher power to come down and take over. I believe that God's dreams for me are bigger than others' expectations of me, or my past failures, or my limitations. Sometimes, when I ponder my dreams, I can hear defeating gibes and taunts usually coming from memories of fears of past failures: "You're too young," or "too old," or too something else. Or, "That'll never work!" "It's never been done that way!" In the spiritual realm, as well as in the world of nature, the singers of the day are more numerous than the singers of the night. It is not hard to look up and cheer up when everything is going well—when health is good, family is happy, and rewards are plentiful—but the real test of the spirit is in the woes unsolicited. At such times, we must endeavor to hope by singing in spite of the dark. Sincerely, if you would learn to keep in tune with who you are, you can sing even in the dark.

I care enough to worry about the posterity of the Igboman — my people at home, and in the Diaspora, vis-à-vis the United States and Canada. Those third sphere Igbos, i.e. the children of the immigrant Igbos in the United States and Canada—the extensions of Africa in the Diaspora — have the unenviable potential of becoming a lost generation. Some of these children who somehow comprehend their social situation and marvel at their predicament, express genuine concern. A part of the problem is that most of their parents are overwhelmed, confused, and in denial.

The possibilities can become scary! Living in the West has strangely become an interesting way of discovering the rest of the Igboman and, in fact, the African man's problems. It has become predictable that the next two generations of Nigerian-Igbo/ African-Americans will only have memories of their "Kunta Kinte"; and, unlike the famous Alex Haley, not be able to actually travel back to their roots. It is this kind of biting reality that ought to prompt one into thinking solutions and preaching concerted action.

I took many such good looks at the Igbo community and documented my emotion and recommendations for action in an address to my people on the occasions of two consecutive conventions of the World Igbo Congress (W.I.C) in 1995 in Los Angeles, and 1996 in Atlanta. The abridged text of my address is reprinted below:

Cockcrow At Noon: A Window Of Hope
Address to W.I.C Conference in Los Angeles, 1995; Atlanta, 1996

Hope in heart puts a smile on the face, for what is the essence of living without hope?
Caught between strands of time stretching two oppo-

site ends of the global time zones, ours is a futuristic landscape of scary places—the geography of nowhere. In this confusing maze of organized chaos, our cock crows at high noon. Alas! we are jarred awake. Thank God we're not all D-E-A-D after all. So, may I say: Good morning, good people! *Mgbe onye jiri teta ura, o buru ututu ya.* (Whenever one chooses to wake up after a night's sleep becomes ones morning.)

We all know what a difference the right action can make. It adds clarity and definition to our goal, while sending the world a message about our history and purpose. And we know how important it is to have the right drivers behind our wheels, those individuals among us whose proactive principles, talents, and vision can help us reach goals and fulfill potentials. As the popular saying goes, "A journey of a thousand miles begins with one simple step." The collective vision of the World Igbo Congress (WIC) is one giant step in the right direction. Congratulations!

We are a special generation of Igbos with special problems under special circumstances. Yes, we are at war for our souls and our posterity. It is spiritual and philosophical; it is economic. It is social and political; it is just. It is for one and for all; it is everything and everywhere. We have the duty to fight it; it is expected of us!

While we may never comprehend the rationale for this war's making, nor ever have privity to the war rooms and decision tables of its makers, we must endeavor to align ourselves against its divergent thrusts and identify with the common people who must fight it. In his play *A Dance of the Dead*, Professor Emeka Nwabueze writes: "The working of a dream sirens the smell of blood, and only the gods may question the fate of man ...." As a people, we must heed to the standard statement of stagecraft that "One cannot win on a bargaining table that which he is unwilling or unable to win on the battle field." The stage is set, and we owe a duty to resurrect and appease the brave souls of the living and dead heroes of our not-so-distant traumatic past. A *tuoro omalu, o malu; a tuoro ofeke, o fenye isi n'ofia*. (A word is enough for the wise.) Advice is what we seek when we already know the answer but wish we didn't. In this our "journey-of-no-return", imaginations run riot. Years of accumulated wisdom and bookery having laid waste long enough in the private chambers of our heads, often erupt into imaginative mind-quake of ideas and ideologies, sometimes dangerously close to collective insanity. We live within a shouting distance of each other's fears, sorrows and pains. Hence, in the quiet bedrock of your mind's eye you can hear *real men* crying, if you dare listen deeply into their heads, our heads. In the sensitive nerve endings of your flesh-and-blood emotional self, you can feel their aching soul, if you dare read between the lines of their thoughts, our thoughts. The rules have changed! Our collective eyes of manhood have stooped so low as to fearing the illusionary impressions of painted devils. Ours have become the great puzzle of the chicken and the egg, which comes first?

So, what's to do? What's to do with *us* — the metamorphosing Igbo turned Nigerians, turned Biafrans, turned Nigerian-Igbo, turned Igbo-Americans in perpetual emotional exile? What about our children and our dreams? What is to be written on our tomb stones when we die? What about history? In our time, there in our homeland, all the basic things we take for granted are costing a bundle to those of us least capable of providing them. For the Nigerian Igbo, especially, the opportunities of living are diminished in direct proportion as what are called the "means" are increased — from politics to drinking water, safety to security, basic health care to, yes, even dying. The last time Dr. Alex Ekwueme was here, I asked him the usual question: "How is home, Sir?" The great one pondered in obvious pain and responded: *"E ji eze ata ndu n'ulo."* Literally, this translates into: "People are biting their teeth, moaning and groaning, to hang on to dear life, day-by-day."

Imagine the likeness! Take a moment and picture your loved ones at home, all that could have been but is not.

My fellow *Onye-Igbo*, are you happy? What if we define happiness, like we should, as an abiding mood of joyful contentment, a deep-down state of peace and hope, not just an upbeat fleeting feeling induced by occasional favorable happenings, nor the drunken highs of our patented, all-seasons, marathon party-celebrations? Now, in the light of this new definition, are you really happy? If not, I urge you to conduct a personal "checkbook checkup": Does your honest self-assessment indicate that you've been putting your heart (and soul) where your real treasures are — in your cultural values, your children, and your future? Sincerely, it's not what you would do with a million if riches be yours tomorrow, but rather, it's what you are doing today with the dollar-and-a-quarter you've got in your pocket. Talk is cheap! It is very easy to, and anybody can, become a 'wise' prophet of doom. In the words of Ella Wheeler Wilcox, "There's always two kinds of people in our world: those who lift; and, those who lean." We must contend with those of us who would stand aloof and greet each venture with reproof. Our world would come to a standstill if things were run by men and women who would always say : "It can't be done!"

Together, we must strive to knock the *"t"* out of *can't*:

- We can look each other in the eye and resolve to unite rather than separate;
- We can resolve to trust and do honest business with one another;
- We can organize and play to win in the political process, both here and at home;
- We can resolve to dump our menacing "African Time Syndrome";
- We can 'set sail' for our kids towards self pride,

partnerships, and marriages;
- We can reshape our image and restore hope for ourselves for a better tomorrow;
- We can... We can... We can...., May it be onto us according to our striving!.

If idealism alone could repair a people or a community, the Igbo people and their communities everywhere ought to be on their way to paradise. It could not, of course! Neither academic degrees nor illusionary wealth, nor even honest individualistic effort, can cure all our woes. But put together and pressed into collective action, they might perk up the patient.

Rather than being stymied by all the problems of human will and human action, we must go at it piece by piece at a time to make something happen in our lifetime, even against all odds. We must avoid the trap of looking back in consternation unless it's to recall a lesson learned, because when we live in the past, we tarnish the present, and ignore the future. For the sake of tomorrow, Ndi-Igbo ought to determine for themselves, and quickly too, why what they predicted yesterday has not happened today.

Imagine the return of hope and zeal to a people with proven pride in history of great deeds. Imagine a collective hope that can be replenished—one wise investment of love and care at a time—by the general population of Ndi-Igbo who happen to live outside the 'war zones' of our beloved country, Nigeria. A concerted community effort is desperately needed. It must start now and must be sustained in order for Ndi-Igbo to achieve a destiny worthy of their past. To be successful, the entire Igbo people in the Diaspora must be mandated, through the WIC and its member regional area organizations, to build on opportunity and success, and not focus on persons, problems and failures. We cannot shy away from controversy; conflict is inevitable, and direct, blunt debate is desirable! In a country that couldn't care less, it's for us to care more. In his book, *The Literature of the American Renaissance*, Thoreau writes: "The best thing a man can do for his culture when he is rich is to endeavor to carry out those schemes which he entertained when he was poor." We may not be 'rich' here in the Diaspora, but we are definitely not poor by any standard of measure at home in Nigeria. Now is the time for us to act upon all those good childhood dreams.

In my capacity as the Executive President of The Igbo People's Congress (IPC), Houston, I bring you mixed tidings from Houston, Texas. On December 9, 1994, we wisely decided to defy the infamous adage, which has continually insulted Ndi-Igbo with its inherent literary implication that we cannot manage ourselves through constructive organizational leadership. God forbid that we can't or wouldn't! On that day, we restructured and re-organized an existing, individual membership Igbo organization—the Igbo People's Congress (IPC)—into an inclusive, nurturing, umbrella organization for the more than 50 localized Igbo organizations in the greater Houston area. By necessity, the new IPC is structured to adhere to the original premise of uniting Igbo people in the Houston area, placing greater emphasis on inclusive participation of Ndi-Igbo in Igbo affairs and keeping away from the usual rigors of political power-play and social fanfare, while providing the broader organizational format necessary for addressing the emerging global problems at home and abroad. A three-tiered functional organization format responds to World Igbo Congress' global vision at the top; IPC's mission statement at the mid-level; and the general needs of the Houston Igbo population at the grassroots.

We are making progress! But not without the thorny land mines of the peculiar Igboman's attitude towards organizational action. In Houston, we have an unhealthy share of Ndi-Igbo who have refused to realize that when a man is wrapped up in himself, he makes a pretty small package. We have the patented diseases of intentional self-alienation, belittling mindset and, of course, the "African Time Syndrome". All these when put together, continue to limit and deprive us of real opportunities. We have an awful lot of 'good men' who choose to remain in their mental shackles; but who perch like preying vultures on the high-grounds of their 'Central Ego Boulevard', on the other side of common sense, ready to usurp public opportunity for personal good. In these men our collective foresight is severely myopic, our hopes minimal, and our tree of life without tap roots. These men scare me pink! They leave holes in my heart.

But we also have giants. Spiritual giants! Men and women who understand that life is an exciting business, and most exciting when it is lived for others and for posterity.

No! Don't go looking for these genuine people brazenly on the high tables of community events. Nor foppishly in big flashy cars, flamboyant chieftaincy regalia, and oversized homes. Rather, look for them in the war trenches and "donkey alleys" of our most troubling issues; and atop our most pressing community service needs. They are the humble donkeys of the Igbo cause who are graciously and religiously tuned to the better angels of their being. For these ordinary folks, their *standard of giving* is more important than their *standard of living;* and their *doing* more important than their *being*. They are, indeed, our true heroes.

Thanks to these uncelebrated heroes, the Houston IPC have surged forward with tangible successes. Pursuant to specific resolutions of the WIC, we have, among other things:

• established a viable children's program to engage in enthusiastic cultural education activities.

• maintained a regular schedule of publication of our newsletter, *Ikoro,* to keep our community connected and informed.

- planned and executed grand IGBO DAY celebrations, replete with symposia and a non-denominational memorial service for the restless heroes and other victims of our civil war; thus establishing an annual 3-day event within and/or around the historically significant 30th day of the month of May to reflect upon our past, celebrate our present, and build hope for our future.
- staked out boundaries on the sand and boldly defended the Igbo image whenever challenged.

My fellow *Onye-Igbo,* when you absorb yourself in criticizing the WIC, IPC, or your local area organization, as the case may be, for its shortcomings; and in waiting to see what happens <u>first</u> before you decide to join in, the solutions and actions you are expecting and waiting to see may well be your own. All Igbo eyes, home and abroad, are upon us. So we may live the moment, but always with eternity in view. We cannot afford to fail! To achieve our goals and vision we must:

- preserve what we have now that is positive — i.e., the link we have created with the home front and the hope we are creating for our home folks, the forward-looking spirit of inclusion rather than exclusion,
- add what we do not have that is positive— i.e., a spirit of camaraderie that removes selfishness and brings forth trust, collective action, and collective self-pride,
- remove what we have that is negative— i.e., selfish attitudes, tardiness, divorce, thievery of all forms and format, and naked arrogance,
- keep out what we do not have that is negative, and,
- empower ourselves collectively to take on the challenge of our time and our generation.

"In all things [hold] yourself to be a pattern of good works." (Titus 2:7). Be your brothers' keeper, for it pays to be meek and humble. God's call to any task includes

His strength to complete it. (*Chi nyere nwa-ogbenye ji ga-enye ya mbazu o ga-eji gwuputa ya.*) "God is able to do exceedingly abundantly above all we ask or think, according to the power that works in us" (Ephesians 3:20). Teamwork divides the effort and multiplies the effect.

The strong among us may be prominent, but the kind-hearted will be lasting. The selfish person, at the expense of others, may be satisfied with what he/she thinks is success, but the meek — those thoughtful of others — will prevail. In our hard-driving, rights-centered world, kind consideration towards others seems out of place. However, eventhough material power may dull the conscience, but it is spiritual power, the renowned resilience of a true Igbo person, that will ultimately overcome. "Whatever your hands find to do, do it with your might, for there is neither work nor wisdom in the grave." Do it now for us, for our children; For culture, and for posterity! The gods are watching.

Notice that I delivered a message of hope, not despair. In service of my people, I can only but become a messenger of hope — active hope, the kind of hope that stirs action and sustains positive thinking. But then for the deeper thinkers, shouldn't I have also asked some hard-probing questions?: Is there intelligent life left out there amongst my people? Now that our ancestors are resfully dead, could it be that we have taken the cumulative wisdom and experience of their being and turned them into toys and twinkies? More so, in the deeper analysis, considering our difficulties in exciting ourselves into prudent remedial collective actions, haven't we all but become terminally stupid?

7

❦

POETRY OF SILENCE

*T*here is more to human life than meets the eye: more to oneself, more to one's neighbor, more to the world that surrounds us. There is more to our past, more to our present—maybe infinitely more. There is more to our interrelationships as persons on Earth's stage. And the further we probe, the deeper the mystery, the reward, and even, the involvement.

Religious leader David McKay taught that the greatest battles of life are fought out daily in the silent chambers of the human soul. He projected the theory that if one wins the battles there, and if one settles the issues that inwardly conflict, one feels a sense of peace, a sense of knowing what one is about. And, also, that one finds that the public victories — where one tends to think cooperatively to promote the welfare and good of other people and to be genuinely happy for other people's successes — would follow naturally.

Like the great battles of life, the poetry of silence also happens in the silent chambers of the human soul, in the language of the woods; a language common to both animate and inanimate objects. We know more from nature than we can communicate at will. Nature is the vehicle of thought that subserves man with language. As Ralph Waldo Emerson has determined, every natural fact is a symbol of some spiritual fact to some first, second or third degree. Thus he writes:

Words are signs of natural facts;
Particular natural facts are symbols of particular spiritual facts;
Nature is the symbol of spirit. [16]

It follows, therefore, that every appearance in nature corresponds to some state of the mind, and that man possesses a universal soul within, wherein as a firmament, the natures of dream, truth, love and freedom arise. That spirit has life in itself, and man embodies it in his meditative state and his thinking language— the language of the woods — whereby all things, both animate and innanimate, preach to us a mute gospel. The moral influence of nature upon every individual is that amount of truth that it reveals to the individual. Hence, DeStael and Goethe called architecture "frozen music;" "a Gothic church," said Coleridge, "is a petrified religion." [17] In God, as well as in nature, every end is converted into a new means, and human spirituality suggests the absolute.

A spiritual person is a thinking person; and may be happiest when he or she learns to worship in silence — soliloquize, dream, meditate. He or she that thinks the most would say the least, as he or she is swallowed up in solemn articulation of his or her petition—his or her poetry of silence—the spiritual relationship of man to his God. He or she, the poet, would find something ridiculous in his or her delight until he or she is out of the sight of men and forms a projection of God in the unconscious. A poet, the orator, the observer bred in the woods, and whose senses have been nourished by their fair and appeasing changes, does not lose his or her lessons altogether, even in the roar of cities and the broil of politics. When natural thoughts flow, miraculously, in the fortunate hours of my early mornings, I stare in awe and I wonder if at all other times I am not blind and deaf. These silent early mornings awake my creative genius. Indeed, my poetry of silence is a wonderful privilege of nature. In this prostrate state, faith is often more fruitful than indisputable affirmation of things of nature by scientific proofs and empirical experiments.

A dream lets me deeper into the secrets of nature than any empirical experiment, because dreams let me find self in everything great and small. They help me set up a tranquil sense of unity, whereby I may rightfully proclaim my human self, lord of all. George Herbert, the British poet (1593 -1633), wrote the following lines on Man:

Nothing hath got so far
But man hath caught and kept it as his prey,
His eyes dismount the highest star,
He is in little, all the sphere,
Herbs gladly cure our flesh, because that they
Find their acquaintance there. [18]

Silence is a powerful religious symbol. The poetry of silence takes only but a moment of silent prayer. "Is not prayer also a study of truth, a sally of the soul into the unfound infinite? No man ever prayed heartily without learning something." [Emerson]. The poet man or woman conforms things to his or her thoughts, esteems nature as fluid, and impresses his or her being thereon. Out of concrete objects he or she molds words of reason. A successful poetry of silence would always conclude by announcing undiscovered regions of thought and, thereby, communicating through hope, new activities to the torpid spirit. The art of prayerful empathic relationship demands patience, courage and consideration, which sum up to mutual understanding. In prayer, as well as in dynamic human relationships, we must first listen to understand, and then pray to be understood. It is not unlike the ideal worship relationship with God.

Patience Is a Virtue

True prayer is a daily conversational relationship with God. We first come to the Almighty with trust and respect. We listen mindfully to hear what God will say to us, confident that He understands us and will prescribe what is best for us. Then we thank God for that love, seek forgiveness for our sins, and then share our needs and the needs of others. A patient interactive prayer or interpersonal relationship is a desirably rich experience of listening and talking to God and man. It touches the soul, stirs the spirit, and awakens the conscience. It is indeed a desirable virtue.

Imagine the depth of the symbolism of silence! A symbolism which connects man directly to the concept of God. God is a patient Being—the most powerful symbol in human history. The concept of God, like other religious and other human symbols, has demonstratedly meant different things to different persons, groups, and ages. Yet, it is hardly too drastic an oversimplification to suggest that this concept has been on the whole, at least, subsumed, integrated, deepened, and made operationally effective in the lives of many hundreds of millions of persons, and in the lives and social cohesion of many thousands of communities. It is, also, in our awareness of the entire range of transcendence with which we are surrounded or endued: grandeur, order, meaning, aspiration, awe, hope, virtue, responsibility, rapport, integrity, worth, and renewal. On the balance, the religious history of the Hindu community, for example, is a history, in part, of traditional ceremonial, ideological, and sociological patterns. Yet in more significant part, it is a history of fortitude and quiet humanness—a history of the conviction that life is worth living and death worth dying; that goals are worth striving for, and, that the immediate is caught up in the eternal.

When I came of age, I thoughtfully picked out an alias to suit and express the person that I am, "Ome-na-nwayo," meaning among other things: "Patience and diligence is a virtue;" "If you fight slow, you win."

- Slow to anger
- Slow to condemn
- Slow to hurt over little things
- Slow to throw the first blow.

And this carries the wisdom that, "About the only thing one

can get in a hurry is trouble. It is the weak who are cruel." Says Leo Roskin. "Gentleness can only be expected from the strong." Patience is learning to cooperate with the inevitable. I condition myself to know that I am always better than what people might criticize me that I am not, and always less than what they might praise me that I am; and, by pressing that understanding into everyday thoughtful action, I always stand to win. In journeying through the minefields and milestones of my life and manhood, I have managed to delve into the many zones of my hitherto unknowns — the much talented, silent, patient self within.

Zones of My Unknowns: The Self Within

Principles are deep! They are fundamental truths, the generic common denominators.   They are tightly interwoven threads, running with exactness, consistency, and strength through the fabric of our lives.   Principles are bigger than people, and/or circumstances. Principles do not die. The more we know of the correct principles to have, the greater is our personal freedom to act wisely.

Each of us is born with our own unique, individual, assortment of potentials and limits.   Some of us reveal early in our lives that we have special talents for athletics, or music, or for dealing with people.   Other of us have more subtle gifts and aptitudes that we must work to develop; aptitudes for science, or drawing, or mechanics, or writing become apparent only as we apply ourselves to learning and developing them.   Whether our gifts and tendencies are dramatic or subtle, God places them within us. For example, the Biblical Samson was given great strength (see Judges 13-16), and David's musical talent caused him to be called into the king's service (see 1 Samuel 16: 14-23). In addition to those whose gifts are dramatic, the Bible also tells us about persons like Bezalel and Oholiab. Of Bezalel, He said:

I have filled him with divine spirit; with ability, intelligence and knowledge of every kind of craft, to devise artistic designs, to work in gold, silver, and bronze; in cutting stones for setting, and in carving wood; in every kind of craft. (Exodus 31:3-5).

Oholiab was chosen to assist Bezalel. Bezalel's and Oholiab's gifts were less flashy than Samson's or David's, but they used them in God's service by working on the Tabernacle, that renowned house of religious symbols.

Most of us are more like Bezalel and Oholiab than we are Samson or David. Many of us have quiet gifts, rather than ones that thrust us into the public eye. One insight to myself has to do with a basic tendency in my personality that is clearly hereditary. My father was very outspoken, very truthful, and a people's man; he was relaxed and carefree. My mother is quiet and reserved, but yet very enterprising. I find both sets of tendencies in me. I am very outspoken. And when I feel angry and insecure, I tend to become quiet, like my mother; then I live inside myself and safely observe.

Also, as I examine my personal scripting more carefully, I find beautiful scripts, positive scripts, that have been passed down to me which I sometimes take for granted. A conscious exercise in self-awareness helps me appreciate those scripts, and to appreciate those who have gone before me and nurtured me in principle-based living, mirroring back to me not only what I am, but also what I can become. I've also come to firm grips with my spiritual dimension, the third dimension. The spiritual dimension is my core, my center, and my commitment to my value system. It is a very private area of my life and of supreme importance. It draws upon the sources that inspire and uplift me, and tie me to the timeless truths of all humanity. However, there remains in my grand design, many more zones of my unknowns, certain of which quake and tremble the soul within.

Fighting "This Thing" That I Have Become

In all my ordeals, in the United States, I have been as much afraid of developing a malicious attitude, as I am of being defeated spiritually. I didn't learn how to live together in the United States, I learned how to live apart. I didn't learn love, I almost learned hate.

Nobody is born a bigot! A poster by the National Conference of Christians and Jews featuring two young boys of about the same age (one White, one Black), both holding themselves in a chest-to-chest happy embrace and smiling into the camera, had the following writing on it:

> There is no mind more open, or heart more willing, to love than that of a young child. But teach a child hatred and prejudice and the mind begins to close, the heart to harden, until, finally, a bigot is born. Sometimes what we don't teach our children [or ourselves] is more important than what we do.

I came to the United State of America with the open mind and the willing heart of a child. Over the years, religion and moral conscience have taught me not to hate White people; but experience has taught me not to trust them. Indeed, I can find my professional self in America, but I still cannot find my spiritual self. This enchanted society has no soul!

I've had the privilege of being a member and a one-time president of Ndi-Ichie Cultural Club, Inc. Houston, Texas; a club which draws its membership primarily from the Igbos in Houston whose hometown origin is in the old Onitsha province in the former Eastern region of Nigeria. The old Onitsha province is the heartland and a heartbeat of traditional Igbo people and Igbo culture.

The preamble to the constitution of Ndi-Ichie Cultural Club, Inc. articulates, precisely, some of the fundamental social principles of the Igbo people from which the club draws its purpose. The preamble is reprinted as follows below:

We salute our ancestors—the forefathers of our land;

the land of our culture. We salute the ancestors of the land on which we stand today. We shall not throw away the beliefs and ideals of our fathers, nor shall we bite the fingers that feed us today.

We have come together like the bunch of brooms, so that we will strengthen each other; we shall avoid being broken one at a time. Hence we will urinate at the same spot and watch it foam. Above all is humanity.

We advocate peace, honesty, unity, wisdom and integrity for all mankind. The visitor must not undo the visited, while the visited must not inflict a hunch on the visitor's back as he leaves. He who washes his hands clean shall eat with the kings. We advocate responsibility for education, and education for responsibility. We shall learn their ways and teach ours. Wisdom is the sharing of cultures.

We come with eagle feathers on our red caps; we bring peace and wisdom. They shall live and we shall live. Let the eagle perch, and let the eaglet perch. If we can help plant the great Iroko tree, there shall be room for all to perch. We advocate the teachings of our forefathers. We advocate a return to the land to seek the solutions to the problems of all people. We advocate seeking it slowly and peacefully.

Is it not said that if one's pebble falls into the river, one must walk slowly into the river searching for it? Is it not said that one who walks slowly does not get hurt? We shall extend our hand of friendship to the short and the tall; male and female; the old and the young. We advocate law and order in any land on which we stand. A stranger has no enemy.

Come close and be our friend, you may learn something new. Something your father could not teach you. The handbag of a stranger contains good and strange things. Together, we will march forward. Long live Ndi-Ichie Cultural Club, Inc.!

(Preamble written by n'Ekwunife Muoneke, Ph.D.)

It is no accident that this preamble borrows from and espouses the general wisdom of the invocations prayerfully adduced in any ritualistic breaking of the Igbo kolanut — that revered spiritual seat of the Igbo cultural symbolism. Such invocations bring man and Spirits in peaceful communion for mutual support and universal coexistence. A sample prayer as our forefathers prayed before the advent of Christianity is necessarily published below in the Igbo language, as it must be, because "the kolanut does not understand English":

Igwe ka ala bia taa oji
Elu n'ala bia taa oji
Eke bia taa oji
Orie bia taa oji
Afo bia taa oji
Nkwo bia taa oji
Onye si m erile, ya erile
Onye si m anuna, ya anukwana
Egbe bere , Ugo bere —
Nke si ibe ya ebela, nku kwaa ya
Obiara be onye a biagbula ya
Mgbe o ga-ala, mkpumkpu apula ya
Ugbua anyi n'ekele obinigwe bu oseburuwa
Olisa bi nelu ma ogodo ya n'akpu n'ala
Onye anyi si n'aka ya n'enweta iheoma n'ile
Anyi nasi gi lekwa oji, biko gozie ya
Obu omenala nna nna anyi ha —
Nke siri n'aka fere aka wee ruo anyi aka

Ebe anyi kwere na oji bu ndu
Mee ka anyi taa oji nkea:
tara ndu .... ise
tara ngozi .... ise
tara ihunanya .... ise
tara omumu .... ise
tara idi n'otu .... ise
tara udo .... ise
K'anyi were nwee ike ibinyere gi n'ihunanya

Mgbe nile, n'oge nile, site na ndudu-ga-ndu; Ruo na ndudu-ga-ndu……….. Iseoooooo!!

Thence, strictly for the education of the non-Igbo person and with a presumption of unanimous consent by the guiding Spirits of my ancestors, I dare to provide an English translation of the foregoing libation literally as follows:

Almighty heaven, come and eat kolanut
Heaven and earth, come and eat kolanut
Eke (first Market Day), come and eat kolanut
Orie (second Market Day), come and eat kolanut
Afo (third Market Day), come and eat kolanut
Nkwo (fourth Market Day), come and eat kolanut
He who says I should not eat, may he not eat
He who says I should not drink, may he not drink
Let the eagle perch, let the eaglet perch —
Whichever should deny the other, may it lose its wings
Visit a friend with goodwill
In return may goodwill follow you when you leave

Now we thank the Almighty God in heaven
The mysterious inhabitant of the heaven, but whose elegance drape the earth
Him from whom we derive all good things
We present kolanut and ask you to bless it
It is the tradition of our forefathers —
Which has passed down to us from age to age

Since we believe that the kolanut is Life
May we eat this kolanut and:
derive Life …………………………….. Amen!
derive Blessing …………………………. Amen!
derive Love …………………………….. Amen!
derive Procreation ……………………… Amen!
derive Unity …………………………….. Amen!
derive Peace ……………………………. Amen!
So that we may direct our lives to follow you in love

Always, and at all time, from eternity to eternity ..... A-A-Amen!!

My value system as an Igboman is rooted in the philosophy of the many riddles and other statements of wisdom as contained in the preamble to the constitution of Ndi-Ichie Cultural Club, Inc. It is within the privileges and treasures of this value system that I find the social strength to strive to get along with other cultures, and the personal discipline to abide by the Divine commandments — to love not hate; to unite not separate.

It's regrettably painful to admit that I do not have all of those treasures anymore. My spiritual vaults have been raided by the devil, and my soul dealt many serious blows. It hurts so badly to know within me that I have acquired the undesirable capacity to hate— that illusionary mind's eye to see things in Black and White. I have to fight "this thing" that I have become, under the circumstances. I must strive to die the same child that I was when I came to the Untied States of America. My ancestors will accept no less, I know!

A dose of reality fighting the City of Houston relegated me to a win/lose, lose/lose mentality. In the long five years of legal war with the city, I became so centered on the "enemy" that nothing else mattered (family included), except the desire to legally change the discriminatory employment policies of the Department of Planning and Development of the City of Houston. I was poised for a WIN, even if it meant losing my professional life as a planner.

Win/lose, Lose/lose are philosophies of war. I lived outside my usual win/win character and maintained this win/lose war paradigm for five years. I was counter-dependently guided by the anticipated 'enemy' actions, while mentally seeing that 'enemy' everywhere around me and in everything I did and thought to do. I had always wondered and tried to second-guess what the City of Houston, by and through the City Attorney's office and its other agents of persecution, was up to with me. I became very defensive, sometimes overactive and, possibly, paranoid. The little power I did have came from anger, resentment and vengeance —

that needed but negative energy that shriveled, destroyed, and left nothing or very little for anything else. For this, I know I can never be the same again!

I was very candid in responding to the investigative questions of the city-contracted psychologist, Carmen Petzold, Ph.D., who published parts of my responses, verbatim, in her report. The constructive portions of that report captured and recorded my inner emotions through the duration of my legal battles with the City of Houston, and extending, unfortunately, to the present day. Part of the report read as follows:

> After Mr. Okpala had reviewed the lengthy allegations about discrimination, harassment, and retaliation which he made against the City, he was asked why he chose to stay in the position. He replied, "I'm standing up for others." However, he did state that he was quite concerned, "I don't know what else might happen to me. I'm in a battle mode most of the time. I don't say things subtly anymore." "Maybe the City has a 'hit-man' out for me. I have a right to have a job with the City. I owe this to the people who will come after me. Happiness is whether or not I did my best after it's all over. I may die doing it, but people die doing things for humanity. It's my duty. Martin Luther King died for other people too...."
>
> Mr. Okpala was also asked to provide a listing of all the changes that have occurred in his life since the time that the first events occurred. Mr. Okpala provided a two page typed list of the changes which had occurred in his life since the events commenced which he was alleging in his lawsuit. Major areas of change which he delineated were; excruciating anger and bitterness, withdrawal, loss of faith, restlessness, hurtful feeling of inadequacy and defeat, stress, mental distress.
>
> Some of the sub-notations he made under <u>excruciating anger and bitterness</u> were reflective of his being resentful, and highly suspicious. "Frustration at the persistence of the culprits and their continued enjoyment of official City support; always in a combatant mode of

watching my back; forced to be always critical of the system; being the odd person out; being definitely stamped a trouble-maker."

Notations made under the heading <u>withdrawal</u> included, "No interest in participating in department's social activities; loss of many friends; constant need to reach inside for strength and sanity; very poor communication with wife." Regarding his loss of friends, Mr. Okpala explained during the interview that, "People are afraid to talk to or be seen with me. I am not keeping up with people like I did before ... I don't have the energy or the willingness. I would rather just be thinking, processing information all the time — what will my next action be? I'm always having to plan my next battle."

Under the heading <u>stress</u>, Mr. Okpala noted aches, frequent fatigue, and loss of appetite. In discussing the changes listed under heading <u>mental distress</u>, Mr. Okpala was somewhat loose or tangential in his descriptions during the interview. Some of this apparent looseness could be due to different cultural expectations. For example he stated, "I have a spiritual obligation to pave the way for other spirits that come after me. I am always operating in the third dimension. There are some holes that I can't explain: feeling inadequate, nothing I can do. A tangible illusion; I can place myself in it. My language is very figurative. Sometimes I can only talk to myself in it. There is a sense of detachment. It is an experience you can't describe (the discrimination). It overwhelms your total self." When he was asked to explain one of his notations under mental distress, he stated, "acquired capacity to hate," "I don't care how many times I die physically, I don't want to be spiritually dead one time. It is a situation where you never know where the enemy is.

According to the records of Dr. Robert bell, a licensed psychologist, Mr. Okpala's present emotional difficulties, including his symptoms of intense anxiety and depression, do not stem from personality defects or from psychopathological causes. Basically, he is a strong person whose hostile and discriminatory treatment in his work environment has resulted in severe emotional suffering.

It is said that wars are won in the general's tent. Meaning that the requisite human strength of character for winning wars must come from within, rather than from without. Thus, relatively, Philip Brooks writes:

> Some day in the years to come, you will be wrestling with the great temptation, or trembling under the great sorrow of your life. But the real struggle is here, now... Now it is being decided whether, in the day of your supreme sorrow or temptation, you shall miserably fail or gloriously conquer. Character cannot be made except by a steady, long continued process. [19]

Peace of mind comes only when life is in harmony with one's true principles and values. Sometimes in the darker hours of our human experience, it is tempting to harbor resentment or to retaliate with the weapon of bitter silence. But it is better to look up in faith and remain prayerfully patient: Thus, praying to our God of surprise and wonder that He would keep us ever aware of His ability to move in many ways we never expected; that we may believe in the impossible which He repeatedly shows us He is capable of; that our God of hope would penetrate our hearts which is often tempted by disbelief; that by the mighty power of His holy spirits, He would help us dare to believe He is the author of a new world order, and make us certain He is bringing change, even as we pray as true believers in the Messiah whom we await. In such times, I look up boldly and call upon my God to come down quickly and take over. I call upon Him directly, neither through some spiritual hierarchy nor some religious denomination, but directly in my privileged capacity as a spiritual being in His own image. Then, and only then, can I silently and sincerely pray: "THY KINGDOM COME, THY WILL BE DONE!"

8

🏵🏵

MEMORIES OF MY TOMORROW

I wish to have the privilege of viewing the occasion of my funeral, aloof from one corner of the space above my casket. It will be one joyous transition experience, I hope, replete with all the unbiased review of my life resumé, tainted only with sincere emotions of my friends and acquaintances; a eulogized testimony of my stewardship, and a preemptive invitation for a return journey, prayerfully ordained by God Himself. Then, and only then, in the third dimension, shall I smile at the memories of my tomorrow.

My tomorrow resides in my past as refined by my present. I know that my tomorrow will be happiest where I am today — serving God and humanity. The road to here has been long, difficult, and sometimes painful, because these are the spring sources of the many winding rivers of my Easter. The new life gained each time is reason for joy, as the journey continues on course.

My Window Is Different Than Yours

The least change in our point of view gives the whole world a pictorial air, the indisputable effect of culture and experience. To the attentive eye, each moment of life has its own beauty; and in the same context, it beholds, every hour, a picture which has never been seen before and which shall never be seen again. The tribes of people, birds and insects, like the plants punctual to their time, follow each other and life has room for all. The silent clock ticks on and contributes something to the mute music of the beautiful nature. But it could all be a mirage, as one looks from the windows of diligence; for "In the fields of observation, chance favors only the prepared mind." [Louis Pasteur].

Our age is retrospective. It builds sepulchers of the fathers and writes biographies, histories and criticism. Simplistically speaking, we live in a primarily left-brain-dominant world, where words, measurements and logic are enthroned; and where the more creative, intuitive, sensing, artistic aspects of our nature are often subordinated. The health of the eye seems to demand a horizon, in which we are never tired, so long as we can see far enough.

And my window is different than yours! The Dawn and the broad Noon is my America of strenuous labor, the understanding and experience; the Midnight and Early-morning is my Africa of mystic philosophies and dreams. I please myself with the quiet observation of the graces of the unseen heroes; and I believe in the spiritual notion that we are touched by it, as by the general notion of traumatic experiences. Moments of emotional pain are only but little milestones to manhood. The events and tribulations of the forced dispersion of my ancestors into slavery have presented, and still present, many such moments of emotional pain to focused view in my window of life. Thence I marvel at the resilience of spiritual men, women, and children under countless challenges of time, man, and environment. I salute the enduring spirits of my ancestors in the Diaspora because they buckled not under the hateful weight of the institution of slavery, nor under the crushing pressure of the divine molding of our human world to a new design. I stand in awe of the many heroes of the grand processes, and genuflect in reverence to the master designers and history makers: the "bad" run-away slaves, the freedom riders, the picket marchers, the ardent Pan Africanists, the surviving social activists. I cannot help but think "back to the future," in deep, deep respect.

From my perspective I can see our world would have been very different without the American Experience of my people, in it and of it. In the United States of America, I can see and comprehend the rest of Africa and the world — all the microcosm of the new content of the Biblical Noah's ark, a wonderful display of all species as God had intended it after the great floods. It's a wonderful world, but only to the extent that we let it be!

The view from my window is different because I look to see with the mind's eye, always beyond the present. I'd rather focus on the beautiful unknowns with hopeful pleasures of the mind and soul. Thus, I look to enjoy my tomorrow in the three dimensional perspective of the body, mind, and soul, qualified only by self-awareness, imagination, conscience, and independent will. In this perspective, the vision cannot be but 20-20, a brand new, mint-mold of a spiritual child's vision that produces the ultimate delight. The power to produce this ultimate delight does not reside in nature but in me, or in a loving harmony of both. One must become a child to use this power with great temperance, opening up the mind to the influence of the kindred impressions of natural objects. This is so because,

> Very few adult persons can see nature; adults have very superficial seeing. The sun illuminates only the eye of the man, but it shines into the eyes and the heart of the child. Nothing is quite beautiful alone, nothing but is beautiful in the whole. A simple object is only so far beautiful as it suggests this universal grace.[20]

Hence, once in view, one would adjust his or her spiritual kaleidoscope to articulate a beautiful "whole" of a world of heroes, angels, and saints. Anyone may go as a friend to another's window to the world and ask questions.

It is within the mindset of such open invitation to my visual world that I once implored the famous Hakeem Olajuwon to review his priorities and re-focus his attention to matters of his relationship with the Nigerian community in Houston. In my article titled, *"Hakeem: Beyond the Dream"*, published in the Houston Punch newspaper, January 1997, and reprinted below, I implored Olajuwon to look to see the real issues in the present and future world of the Nigerian-Americans in Houston. I implored Mr. Olajuwon to indeed see beyond the dream that:

Yes, indeed, for millions of Nigerians and Nigerian-Americans, especially the tens of thousands in Houston, the story of Hakeem, the Nigerian-American, is already a story far beyond basketball. One can watch Hakeem and see the typical work ethics of the average Nigerian or Nigerian-American. Typically, their motto is 'steady eye on the ball' and steadfast struggle for proscribed results. While he, Hakeem Olajuwon, personifies professional excellence in his sport, the rest of deserving Nigerians and Nigerian-Americans, are due a fair shake from their contributing work ethics outside and beyond the proud symbol of "Hakeem the Dream" and basketball.

It's always a common practice that after the fire, when the dust is settled and cool, people search the rubble for any un-answered questions. We, the Nigerians and Nigerian-Americans in Houston, should act no differently. After the marvel and luster of a "Twoston" (1994 and 1995 Houston back-to-back NBA Championship victories) performances at the NBA championship basketball under Hakeem (the Dream) Olajuwon, the Nigerian-American, comes the right time for us to ponder at some yet un-answered questions about our social, economic, and political existence in Houston:

• What is it, exactly, does the City of Houston claim to celebrate in cultural diversity, when well-educated, hard-working Nigerians and Nigerian-Americans, cannot secure decent jobs or, are denied the right to fair competition for promotions in their respective places of employment?

• What *really* would it take for the Nigerian community in Houston to "belong" in the City's social, economic, and political mainstream?

• What is it in the Nigerians' speaking voice and/or native accent that renders us almost unilaterally unemployable, and/or unpromotable, usually for purported *"lack of organization and communication skills"*?

There is a special pleasure in watching Hakeem the Dream in and outside the basketball court. But, considering the fact that when it comes to his getting a fair share of the ultimate proceeds of his selfless contribution to the sport of basketball, he, Hakeem Olajuwon, is still left outside the mainstream of the money wagon, that pleasure is short lived. We Nigerians and Nigerian-Americans cannot but wonder whether we must give up our cultural identity in order to belong in, and benefit from, this society we now call home. The Mayor and City Council of the City of Houston are yet to respond to the above questions that were put to them at the occasion of my address to the council session of August 20, 1994.

While we must await an official answer from the city, we should also endeavor to search our souls, and such rubble as the NBA Championship, Houston-proud, celebrations, for more personal and realistic answers. As for Hakeem, the dream, Olajuwon, he should take a quiet-time, wide-eyed look through his mind's window, on the *other* side of his NBA trophies, and ask himself a personal question: If he, Hakeem the Nigerian-American, can take such good care of Houston and America, why don't Houston and America take good care of deserving Nigerians and Nigerian-Americans in Houston? Equity and good faith demand an answer!

Tracing The Cycle:

The Child I Shall Become

Is there a cycle of life? Is there a cycle of learning where no point is either the beginning or an end, and lines can be drawn from any one point to another? Supposing that some line can clearly be drawn to divide the concept of life from the reality of death, the problem, for those of us who conceive the universe as one, would be whether it is then one world or two; whether the rift or chasm that separates life from death would involve an iron curtain or a great wall of China. If that should be, it would prevent communication between the two worlds.

Nonetheless, an answer appears to be suggested by the conception that the human body, mind, and soul are but one union— an organized whole. This conception serves to favor the view that, in any natural system that survives and recycles itself, there can be no impenetrable barriers to communication, or unbridgeable breaks in continuity within that system. Such is the cycle of human life. Underscoring it, is the human faith that the whole encyclopedic concept of man's being is a single universe of discourse.

Every year, in the middle of the month of June, I think a little more seriously about a topic that interests everyone but concerns only those who have reached certain age plateaus. The topic is, "getting older." The reason I think about it at this time of the year is because I celebrate another year of life in the month of June. The interesting thing about this aging process is that each of us faces the same inescapable prospect, yet we all handle it differently. It all depends on one's perspective.

Our lifetime passes quickly, as the writer of Psalm 90 pointed out so bluntly (v.10): "The days of our years are threescore years and ten (70). And if by reason of strength they be fourscore (80) years, yet their strength is achieved through labor and sorrow, for it is soon cut off, and we fly away." Because the foregoing is true, we need the kind of attitude and positive expectation poet Robert Browning displayed when he wrote: "Grow old with me! The best is yet to be, the last of life for which the first was made." Life is cumulative, Browning was saying, and each of our days is a foundation for tomorrow. As we maintain this perspective, we will enjoy the passage of time. My prayer is for a youthful old age. The true substance of my fated experience is in my faith that as God adds years to my life, He will add life to my years.

I am not solitary in my quiet time though nobody is with me. I am a man in love with nature— those essences unchanged, and unchangeable, by man: space, the air, the rivers, the animals, and the woods—the integrity of impression made by manifold natural objects. Nature, in its service to man, is not only the material, but is also the process and the result. To my adult body and mind, which will have been cramped by noxious work or company, nature is medicinal and shall restore my tone. The natural man in me belongs in the woods, the very first laboratory of my childhood years to which I shall return.

"In the woods, a man casts off his years, as the snake his slough, and at what period so ever of life, is always a child. In the woods is perpetual youth." [21] In the woods, I shall return to reason and faith. There, nothing can befall me: no disgrace, and no calamity which nature cannot repair. I shall become nothing but shall see all things. The currents of the universal Being shall circulate through me, for I am part and particle of God. I shall have no questions to ask which are unanswerable, and no personal needs which are insatiable. The two lasting bequests I shall have are roots and wings—a strong intergenerational family and the freedom to rise above any negative scripting that may have been passed down to me. I shall become a "transition" person, the person who can change and transfer better scripts to the next generation. I shall become the refined link between the past and the future. My transitional changes shall affect many, many lives to come.

The child I shall become is a spiritual being with human experience, rather than a human being with spiritual experience. It will give meaning to my life, and enable me to love, to serve, and to try again; the cycle of my childlike life shall continue in perpetuity. Death will be only but a process similar to my birth as a child. I'm sure I didn't ask or want to be born, therefore I cried in apparent protest. I'm sure if you could ask any infant still in the womb if it wants to be born, it would say: "No way! I'm warm, protected, and nourished in here. I've heard that the process of being born, and the act of living, are very stressful. And besides, I don't know what it's like out there on the other side."

Similarly, nobody wants to go through the process of death.

We become comfortable here, and we don't really know much about what lies beyond this life. But it is conceivable that death is far beyond what we know as our present life and, by faith, we can prepare for death by living as fully in life as fate allows. Then, when the time comes, we can die as children of God, confirmed in the eternal cycle of our being. And so shall it be!

Integrity: Measuring Success

"When what we do become more important than who we are, we are in trouble. Big trouble!" [Richard Dortch.] [22]

The reason that the game of politics will always elude me is because I have not learned to put up a public face while thinking a private thought — that art of educated mass deceit. Integrity is, fundamentally, the value we place on ourselves. It is our ability to make and keep commitments to ourselves; the guts to "walk our talk".

Is it ever right to stretch the truth? Is it right to slant it and make it serve some predetermined goal? Is it ever judicious to tell a lie to protect someone or something? Does the end ever justify the means? Considering the foregoing questions, Richard Dortch writes, in compendium:

Objectivity and credibility are important but dying issues in today's world. In relationships, in the workplace, at home, or at church, we have become too concerned about success, bigness, and its related issues. Producing character and knowing how to live no longer seem to be essential in our modern society. The catch phrase may well have become: "The Shifting of Value-system Syndrome," the shrewd survival of the fittest.

There is integrity and honor in truth! When we practice deceit, we lie. The problem becomes that a general suspicion and distrust accumulate in society, and so we find ourselves in a state of affairs where hardly anyone believes what they hear. Lying betrays a lack of courage. It says, " I don't have the guts to stand up for what is right."

Quite often, the bigger problem is not what we do, but what we fail to do. Often, when we fail, it is not the result of ignorance. Most people know what they are supposed to do and the importance of why they should do it. Therefore, when it comes to moral misjudgment, they cannot plead ignorance. More knowledge won't help because they are already capable of discerning right from wrong. What's needed is the will to live up to what they already know. Failure results because they are unwilling to follow through on what they know to be right. Integrity is telling the truth and not picking and choosing the facts. It's always easy to alter our integrity to meet our own set of circumstances. This is selective integrity. Selective integrity is doing evil and expecting good to come out of it. Each time we experience selective integrity, whether as the one who is doing it or being harmed by it, we lose respect for each other and, ultimately, ourselves.

All this means that the significance of a life of integrity is in its wholeness, its completeness. What's dirty on one side is dirty on the other. What's clean on one side is clean on the other. There cannot be a two-faced, double meaning to things we do. Our lives are complete in detail, without duplicity.

In today's society, we are challenged by a growing degree of cynicism and sophistication, a sense that all things are relative and nothing is absolutely right or wrong. We are challenged further, therefore, to come up with a common empirical formula for measuring success. [23]

My take is that "success" is illusive, and the real test of who a person is resides in his or her character. What God intended for me to become is more important than what I do or own in life. To me, this element of personal truth is essential to living a life of integrity, and in measuring success afterwards.

Generally, according to Steven Covey, an author and renowned motivational speaker, the old "Character" ethic taught that there are basic principles of effective and fulfilled living, and that people can only experience true success and enduring happiness as they learn and integrate these principles into their basic characters. Aspects of these basic principles include integrity, humility, fidelity, temperance, courage, justice, industry, modesty, and the Golden Rule: "Do unto others as you would like them do unto you." The more modern "Personality" ethic teaches differently that, "Your attitude determines your altitude"— survival of the shrewdest. Although part of this social paradigm stresses the importance of positive mental attitude—"Whatever the mind of man can conceive and believe, it can achieve"—its fundamental approach to success is clearly manipulative, or even deceptive. It encourages people to use techniques to get other people to like them, or fake interest in the hobbies of others to get out of them what they wanted for themselves; or, to use the "power look" or "power walk" to intimidate their way through life.

Both Character ethic and Personality ethic are social paradigms of success. I belong and subscribe fully to the Character ethic. My social paradigms determine my definition of success. I have searched my heart diligently and seen the issues of life that flow from it. Life is a natural system, "You always reap what you sow." There are no shortcuts! Mr. Covey points out that many people with secondary greatness, such as social recognition for talents and personality, lack primary greatness or goodness in their character. But it is character that communicates most eloquently the ultimate value of success.

The more aware I have become of my basic notions of life, maps, and/or assumptions, and the extent to which I have been influenced by my life experiences, the more I take responsibility for those notions, examine them, test them against reality, listen to others, and, thereby, get a larger and a far more objective view of success. "We are what we repeatedly do." "Excellence (as well as success) is not an act (or occurrence), but a habit." [Aristotle]. Our character, basically, is a composite of our habits. Thus, sequentially, the common maxim goes: "Sow a thought, reap an action; sow an action, reap a habit; sow a habit, reap a character;

sow a character, reap a destiny". [24] "Habits are essential factors in life because they are consistent, often unconscious patterns. They constantly express our character and produce our effectiveness (success), or our ineffectiveness (failure)." [25] Developing personal habit involves a rigorous process and tremendous self-commitment. It is a painful process of change and consolidation that must be motivated by a personal and higher purpose in life. And, in my case, by a willingness to subordinate what I think I want now, for what I want in eternity. But even then, the process produces genuine happiness — a fruit of the desire and ability to sacrifice personal pleasures for effective living. It enhances true independence of character, which in turn matures into a highly interdependent paradigm of a natural life, and, thence, to the maximum effectiveness of a successful living.

There is also the intrinsic security that comes from effective interdependent living. I have come to know myself in deeper, more meaningful ways, understand my deepest values, and recognize my unique contribution capacity. As I live my values, my sense of identity, integrity, control, and inner-directness infuse me with both exhilaration and peace. I have defined myself from within, rather than from without, not through people's opinions, or by comparisons of myself to others. At my core, "Right" and "Wrong", "Success" and "Failure" have very little to do with my operational mental attitude. I subscribe to the wisdom of Victor Frankl, a Jewish psychiatrist and a survivor of Nazi death camps during World War II, who used the known human endowment of self-awareness to discover a fundamental principle about the nature of man. Mr. Frankl writes:

> Between stimulus and response, man has the freedom to choose. Within this freedom to choose are those endowments that make us uniquely human. In addition to self-awareness, we have imagination — the ability to create in our minds beyond our present reality. We have conscience — a deep inner awareness of right and wrong; of principles that govern our behavior, and a sense of degree to which our thoughts and action are in harmony with them. And we have independent will — the ability

to act based on our self-awareness, free of all other circumstantial influences. [26]

It is when this independent will is elevated to a higher level, and applied in cycle to imagination and conscience in natural-law interdependent living, that success is literally guaranteed. No matter the context and the measuring parameters, a balanced, win/win life is achieved; a value-driven cycle of fulfilled life, death, and rebirth that equals SUCCESS in any human language and/or social culture. In his book *The Seven Steps of Highly Effective People*, Steven Covey comments further on Frankl's findings:

> We don't have to go through the death camp experience of Frankl to recognize and develop our own proactivity. It is in the ordinary events of every day that we develop the proactive capacity to handle the extraordinary pressures of life. It's how we make and keep commitments, how we handle traffic jam, how we respond to an irate customer, a critic, or a disobedient child. It's how we view our problems and where we focus our emergencies. It's the body language and attitude we use and display in our everyday living. [27]

It is solely in the way we measure "success"! It is the extents to which we take responsibility for our own effectiveness, develop our own mode of happiness, and, ultimately, take control of our life's challenging circumstances. As Samuel Johnson observed:

> The foundation of content (and success) must spring up in the mind; and he who has so little knowledge of human nature as to seek happiness (and success) by changing anything but his own disposition, will waste his life in fruitless efforts, and multiply the grief he proposes to remove. [28]

Life is truly effective only when we begin with the end in mind — the schematic painting of the total picture, the preemptive conceptualization of the whole. If you would carefully consider what you want to have said on your tombstone, you will find your personal definition of SUCCESS.

Truly, the only real success is the success with self, the self that one has discovered and understood over one's life experiences and fate. For me, success is not in having things, but in having mastery and victory over the aspects of me not suitable for life after death. My success is measured and guaranteed in any principled upholding of my personal values and established mission statement, that central part of my being so principle-based that it is immune from short-term circumstantial changes in life; those basic paradigms at my core. By centering our lives on timeless, solid, unchanging principles, we create a fundamental paradigm for effective living. It is this center that puts all other "centers" of our lives in perspective, and allows us to measure true success. In this proper context, therefore, "Success," said IBM founder T. J. Watson, " is on the far side of Failure." And, if I may add, ONLY YOU CAN BE YOUR OWN JUDGE!

When we examine the human endowment of independent will in the context of effective self-management, we realize it's usually not the dramatic, the visible, the once-in-a-lifetime, up-by-the-bootstraps effort that brings enduring success. Rather, success is measured ultimately by the degree to which we have developed our independent will in our everyday lives, which is itself measured by our personal integrity. This integrity is our ability to make and keep commitments to ourselves, to "walk our talk." It is honor with self, a fundamental part of the character ethic and the essence of a proactive life. Success and satisfaction, therefore, become a function of personal expectation, as well as personal realization, both in spiritual and concrete terms. The key is a life-long scheduling and achievement of value-driven goals and priorities. I hope you agree.

Hip! Hip! Hip! Hooray!!

I rejoice in life for its own sake. Life is no brief candle to me. It's a sort of splendid torch which I've got to hold up for the moment, and want to make burn as brightly as possible, before handing it on to future generations. I celebrate in advance the victory of my service to nature and mankind — personal victories, public victories; known, and yet unknown.

The human animal would always seek ways, and find reasons, to celebrate for assorted happenstances of big and small victories or successes in life, however they may have been articulated or defined. Feasts and festivals are often the preferred vehicles for proclamations of joy and/or elated excitement for personal or community victories, successes and achievements. Throughout the history of human cultures, certain days or periods of time have been set aside to commemorate, ritually celebrate, re-enact, or anticipate events or seasons—be it national, religious, political, or socio-cultural—that give meaning and cohesiveness to an individual and his or her religious, political, or socio-cultural community.

Feasts and festivals usually—though not always at all times—involve eating or drinking or both, in connection with specific kinds of rites, such as passage rites, seasonal observances, and commemorative observances. Festivals often include not only feasting, but also dramatic dancing and athletic events, as well as revelries and carnivals that at times border on the licentious. By their very nature, feasts and festivals are special times. Not just in the sense that they are extraordinary occasions, but in the sense that they are separate from ordinary times. Through ritualistic re-enactment of the events that inform an individual about his or her identity, achievements and destiny, that individual participant in a festival identifies him or herself with the sacred time. The religious individual feels the need to plunge periodically into this sacred and indestructible time. For him or her, it is the sacred time that makes possible the other time — ordinary time, the profane duration in which every human life takes its course. It is the eternal present of the mythical event that makes possible the profane duration of historical events. In religious cultures, sacred times occur for sacred reasons. For example:

• In Chinese religions, New Year festivals (January to February) celebrate the victory of order in nature over chaos.

- In Christianity, the festival of Easter or Feast of the Resurrection is the ritual re-enactment of the event of Christ's victory over death, every year (March to May), in order that the believer might participate in the present and future kingdom of peace.
- In Judaism, Hanukkah (December to January), the Feast of Dedication, also called the Feast of Lights, the eight-day commemoration of the victory of the Jewish Maccabees over the Syrians and the redemption of the Temple at Jerusalem.
- In Islam, The Great Festival (occurs at variable times) inaugurates the pilgrimage to Mecca.

More so, national festivals of independence commemorate national socio-political freedoms from their erstwhile colonial masters. Other sacred times commemorating crucial stages of personal victories in life, such as birth, puberty, marriage, and death have been times of sacred significance for peoples of all races, from time immemorial.

Some feasts and festivals provide psychological, cathartic, and therapeutic outlets for people during periods of seasonal depression. In Africa, for example, the natural urge to express joy and emotion is also satisfied in the ritual dance on the proper occasions. In modern sports, for another example, winning is everything and is celebrated to the ultimate: "A win is a win and all that matters," the maxim goes. On the chalkboard of modern competitive sports, the only mathematics or logic that matters is that the sum total of numbers on the win column, be greater than that on the loss column. In sports, winners and losers belong in different worlds, much like day and night on the opposite sides of the earth in the sun's orbit. This separation by numbers is absolute, and it frowns seriously at any non-quantifiable rationalization or subjective wisdom to the contrary.

Next to numbers, however, there is statistics — a higher order of mathematics—which, though it allows certain rationalization and also, by necessity, allows subjective insights into the more complex and unreal areas of the number system, yet advances separation to dangerous levels. In a rigid world of statistical probability, the separation between win and lose is only but a thin line of chance of action or inaction, success or failure, hope or despair— a 50/50 rigid artificial parameter for determining human fate. Thus, in our world of labor and chance, there are exactly as many winners as there are losers; meaning that, possibly, in this matter, a simple arithmetic operation of subtraction would hypothetically resolve and equate the whole universe of human fate and human endeavor to an empirical zero. Wherefore, in that case, the whole universal theory of being would have become but a gigantic lie.

Therefore, Mark Twain, the famous American writer and philosopher, may have been technically correct when he once commented that "There are lies, damn lies, and then there is statistics," presumably, according to him, in that order of inherent iniquity. But we now know that life is much more than real numbers and statistics. Thus, in the fated universe of spiritual living, there are only winners, and any serious, conscious striving by one at stepping into this spiritual universe, guarantees one the everlasting occasion to shout for oneself, three happy cheers of joyful exhilaration: Hip! Hip! Hip! Hooray!!

"A good name is better than precious ointment; and the day of death better than the day of one's birth." (Ecclesiastes 7:1). If not, why is it that we don't always recognize when life begins, but we think we always know when it ends? I leave you with a personal poem to share:

One For Me

BLESSED ARE ALL THE TEARS THAT FALL
CLEANSING THE WINDOWS OF SOULS THAT HURT
THEY USHER IN A CHANGE OF HEART ANEW
PRAYING THIS WORLD A BETTER PLACE FOR ALL

LIFE'S NOT FAIR BUT GOD IS GOOD I KNOW
SO I'LL KEEP THE FAITH ALIVE
WITH ALL THE TRUST OF A SPARROW ALIKE
STILL TRUSTING PEOPLE I DON'T EVEN KNOW

LIFE'S NOT FAIR BUT GOD IS GOOD I KNOW
SO I'LL KEEP THE FAITH ALIVE

WITH ALL THE CONTENTMENT OF A DOVE ATOW
NOT WORRIED A HAIR ABOUT OUR MAN-MADE WORLD

LIFE'S NOT FAIR BUT GOD IS GOOD I KNOW
SO I'LL KEEP THE FAITH ALIVE
WITH ALL THE COURAGE OF AN EAGLE ASOAR
SMOOTH THROUGH, THOUGH TOUGH UNDER PRESSURE

LIFE'S NOT FAIR BUT GOD IS GOOD I KNOW
SO I'LL KEEP THE FAITH ALIVE
WITH MUCH HOPE FOR COMFORT ABOUND
STILL MINE, THE GOSPEL ACCORDING TO THE BIRDS

BLESSED ARE ALL THE TEARS THAT FALL
CLEANSING THE WINDOWS OF SOULS THAT HURT
SO LORD GOD WHEN NEXT YOU MAKE THE DAYS AMORE
PLEASE CUT OUT ONE QUIET, PEACEFUL DAY FOR ME.

Thank you for taking the time and interest to meet me. May our hopes endure!

...Ome-na-nwayo....

Endnotes

1. Guide to Encyclopaedia Britannica. The Mysteries of life: Introduction to Part Three, Life on Earth; page 127
2. Guide to the Britannica. The Point and Pleasure of Reading History: Introduction to part Nine; page 560
3. Serfontein, J.H.P. Brotherhood of power: An Expose of the Secret Afrikaner Broederbond. Bloomington, Indiana: Indiana University Press, 1978.
4. Wilkins, Ivory and H. Strydom. The Broederbond. New York: Paddington Press, 1979.
5. Durkeim, Emile. "Education and Society" In Power and Ideology in Education, New York: Oxford, 1977.
6. Van Sertima, Ivan, ed. Egypt Revisited: Journal of African Civilization. New Brunswick: transaction Press, 1982.
7. Diop, Chikh. The cultural Unity of Black Africa. Chicago: Third World press, 1978.
8. Rashidi, Runoko, ed. African Presence in Early Asia: Journal of African Civilization. New Brunswick: Transaction press, 1988.
9. Asa G. Hillard, III. The Maroon Within Us. Baltimore, MD: Black Classic Press, 1995; page 192.
10. Budge, 1973; Hilliard in The Maroon Within Us, 1995; page 188.
11. The Book of Hope. Florida: Life Publishers International, 1994.
12. Ngubane, Jordan K. Conflict of Minds: Changing Power Distributions in South Africa. New York: Books in Focus, 1979.
13. Bradley/Beatty/Long/Perkins. (Emerson Ralph Waldo on Fate). The American Tradition in Literature, 5th Edition. New York: Random house, 1956

14. Power Thoughts from the World's Greatest Power Thinkers. Garden Grove CA: Crystal Cathedral Ministries, 1996.
15. Covey, Steven. *The Seven Steps of Highly Effective People.* New York: Simon & Schuster, 1989. Page 299.
16. Bradley/Beatty/Long/Perkins. (Emerson on Nature), page 574.
17. Bid, page 583.
18. Bid (Herbert, George. "Man" stanza 4), page 594.
19. Covey. Page 297.
20. Bradley/Beatty/Long/Perkins; (Emerson on Nature).
21. Bid, page 568.
22. Dortch, Robert. Integrity: How I Lost it and My Journey Back. Green Forest, Arizona: New Leaf Press, 1993. Page 40.
23. Bid, pages 291-320.
24. Schuller, Robert. Power Thoughts from the World's Greatest Power Thinkers. Garden Grove CA: Crystal Cathedral Ministries, 1996
25. Covey. Page 46.
26. Covey on Victor Frankl; *The Seven Steps of Highly Effective People,* page 70.
27. Covey. Page 92.
28. Covey on Samuel Johnson; *The Seven Steps of Highly Effective People.* Page 93.

APPENDIX A

Text of first (discrimination) lawsuit against the City of Houston

IN THE UNITED STATES DISTRICT COURT
FOR THE SOUTHERN DISTRICT OF TEXAS
HOUSTON DIVISION

BENNETH E. OKPALA	§
Plaintiff,	§ C.A.NO H-
92-1867	
Vs.	§
	§
MAYOR BOB LANIER,	§
CITY OF HOUSTON, DEPARTMENT	§
OF PLANNING AND DEVELOPMENT,	§
MARINA SUKUP, CHARLES SETTLE,	§
MARLENE GAFRICK, J. HAL CATON,	§
DONNA R. KRISTAPONIS, BOB LITKE,	§
PATRICIA RINCON-KALLMM, and	§
CHRISTINE BALLARD;	§
Defendants	§

PLAINTIFF'S SECOND AMENDED COMPLAINT TO THE
HONORABLE JUDGE OF SAID COURT:

COMES NOW, BENNETH E. OKPALA and files this his
Plaintiff's Second Amended Complaint against BOB

LANIER as the MAYOR OF THE CITY OF HOUSTON, THE CITY OF HOUSTON DEPARTMENT OF PLANNING AND DEVELOPMENT, MARINA SUKUP, CHARLES SETTLE, MARLENE GAFRICK, J. HAL CATON, BOB LITKE, PATRICIA RINCON-KALLMAN, and CHRISTINE BALLARD, hereinafter referred to as Defendants, and would respectfully show the Court the following:

I.

Plaintiff, BENNETH OKPALA, complains against the Defendants and alleges that Defendants discriminated against him with respect to employment on the basis of race and national origin, in contravention with the mandates of Title VII of the Civil Rights Act of 1964, as amended, 42 U.S.C. 2000e et. seq., and in violation of the Civil Rights Act of 1866, as amended, 42 U.S.C. 1981.

II.
JURISDICTION

(1) This action is of a civil nature for injunctive relief and damages, and to secure the protection of and to redress deprivation of rights secured by Title VII of the Civil Rights Act of 1964, as amended, 42 U.S.C. 2000e et seq., providing for relief against discrimination in employment on the basis of race and national origin; and 42 U.S.C. Sec. 1981 providing for the redress of deprivation of the right to make and enforce contracts and to the full and equal benefit of all laws as enjoyed by white citizens.

(2) The jurisdiction of this court is invoked under 28 U.S.C. 1343, 42 U.S.C. 2000e et seq., and 42 U.S.C. 1981.

(3) The unlawful employment practices alleged below were and are being committed within the Southern District of the State of Texas, Houston Division.

(4) The City of Houston, through its grievance proceedings has failed to provide relief to BENNETH OK-

PALA and has equally failed to control the discriminatory practices of the department against BENNETH OKPALA.

III.
PARTIES

(5) Plaintiff, BENNETH OKPALA, is an African American male citizen of the United States and is a resident of Harris County, Texas.

(6) Plaintiff, BENNETH OKPALA, was born in Nigeria and was a citizen of Nigeria until August 25, 1989, when he became a naturalized citizen of the United States of America.

(7) Defendant, CITY OF HOUSTON, is a municipal corporation organized under the constitution, general and special laws of the State of Texas in 1837, and service can be had by serving Anna Russell, City Secretary, City Hall, 901 Bagby, Room 203, Houston, Texas 77002.

(8) Defendant, CHARLES SETTLE is a resident of Harris County Texas, and was the manager of the Comprehensive Planning Division of the Department of Planning and Development within the City of Houston, and was Plaintiff, BENNETH OKPALA's supervisor at all material times relevant to the discriminatory practices alleged in BENNETH OKPALA's Original Complaint and also herein complain of, and process can be had upon him at 900 Bagby, Houston, Harris County, Texas 77002.

(9) Defendant, MARINA SUKUP, is a resident of Fort Bend County, Texas, and was the Assistant director of the Department of Planning and Development of the City of Houston, and was BENNETH OKPALA's Assistant Director at all time material to the discriminatory practices alleged in "Plaintiff's Original Complaint," and process can be had upon her at 39 Epping Forest Way, Sugar Land, Texas 77479.

(10) Defendant, MARLENE GAFRICK, a supervisor with the Department of Planning and Development at all

time material to discriminatory practices alleged in "Plaintiff's Original Complaint", interviewed BENNETH OKPALA for the Planner III position, and can be served at 900 Bagby, Suite 4001, Houston, Texas 77002.

(11) Defendant, DONNA H. KRISTAPONIS, is a resident of Harris County, Texas, and is the Director of the Department of Planning and Development of the City of Houston, and is BENNETH OKPALA's director at all times material to the discriminatory practices alleged below, beginning from the date of Defendant's employment with the city of Houston as a Director of the Department of Planing and Development of the City of Houston, and process can be had upon her at 1801 Main Street, 7th Floor, Houston, Harris County, Texas 77002.

(12) Defendant, BOB LITKE, is a resident of Harris County, Texas, and is the Deputy Director of the Department of Planning and Development of the 'City of Houston, and is BENNETH OKPALA's Director at all times material to the discriminatory practices alleged below, beginning from the date of Defendant's employment with the City of Houston, and process can be had upon him at 1801 Main Street, 7th Floor, Houston, Harris County, Texas 77002.

(13) Defendant, PATRICIA RINCON-KALLMAN, is a resident of Harris County, Texas, and is the Assistant Director of Comprehensive Planning Division, Department of Planning and Development of the City of Houston, and is BENNETH OKPALA's Assistant Director of Comprehensive Planning Division at all time material to the discriminatory practices alleged below, beginning from the date of Defendant's employment with the City of Houston as an Assistant Director of Comprehensive Planning Division, and process can be had upon her at 1801 Main Street, 6th Floor, Houston, Harris County, Texas 77002.

(14) Defendant, CHRISTINE BALLARD, is a resident of Harris County, Texas, and is the Manager, Comprehensive Planning Division, Department of Planning and

Development of the City of Houston, and is BENNETH OKPALA's Manager at all time material to the discriminatory practices alleged below, beginning from the date of Defendant's employment with the City of Houston, and process can be had upon her at 1801 Main Street, 6th Floor, Houston, Harris County, Texas 77002.

(15) Defendant, J. HAL CATON, is a resident of Harris County, Texas, and is the Acting Director of the Department of Planning and Development of the City of Houston, and was BENNETH OKPALA's Acting Director at all time material to the discriminatory practices alleged in the Original Complaint, and service can be had upon him at 1801 Main Street, 2nd Floor, Houston, Harris County, Texas 77002.

IV.
CONDITIONS PRECEDENT TO FILING SUIT

(16) On or about December 22, 1992 BENNETH OKPALA received another "Notice of Right to Sue" from the District Office of the EEOC.

(17) All conditions precedent to filing suit under Title VII of the Civil Rights Act of 1964, 42 U.S.C. 2000e et. seq. have been satisfied. Upon the occurrence of the factual circumstances constituting the basis for this claim, BENNETH OKPALA timely filed complaints with the Equal Employment Opportunity Commission (EEOC)

V.
FACTUAL ALLEGATIONS

On or about March 27, 1992, BENNETH OKPALA received Notice of Right to Sue from the District Office of the EEOC.

(18) BENNETH OKPALA sought to be promoted to a better job position but was denied such promotion solely because of his race and national origin.

(19) On or about September 1989, BENNETH OKPALA applied for the then open positions of Planner III,

within the Comprehensive Planning and Current Planning Divisions of the Department of Planning and Development, but Defendants refused to hire him for the positions and instead hired two white males and a white female with less experience and/or seniority.

(20) Three times in 1990, BENNETH OKPALA applied for the then open positions of Planner III within the Department of Planning and Development in the City of Houston, but Defendants refused to hire him and in each instance, hired white male or female employees with less experience and/or seniority.

(21) During the above said occasions, BENNETH OKPALA, along with Michael Kramer, was interviewed for Planner III Positions that were then open. The position was offered to Michael Kramer (white male), and Michael Kramer was promoted to Planner III position.

(22) Prior to the posting of the above positions, Margaret Wallace was hand-picked by MARINA SUKUP to fill a Planner III position in the Comprehensive Planning Division. That position was never posted for competition. Margaret Wallace was an Administrative Assistant in the Housing and Economic Development Division. She does not have a degree in planning and had no planning experience prior to her selection. Ms. Wallace was subsequently promoted to Planner Leader, and was recently selected by PATRICIA RINCON-KALLMAN for promotion to Administrative Manager position.

(23) At about the same period as in number 20, Rebecca Thompson (white female) was promoted to the position of Planner III in the Current Planning Division of the Department of Planning and Development.

(24) At about the same period as in number 20, and number 21, Michael Johnson (a white male) was subsequently hired from outside of the Department to fill the remaining Planner III position in the Comprehensive Planning Division.

(25) BENNETH OKPALA's record of employment was rated as above standard and had been previously rec-

ommended for the promotion by his previous supervisor, Madan Mangal. The promotion was suspended until the budget constraints could be worked out with the city government.

(26) BENNETH OKPALA contends that he is more qualified and has more experience in areas such as planning than Michael Kramer, Rebecca Thompson, and Michael Johnson, respectively.

(27) BENNETH OKPALA was denied the promotional opportunities in violation of departmental policies because of his race and national origin.

(31) BENNETH OKPALA contends that MARINA SU-KUP, CHARLES SETTLE, J. HAL CATON and MARLENE GAFRICK conspired to hire and promote MICHAEL KRAMER because of his social affiliations with MARINA SUKUP who was the then Assistant Director, and also because of his color (white), in violation of equal employment opportunity clause of the Civil Rights Act of 1964.

(32) On or about December, 1991, or early during January 1992, BOB LITKE and PATRICIA RINCON-KALLMAN approached Mr. Mangal, BENNETH OKPALA's former Supervisor, in Mr. Litke's office; the substance of their conversation was to use influence and their superior position to influence Mr. Mangal to reconsider his favorable evaluation of Mr. Okpala. Mr. Mangal was concerned enough to communicate such approach to Mr. Okpala.

(30) Following BENNETH OKPALA's filing of a grievance against the Department, he was openly and constructively ostracized and excluded from department activities, causing him great emotional and mental anguish and professional degradation, which further denied him valuable opportunities to grow and become even more qualified to earn higher positions within the department and the city, all of which constituted harassment, retaliation, and further discrimination against Mr. Okpala on the part of Defendants.

(31) BENNETH OKPALA contends that the reasons advanced were fabricated after-thought and were offered only after a protracted period of continuous request for an explanation for his being passed up for promotions.

NEW ALLEGATIONS PURSUANT TO PLAINTIFF'S NOTICE OF RIGHT TO SUE OF DECEMBER 22, 1992.

Whenever the word(s) "Defendant" or the word "Defendants" is used with respect to paragraphs (32) to (39), only the following Defendants are meant: DONNA H. KRISTAPONIS, BOB LITKE, PATRICIA RINCON-KALLMAN, and CHRISTINE BALLARD.

BENNETH OKPALA adopts all the forgone allegations into this paragraph as if fully set forth here in details and further alleges the following new acts:

(32) On or about March, 1991, two positions, Senior Planner (PN#22250) and Planner Leader (PN#22245) became open and posted. MR. OKPALA applied for the two positions and was referred for interviews for the said positions by the Personnel Department; however, BENNETH OKPALA was denied interview.

(33) Following the denial of interview as alleged in paragraph (33), MR. OKPALA noticed more hiring beyond the two originally posted positions (positions similar to those for which he had applied). Such hirings for the said positions were executed without notice being posted on the Department Bulletin Board, as is required by city hiring policies. MR. OKPALA, on or about December 16, 1991, challenged the act of secrecy in job openings in writing. The memorandum was addressed to Defendant, PATRICIA RINCON-KALLMAN, Assistant Director.

(34) Following BENNETH OKPALA's memorandum of December 16, 1991, challenging the secrecy in job openings (jobs for which BENNETH OKPALA qualified

and positions in which he had demonstrated interest), Defendant, PATRICIA RINCON-KALLMAN, on January 10, 1992, wrote and denied the fact that Defendants had failed to post subsequent job openings and in her memorandum of January 10, 1992, also supplied MR. OKPALA the list of job openings beyond the only two positions for which he had earlier applied. MR. OKPALA continues to assert that the subsequent positions which were supplied him as a result of his memorandum were never posted before the date of his memorandum to Ms. Rincon-Kallman.

(35) On or about February 27, 1992, BENNETH OKPALA was interviewed for Senior Planner Position, but was not hired. MR. OKPALA contends that the interview was a sham and was not conducted in good faith, but rather, was conducted for the evidential benefit that it might provide for the Defendants. For example, prior to interviewing BENNETH OKPALA, Defendants had interviewed and/or hired thirty-two (32) persons for the types and similar positions. Defendants have continued to interview more persons for the Senior Planner and Principal Planner positions, even after MR. OKPALA was interviewed for Senior Planner position.

(36) BENNETH OKPALA further contends that the acts of secrecy alleged in paragraphs (31) through (35) were done intentionally, and were designed for the express purposes of depriving him of any and all knowledge of those job openings until they were filled.

(37) On or about October 1991, at a management meeting, Defendant, BOB LITKE, strongly suggested that Nigerian Planners should be excluded from Planner of the Day Program. Such suggestion was accepted by Defendant, PATRICIA RINCON-KALLMAN and Kathy Striver, then Assistant Director for the Zoning Division, and was subsequently adopted as a Department Policy.

(38) On or about October, 1992, Mrs. Sheila Strain-Bell, then Principal Planner and direct Supervisor of BENNETH OKPALA gave a favorable evaluation of his work

performance and rated his work performance "above average," among other favorable comments. Defendants PATRICIA RINCON-KALLMAN and CHRISTINE BALLARD, sought to use their superior positions to pressure and influence Mrs. Strain-Bell to change her evaluation of BENNETH OKPALA, and when Mrs. Strain-Bell refused out of principle, self-respect, and in obedience to the laws of the land, the above-named Defendants threatened her with serious consequences. When Mrs. Strain-Bell failed to reverse her evaluation of BENNETH OKPALA, Defendants, DONNA H. KRISTAPONIS, BOB LITKE, PATRICIA RINCON-KALLMAN and CHRISTINE BALLARD, conspired to terminate Mrs. Strain-Bell's employment with the City of Houston.

(39 The new allegations asserted in paragraphs (31) to 38) constitute continued (i) constructive ostracization, (ii) exclusion from department activities, (iii) infliction of great emotional and mental anguish, (iv) infliction of severe emotional distress, (v) professional degradation, (vi) denial of valuable opportunities to grow and become even more qualified to earn higher positions within the department and the city, (vii) harassment, (viii) retaliation, and (ix) further discrimination against BENNETH OKPALA on the part of Defendants.

(40) The design, intent, purpose and effect of Defendants' policies and practices as described above has been to deprive BENNETH OKPALA of equal employment opportunities and to deprive him OKPALA of the same right to make and enforce contracts as is enjoyed by white citizens of the United States.

(41) BENNETH OKPALA has worked for Defendants from June 1987 to present. MR. OKPALA's record of employment was rated above standard during that period and indicated a consistent pattern on his behalf to self-improve and to establish qualifications for advancement. MR. OKPALA's work record and accomplishments clearly indicated that he was qualified for the respective positions enumerated above. Yet, due to the inherently

discriminatory system of promotion, hiring and advancement used by Defendants, BENNETH OKPALA was never hired for the positions.

Due to Defendants' discriminatory hiring, promoting, transferring and advancement practices, BENNETH OKPALA was denied all of the positions enumerated above for which he applied and other persons with less experience, seniority and education, and with no higher qualifications than MR. OKPALA were hired for the positions.

(42) As a direct and proximate result of Defendant's racially motivated discriminatory acts, BENNETH OKPALA has suffered great and irreparable economic and other loss. He has been and is now being deprived of income including wages, progressive retirement benefits, and other fringe benefits due him solely because of his race and national origin, in an amount to be proved at trial.

(43) BENNETH OKPALA is now suffering and will continue to suffer irreparable harm and injury from Defendants' discriminatory policies, practices, customs and usage as set forth herein.

(44) As a further result of Defendants, discriminatory and wrongful acts as set forth herein, BENNETH OKPALA has suffered severe emotional distress, humiliation, embarrassment, and mental anguish for which he seeks redress in an amount to be proved at trial.

(45) Defendants at all times relevant to this action acted with malice towards BENNETH OKPALA. Defendant acted intentionally with conscious disregard and indifference to the protected rights of the Plaintiff, BENNETH OKPALA.

(46) MR. OKPALA's marriage was nearly completely destroyed by reason of the severe injuries Defendants had inflicted upon MR. OKPALA's state of mind, which in turn affected the manner and nature of relationship with his wife in adverse fashion.

(47) BENNETH OKPALA's constitutional rights were openly abused and deprived of, including but not limited to the rights also guaranteed him under the Equal Protec-

tion clause of the 14th Amendment to the US Constitution as amended to apply to the states.

VI.
DAMAGES

All the relevant paragraphs for damages are re-stated herein as if re-stated verbatim, and fully.

(48) BENNETH OKPALA is entitled to recover all of the damages mandated by law under both Title VII and Section 1981. Such damages include, but are not limited to back pay, fringe benefits loss in holiday pay, vacation pay, insurance benefits, compensation for lost promotional opportunities, wage increases denied, and punitive damages as allowed under Title VII and Section 1981, as amended. Said damages to be awarded jointly and severally against the Defendants for the respective periods (applicable notices of Right to Sue March 27, 1992, and December 22, 1992, respectively) each participated in the above-enumerated acts alleged, respectively.

(49) In addition, no amount of legal remedy will fully redress the injury suffered by BENNETH OKPALA. MR. OKPALA suffered and is now suffering, and will continue to suffer, irreparable injury as a result of the racially discriminatory practices of the Defendants. MR. OKPALA has endured a great deal of severe mental and emotional distress. Defendants acted willfully and with reckless disregard for the rights of the BENNETH OKPALA. Defendants should be taught that the laws of our land would not tolerate flagrant circumvention and violations of the Civil Rights of others.

CONTENTIONS OF THE PARTIES
A.
DEFENDANTS' CONTENTIONS

1. Defendants deny that Plaintiff was treated differ-

ently because of his race.

2   Defendants contend that the reason for not promoting Plaintiff to the Planner III positions was because of Plaintiff's oral communications and work organization skills.

3.   Defendants deny that the City of Houston grievance procedures were inadequate to mediate Plaintiff's grievance.

4.   Defendants contend that the Caucasians hired over Plaintiff were more qualified than Plaintiff.

5.   Defendants deny that any knowing conspiracy was ever directed towards Plaintiff.

6.   Plaintiff was denied the Senior Planning (PN #22250) and Planner Leader (or Principal Planner) (PN #22245) positions because he did not possess the requisite "zoning" experience for the positions sought.   Furthermore, several of the successful candidates for the Senior Planner position were African-American (Gwen Campbell) and of Nigerian descent (Akinyele Akinsanya). Also, one of the successful candidates for the Principal Planner was African-American (Sheila Strain-Bell).

7.   Defendants contend that the Planner III position, PN #18372, required that a candidate possess oral communications and work organizational skills.

8.   Defendants contend that their decision not to promote Plaintiff was not racially motivated.   Defendants vehemently deny that an intra-corporate conspiracy existed to deny Plaintiff 's promotability to either position and further deny the numerous allegations contained in Plaintiff's amended complaint regarding the management of the Department of Planning and Development.

B.
PLAINTIFF'S CONTENTIONS

1.   Plaintiff contends that he was denied the promotions to Planner III (PN #18372 and #19800) because of his race/national origin (Nigerian).

2. Plaintiff contends that he was denied promotion to Planner Leader or Senior Planner (PN #22245 and #22250) because of his race/national origin, Nigerian, and also as retaliation for filing a discrimination complaint with the EEOC.

3. Plaintiff further contends that the positions occupied by individuals listed under Plaintiff's Statement of Facts, No. 20, were also positions denied him because of his race and national origin.

4. Plaintiff asserts also that as part of the design and scheme to deny him a promotion to a Planner III, his application for promotion consideration was not acted upon forthwith, rather his applications were invariably always received and acted upon last and late.

5. Plaintiff contends that persons were hired for positions that were not posted and advertised to the general staff, and that Caucasians were preferred over non-whites.

6 Plaintiff further contends that cronyism and favoritism plays a significant factor in determining which employees are considered for promotion in the City of Houston Planning Department.

7. Plaintiff asserts and contends that certain members of the management committee acted in cohort to exclude Plaintiff and employees of Nigerian extraction from the Planner of the Day Program.

8. Plaintiff asserts and contends that Defendants' continual denial of a promotion to him to Senior Planner and Planner Leader, is retaliatory, racially based and racially motivated.

9. Plaintiff asserts and contends that he was denied interviews at least five (5) times for the Planner III, Planner Leader, and/or Senior Planner positions.

10. Plaintiff asserts and contends that he didn't need any written or oral courses in order to effectively perform the duties of a Planner III, and that this issue is a deliberate ruse by higher management in the Planning Department.

11.   Plaintiff further contends that the persons promoted to Planner III over him: Michael Kramer, Rebecca Thompson and Michael Johnson were no more qualified than himself.

12.   Plaintiff contends further that he possessed seniority and qualification over Margaret Wallace who was appointed to Planner III.

13. Plaintiff contends that Michael Johnson applied and was hired for PN #19800 in November 9, 1990, well after the deadline of October 23, 1990.

ADMISSIONS OF FACT

1   Plaintiff was hired by Defendant, City of Houston, sometime in June 1987 as a Planner II.

2.   Plaintiff is still employed by Defendant City of Houston in the Planning Department as a Planner II (now classified as Planner)

3.   Plaintiff was denied interview at least five (5) times by Defendants for Planner III, Planner Leader, and Senior Planner positions.

4.   Plaintiff admits that Michael Kramer, Rebecca Thompson, and Michael Johnson were promoted over him.

5.   Defendants have not denied that Plaintiff was otherwise qualified for position PN #19800 and PN #22250.

6.   Defendants have not denied that Plaintiff pursued the employee grievance procedure in an attempt to find a solution to Plaintiff's complaint.

7.   Defendants have not explicitly denied that there was a management committee meeting, in which Bob Litke, Patricia Rincon-Kallman, Gwendolyn Campbell and Kathy Striver were present when Bob Litke said, without opposition from Patricia Rincon-Kallman that Nigerian planners should be excluded from Planner of the Day Program.

8.   Defendants have consented to suit under Title VII,

42 U.S.C. 2000e et. seq. and Section 1981.

9. Plaintiff admits that Margaret Wallace does not possess a zoning or comprehensive planning background but was appointed to Planner III, now classified as Senior Planner.

CONTESTED ISSUES OF FACT

1. Whether the reasons given for Plaintiff's non-selection for the Planner III, Senior Planner, and Planner Leader positions were legitimate nondiscriminatory business reasons which warranted the denied promotions.

2. Whether Plaintiff's own conduct, i.e., his failure to take advantage of course study to improve his oral and communication skills as suggested by Defendants, contributed to his denial of a promotion for a Planner III position.

3. What damages, if any, resulted to Plaintiff if Defendants' violated any of the acts alleged.

4. Whether Plaintiff failed to mitigate his damages.

5. What offsets or credits are due to the City.

6. Whether Defendants acted in conformance with the Affirmative Action Policy of the City of Houston in its actions relating to promotions.

7. Whether Defendants had a policy to discriminate against Plaintiff, an African American employee of Nigerian descent.

8. Whether Defendants' actions were intentional.

9. Whether Defendants were justified in not promoting Plaintiff, because he was not the best-qualified candidate for the positions sought: Planner III, Senior Planner and Planner Leader positions.

10. Whether the Department of Planning and Development denied Plaintiff any due process or equal protection rights in their decision not to promote him.

11. Whether Plaintiff was denied any rights or privileges as are enjoyed by white persons by the Department

of Planning and Development.

12.   Whether Plaintiff has proven the existence of an intra-corporate conspiracy initiated by the named party Defendants against Benneth Okpala.

13. Whether the denial and refusal to promote Plaintiff to Planner III, under job postings PN #18372 and 919800, was racially motivated.

14. Whether the denial to promote Plaintiff to Planner Leader and Senior Planner positions, under job postings PN #22245 and #22250, was racially motivated.

15. Whether the statement made by Defendant BOB LITKE, with the acquiescence of Defendant PATRICIA RINCON-KALLMAN, in a management committee meeting that Nigerian planners be excluded from the "Planner of the Day" program was racially motivated.

16. Whether the repeated insistence and denial by Defendants to promote Plaintiff because of a purported communications deficiency and a lack of work organization skill was a subterfuge, and therefore racially motivated.

17. Whether Defendants discriminated against Plaintiff because of his race and national origin.

18. Whether Defendant PATRICIA RINCON-KALLMAN applied inordinate pressure and aped Ms. Strain-Bell to revise her high, favorable ratings of Plaintiff's job performance.

19. Whether Defendants BOB LITKE and PATRICIA RINCON-KALLMAN attempted to negatively influence Mr. Mangal to do a revision of his earlier favorable review and evaluation of Plaintiff's job performance.

20. Whether Plaintiff had more seniority and was similarly, if not more qualified, particularly, than Michael Kramer and Michael Johnson, and comparably qualified to Rebecca Thompson.

21. Whether Defendant MARINA SUKUP personally orchestrated and masterminded the hiring of Margaret Wallace as a Planner III for an opening that received no job posting.

22. Whether candidate Margaret Wallace, who was hired and promoted to a Planner III, was degreed in the planning discipline at the time she was appointed to a Planner III position

23. Whether Margaret Wallace was more qualified than Plaintiff at the time she was appointed to Planner III position.

24. Whether any other candidates competed with Margaret Wallace for the Planner III position for which she was eventually hired.

25. Whether Plaintiff's job performance was at or exceeded department guidelines.

26. Whether Defendants MARINA SUKUP, CHARLES SETTLE, J. HAL CATON , and MARLENE GAFRICK were in cohort and conspired to hire and promote Michael Kramer because of the social affiliations between Ms. Sukup and Michael Kramer.

27. Whether Plaintiff was treated as an outcast and outsider after he filed a grievance against the department.

AGREED UPON PROPOSITIONS OF LAW

1. Defendants accept Plaintiff's Title VII claim arising under 42 U.S.C. Section 2000e et. Seg. Defendants also accept and recognize Plaintiff's Section 1981 claim. Title VII of the Civil Rights Act of 1964 proscribes discrimination by an employer based on an individual's race, color, religion, sex, and/or national origin. Section 2000e-2(a) provides in pertinent part that:

It shall be unlawful employment practice for any employer: (1) to fail or refuse to hire or to discharge any individual, or otherwise to discriminate against any individual with respect to his compensation, terms, conditions, or privileges of employment, because of such individual's race, color, religion, sex, or national origin; or (2) to limit, segregate, or classify his employees or applicants for

> employment in any way which would deprive or tend to deprive any individual of employment opportunities or otherwise adversely affect his status as an employee because of such individuals race, color, religion, sex, or national origin.

Defendants have also recognized Plaintiff's claim arising under 42 U.S.C. S 1981. Section 1981 provides in pertinent part that:

> All persons within the jurisdiction of the United States shall have the same right in every state and territory to make and enforce contracts, to sue, be parties, give evidence, and to the full and equal benefit of all laws and proceedings for the security of persons and property as is enjoyed by white citizens, and shall be subject to like-punishment, pains, penalties, taxes, licenses, and exactions of every kind, and no other.

2. Title VII case analysis embody the concept of either disparate treatment or disparate impact. Plaintiff's case proceeds under the analytical framework of the former. In Title VII cases, the United States Supreme Court has established a four prong test that lower courts must follow. In establishing a prime facie employment discrimination case by a preponderance of the evidence, a Plaintiff must show that: (1) he is a member of a protected group; (2) he was qualified for the job that he held; (3) he was discharged; and (4) persons who are not members of the protected class remained in similar positions. (Vaughn v. Edel, 918 F. 2d 517, 521, (5th Cir. 1990)., quoting McDonnell Douglas Corp. v. Green, 411 U.S. 792, 802 n. 13, 93 S. Ct. 1817, n. 13 1824 (1973).) Plaintiff, however, remains employed by Defendant City of Houston in the Planning and Development Department. Hence, prongs two (2) through four (4) of the McDonnell test is inapplicable given the facts of Plaintiff's case. In the instant case, therefore, the disparate treatment analysis of national origin discrimination delineated

by the United States Supreme Court in Texas Dept. of Community Affairs v. Burdine, 450 U.S. 248, 101 S. Ct. 1089, 67 L. Ed. 2d 207 (1981) is applicable.

3. To establish a prima facie case, a Plaintiff as here, must show: (1) that he has an identifiable national origin; (2) that he applied and was qualified for a job for which the employer was seeking applicants; (3) that he was rejected despite his qualifications; and (4) that, after his rejection, the position remained open and the employer continued to seek applicants from persons of complainant's qualifications. If the Plaintiff establishes a prima facie case, the burden then shifts to the Defendant who must articulate legitimate non-discriminatory reason for its action. McDonnell Douglas, supra, 411 U.S. at 802 n. 13, 93 S. Ct. n. 13 at 1824.

4. The burden of establishing a prima facie case is not onerous. Burdine, supra, 450 U.S. at 253, 101 S. Ct. at 1093-94. Also, the McDonnell Douglas test is inapplicable where the Plaintiff presents direct evidence of discrimination. When direct credible evidence of employer discrimination exists, a different process appertains. Vaughn, supra, 918 F. 2d at 521; TransWorld Airlines, Inc. v. Thurston, 469 U.S. 111, 121, 105 S. Ct. 613, 62122, 83 L. Ed. 2d 523 (1984).

5. A finding of intentional discrimination, or its absence, is a finding of fact. Vaughn, 918 F. 2d at 520.

6. To succeed in carrying the ultimate burden of proving intentional discrimination, a Plaintiff may establish a pretext directly, by showing that the employer was more likely motivated by a discriminatory reason unworthy of credence. Burdine, 450 U.S. at 256, 101 S. Ct. at 1095.

7. The Equal Employment Opportunity Commission holds that a Plaintiff who proves he has been discriminated against solely because of his accent does establish a prima facie case of national origin discrimination. Bell v. Home Life Insurance Co., 596 F. Supp. 1549, 1544-55, (M.D.N.C. 1984). EEOC guidelines define discrimination to include: "the denial of equal employment op-

portunity ... because an individual has the.... linguistic characteristics of a national origin group." 29 C.F.R. S 1606.1 (1988). The EEOC cautions that denying employment opportunities because of an individuals foreign accent insofar as it creates an inability to communicate well in English may be a "cover" for unlawful discrimination. An adverse employment decision may be predicated upon an individuals' accent when, but only when, it interferes materially with job performance. Fragante v. City and County of Honolulu, 888 F. 2d 591 (9th Cir. 1989).

8. A foreign accent that does not interfere with a Title VII claimant's ability to perform duties of the position he has been denied is not a legitimate justification for adverse employment decisions. Carino v. The University of Oklahoma Board of Regents, 750 F. 2d 815 (10th Cir. 1984); Berke v. Ohio Department of Public Welfare, 628 F. 2d 980, 981 (1980).

9. Title VII charges can be brought against persons not named in an EEOC complaint as long as they were involved in the acts giving rise to the EEOC claims. Sosa v. State Center F.2d 1451, (9th Cir). F.2d 1346, 1352F (9th Community College District, et. al.; 920 1990); Wrighten v. Metropolitan Hosp., 726 Cir. 1984). Where the EEOC or Defendants anticipated that the claimant would name themselves or should have those Defendants in a Title VII suit, the Court has jurisdiction over those Defendants even though they were not named in the EEOC charge. Sosa, 920 F. 2d at 1458; Chung v. Pomona Valley Community Hosp., 667 F. 2d 788, 792, (9th Cir. 1982); Danner v. Phillips Petroleum Co., 447 F. 2d 159, (5th Cir. 1971). "It is now too well settled to discuss that no EEOC effort to conciliate is required before a federal court may entertain a Title.VII action." Id. at 160. An effort to conciliate by the EEOC is not in any sense a condition precedent to the charging party's right to seek judicial consideration of his grievance. Miller v. International Paper Co. , 408 F. 2d 283, 288291, (5th Cir.

1969).

10. Charges upon which complaints of discrimination are based should be construed liberally. Danner, supra, 447 F. 2d at 161. To compel the charging party to specifically articulate in a charge filed with the panoply of discrimination which he may have suffered may cause the very persons Title VII was designed to protect to lose that protection, because they are ignorant of or are unable to thoroughly describe the discriminatory practices to which they are subjected. Id. The complaint in the civil action ... may properly encompass any ... discrimination like or reasonably related to the allegations. King v. Georgia Power Co. , 295 F. Supp. 943, 947 (N.D. Ga. 1969); United States v. Mayton, 335 F. 2d 153, 161, (5th Cir. 1964) ; Jenkins v. United Gas Corp., 400 F. 2d 28, 30 n. 3, (5th Cir. 1968); Herbert v. Monsanto Company and Texas City, 682 F. 2d 1111, 1133, (5th Cir. 1982). Title VII was designed to protect the many who are unlettered and unschooled in the nuances of literary craftsmanship. It would falsify the Act's hopes and ambitions to require verbal precision and finesse from those to be protected, for we know that these endowments are often not theirs to employ. Since the act involves a "lay initiated proceeding," it would be out of keeping with the Act to import common law pleading niceties to the charge of discrimination or in turn to hog-tie the subsequent lawsuit to any such concepts. Jenkins, supra, 400 F. 2d at 30, n.3.

a) DEFENDANTS' AGREED PROPOSITIONS OF LAW

Title VII of the Civil Rights Act of 1964 makes it unlawful for an employer to fail or refuse to hire or to discharge any individual, or otherwise to discriminate against any individual with respect to his compensations, terms, conditions, or privileges of employment, because of such individual's race, color, religion, sec, or national origin; or (2) to limit, segregate, or classify his employees or applicants for employment in any way which would deprive any individual of employment opportunities or otherwise adversely affect his status as an employee, because of such individuals race, color, religion, sex, or national origin. 42 U.S.C. S 2000e-2.

1. Plaintiff is an employee within the meaning of Title VII.

2. This is a disparate treatment case under Title VII.

3. The elements establishing race/national origin discrimination are enunciated in McDonnell Douglas Corp. v. Green, 411 U.S. 792, 93 S. Ct. 1817 (1873); Texas Department of Community Affairs v. Burdine, 450 U.S. 248, 101 S. Ct. 1089 (1981).

4. The McDonnell Douglas/Burdine four prong test for asserting race/national' origin discrimination also applies to claims brought under 42 U.S.C. S 1981. Patterson v. McLean Credit Union, 109 S. Ct. 2363, 49 U.S. 164, 186 (1989). To establish a S 1981 prima facie case, the Plaintiff must further satisfy the requirements of Jett v. Dallas Independent School District, 491 U.S. 2701.

5. Under the McDonnell Douglas standard, the ultimate burden of establishing a case of race/national origin discrimination rests with the Plaintiff at all times. McDonnell Douglas, 93 S. Ct. 1817.

6. Once the Plaintiff established a prima facie case, the Defendant must then articulate some legitimate, nondiscriminatory reason for its actions. Burdine, 101 S. Ct. at 1094; McDonnell Douglas, 93 S. Ct. at 1,824.

7. Once the Defendant articulates its reason, the Plaintiff must then prove by a preponderance of the evidence that the Defendant's proffered reasons are pretextual. McDonnell Douglas, 93 S. Ct. at 1825, 1826.

b) *CONTESTED PROPOSITIONS OF LAW*

1. Whether Defendants' acts, treatment of Plaintiff's application for promotions to Planner III, Planner Leader, and Senior Planner positions constitute acts that are pro-

scribed by Title VII of the Civil Rights Act of 1964, and 42 U.S.C. S 1981.

2. Whether Defendants, denial of Planner III to Plaintiff under PN #18372, #19800, and Planner Leader, Senior Planner position PN #22245 and #22250 constitute acts that are proscribed by Title VII of the Civil Rights Act of 1964.

3. Whether Defendants can meet their burden under Vaughn, McDonnell Douglas, and Burdine in light of the affidavits and evidence proffered by Plaintiff.

4. Whether Plaintiff has established a prima facie case under Title VII.

5. Whether Plaintiff's complaint fails to state any claim upon which relief can be granted under 42 U.S.C. S 1981.

6. Whether Plaintiff's claim of incorporate conspiracy involving the named party Defendants is actionable under Title VII or 42 U.S.C. S 1981.

7. Whether Plaintiff has failed to allege any facts showing that he has been denied any rights to which he is entitled.

APPENDIX B

Text of second (retaliaton) lawsuit against the City of Houston

IN THE UNITED STATES DISTRICT COURT
OF THE SOUTHERN DISTRICT OF TEXAS
HOUSTON DIVISION

BENNETH E. OKPALA,	§	
Plaintiff,	§	ACTION H-95-5249
V.	§	JURY REQUESTED
	§	
CITY OF HOUSTON,	§	
Defendant.	§	

PLAINTIFF BENNETH E. OKPALA'S OPPOSITION TO DEFENDANT
CITY OF HOUSTON'S MOTION FOR
SUMMARY JUDGMENT

Plaintiff Benneth E. Okpala ("Okpala") files this his opposition to the motion for summary judgment filed by Defendant City of Houston ("the City") and therein responds as follows.

BACKGROUND

Okpala brings this case under 42 U.S.C. Section 2000e et seq. ("Title VII") alleging retaliation for engaging in protected activity. Okpala has suffered retaliation by being denied promotion from Planner to the position of Principal Planner. Such positions were given to Philip Imoisi ("Imoisi") and Kathy Goode ("Goode"). Additionally, Okpala suffered retaliation in the form of unwarranted reprimands and being falsely charged and disciplined for alleged use of profanity and racial slurs. Retaliatory reprimands affected Okpala's career with the City according to the Assistant Director, Patricia Rincon-Kallman.

STATEMENT OF THE CITY'S MOTION

The City contends it is entitled to summary judgment for the following reasons:

A. Promotion Claims

1. The City contends that because the individuals who were promoted over Okpala are Nigerian (Imoisi) and African American (Goode), and Okpala is Nigerian, ipso facto, Imoisi and Goode are in the protected group. The City cites no law for this proposition. There is no law to support such a rationale.
2. The City contends that Imoisi and Goode, unlike Okpala, had experience as Senior Planner and therefore were "more" qualified.
3. The City argues that Okpala failed to establish the element of causal connection necessary to prove retaliation.

B. Miscellaneous

1. The City contends that harassment complained of by Okpala is not actionable under Title VII because it did not affect promotion or salary.
2. Page 16 of the City's motion bears a captioned, Ib) "Defendant is entitled to summary judgment on the re-

maining retaliation claims asserted under paragraphs 2 through 5 because each asserted claim is time-barred." This section of the City's motion borders on gibberish. Okpala is unable to respond. Excepting those claims previously dismissed by this Court, Okpala notes the following for the Court's information:

a) EEOC charge #330-94-2441 was filed 5/23/94, re occurrence of 2/22/94.

b) Should any of the claims for EEOC charge #330-94-2441 not be timely, such claims are admissible as to the issue of intent and motivation. <u>United Air Lines v. Evans, Infra</u>.

c) EEOC charge #330-95-0339 was filed 11/l/94 re August and September 1, 1994 occurrences.

d) EEOC charge #330-96-1029 was filed 2/9/96 re occurrence of 2/16/96.

e) When there is retaliation under Title VII and a charge or lawsuit is pending, it is unnecessary for an employee to exhaust administrative remedies. <u>Gupta v. East Texas State University</u>, 654 F.2d 411, 414 (5th Cir. 1981, Unit A). The instant case was filed November 15, 1996. The City's reference to a two-year statute of limitation has no relevance.

OKPALA'S STATEMENT OF OPPOSITION

1. It is not disputed that Okpala suffered denial of promotion while engaged in protected activity. In a retaliation claim under Title VII, the protected group consists of individuals who have filed EEOC charges or filed civil rights lawsuits. Those not in the protected group are individuals who have not filed EEOC. Okpala incorporates by reference exhibit A of the City consisting of the above-discussed EEOC charges. Fed. R. Civ. P. 10. charges or civil rights lawsuits. The race or the national origin of the individual is not relevant. Okpala has established a prima facie case of retaliation.

2. The factual record demonstrates that at a minimum

the candidates for the Principal Planner positions was the more qualified.

3. Okpala's supervisor testified that the reprimand Okpala received could be detrimental to Okpala's career. Such harassment is actionable under Title VII. The retaliation beyond denial of promotion is actionable. Even if such harassment were not actionable for damages purposes, such behavior is relevant and admissible to establish intent and motivation. United Air Lines v. Evans, 431 U.S. 553, 558, 52 L.Ed.2d 571, 578, 97 S.Ct. 1885 (1977).

4. Certain alleged acts of retaliation by Charles Frederiksen set out by Okpala in his EEOC charge filed 5/.29/94 [exhibit A attached to the City's motion, charge #330 94 2441] in those instances not within the 300 day period go to the issue of motivation and intentional retaliation. United Air Lines v. Evans, 431 U.S. 553, 558, 52 L.Ed.2d 571, 578, 97 S.Ct. 1885 (1977).

Attachments

In order to assist the Court in its ruling, Okpala attaches exhibit 1 through exhibit 25. Such exhibits are more fully described in the Appendix attached hereto.

FACTS
Prefatory

Plaintiff Benneth E. Okpala ("Okpala") has been employed since June 1987 by Defendant City of Houston ("the City") in the position of Planner in the City's Comprehensive Planning Division, Department of Planning and Development. Exhibit 1.

Okpala filed a number of EEOC charges against the City, including charge numbers 330-91-1896, 330-92-1846, 330-94-2441, 330-95-0339 and 330-96-1029. Additionally, Okpala sued the City in the matter of Benneth E. Okpala v. Bob Lanier, Mayor, City of Houston, et al., United States District Court, S.D. Texas, Houston Div., C.A.

No. H-92-1867 ("Okpala"), therein alleging racial and national origin discrimination. Id.

As a consequence of Okpala's protected activity, he suffered adverse employment actions by the City. Okpala was denied promotion to two positions as Principal Planner. Position number 55621 was given to Kathy Goode ("Goode"). Position number 52388 was given to Philip Imoisi ("Imoisi"). Id. Neither Goode nor Imoisi filed EEOC charges or lawsuits against the City. Philip Imoisi and Kathy Goode, had not filed EEOC charges or a civil rights lawsuit.... 11 p. 18. Patricia Rincon-Kallman ("Kallman") is Assistant Director of the City's Planning and Development Department. Exhibit 2, Kallman, 8. Miguel Angel Garcia ("Garcia") is Assistant Director for Neighborhood Services. Exhibit 3, Garcia, 9-10. Kallman selected Goode over Okpala; Garcia selected Imoisi over Okpala. Exhibit 4. At the time Kallman selected Goode over Okpala for the position of Principal Planner, she knew Okpala had filed his previous lawsuit and certain EEOC charges. Exhibit 2, Kallman, 17, 18. In fact, Kallman had given an affidavit in Okpala I. Id. At the time Garcia selected Imoisi over Okpala for the position of Principal Planner, Garcia knew that Okpala had sued the City for employment discrimination in Okpala I. Exhibit 3, Garcia, 42-43.1

In addition to being denied the promotions to Principal Planner which were given to Goode and Imoisi, Okpala was subjected to constant retaliatory action in the form of being falsely accused of using abusive profanity and racial slurs, being given an extra workload, and being given unwarranted reprimands.

Retaliatory Harassment

Okpala I was tried in April 1995. During the EEOC stage and the pretrial stage of Okpala I, Okpala was constantly harassed by Charles Frederiksen ("Frederiksen"), Administrative Manager, who for part of the time period of this case was over Okpala. Exhibit 2, Kallman, 37-38. Okpala complained to Kallman without significant relief. Exhibit 1.

By January 1994, the harassment worsened. Frederiksen, with the expressed approval of Kallman, increased Okpala's work by the estimate of Kallman and Frederiksen of something less than 15%. Defendant does not dispute that Plaintiff has established ... that Okpala was engaged in protected activity.... 11 Defendant's motion, p. 9. Exhibit 2, Kallman, 107. In addition to working a full assignment on the Utilities Profile with Solid Waste, Gas and Electricity, along with special projects in Landfill Permit Review, Okpala was assigned by Frederiksen to assume work previously done by Scott Neitzel, a Senior Planner. Exhibit 6; Exhibit 2, Kallman, 122-123. Despite Kallman's acknowledgment that Okpala had to do his full work assignment plus the work formerly done by Neitzel, Kallman testified she denied Okpala's request for relief from the overload. Exhibit 2, Kallman, 46. Because the job harassment continued unabated with instances such as being singled out for extra work assignments, Okpala filed EEOC charge 330 94 2441. Exhibit 5.

The pattern of retaliatory harassment continued into the summer and fall of 1994, and after. On September 1, 1994, Kallman gave Okpala an unwarranted formal oral counseling. Kallman called Okpala in the office and in the presence of supervisors Meleka Meleka and Frederiksen, Kallman talked to Okpala for what Kallman remembers as being fifteen minutes. Exhibit 2, Kallman, 37-38, 92-93. The counseling concerned a night meeting Kallman and her staff held in the field at a local school. Kallman contends that on 8/23/94, Okpala failed to follow orders to arrive at the site at 6:00 p.m. and remain after the meeting to clean up. Exhibit 7. The tone of Kallman's "counseling session" on 9/1/94 was accusatory, dictatorial, and did not lend itself to interchange between employee and employer. Exhibit 1.

Although Okpala did explain in the 9/1/94 meeting that he had not understood the instructions as to cleaning up [as evidenced by Kallman's memo of 11/3/94, exhibit 7], Okpala chose to put his response in writing to the charges leveled by Kallman. Because of the harassment from the pending lawsuit and EEOC charges and because of the tone of Kallman's meeting, Okpala wanted the protection of a written response. Exhibit 1. The day after the 9/1/94 counseling, on 9/2/94, Okpala delivered a memo to Kallman explaining that: 1) he was late to the meeting because of a flat tire; and 2) he did not wait to clean up because he was not on the Moving Team for that day. Exhibit 8.1

Kallman insists that she gave Okpala notice of clean-up duty at a staff meeting prior to the 8/23/94 on-site school meeting for which Kallman counseled Okpala. Such protestation does not withstand the credibility test. In deposition, Kallman places the meeting where she allegedly announced the new clean-up rules three days prior to 8/23/94. ("It would have been a couple of, three days before the meeting was our normal procedure, to meet a few days before the meeting to discuss the details.") Exhibit 2, Kallman, 34-35. In her counseling notes, Kallman places the staff meeting where she allegedly gave new instructions about cleanup as 8/23/94, the morning of the on-site meeting. Exhibit 9. At meetings such as the one on 8/23/94, Kallman had a pattern of selecting certain individuals to clean up. Such individuals were called the Moving Team. Exhibit 2, Kallman, 32-33. Kallman testified that there was no record of Okpala ever refusing to serve on the Moving Team. Exhibit 2, Kallman, 117. Kallman contends that on 8/23/94, all employees were part of clean up. Exhibit 2, Kallman, 89-90. Kallman's reply memo of 11/3/94 to Okpala does not make a direct reference to any such staff meeting. Exhibit 7.1

By letter dated 8/24/94 [one day after the 8/23/94 on-site school meeting discussed above], Gwendolyn J. Cox ("Cox"), who acted as a secretary to Kallman, wrote Kallman charging that Okpala had used profane, abusive language towards Cox and further, had used the racial slur "nigger" to characterize Cox. Exhibit 11. Kallman testified that at the time of the charges by Cox, Kallman was aware of the on-going lawsuit in Okpala I. Exhibit 2, Kallman, 111. Kallman testified that she had never heard Okpala use profanity; nor had Kallman ever heard Okpala use a racial slur. Exhibit 2, Kallman, 18-19. Cox indicated that there were three employees who were witnesses, namely, Maria Lara ("Lara"), Katherine Bryant ("Bryant"), and Kathy Goode. Despite Cox's accusation that the other employees were witnesses, the statements of Lara, Bryant and Goode do not corroborate Cox's charges. [E.g., Cox stated: " ... Lara was sitting at the typewriter near my work area and heard.... Exhibit 11. Lara stated: I don't remember him using any profanities ... Exhibit 12. Bryant stated: "I don't remember him using any profanities... Exhibit 13. Nor do any of the witnesses make any reference to racial slurs."

On 11/9/94, despite never having heard Okpala use profanity or racial slurs and after having reviewed the statements of Lara, Bryant and Goode, Kallman gave Okpala a written counseling letter.

On 10/7/94, Okpala requested by memo that the counseling of 9/l/94 be withdrawn. Exhibit 10. Kallman took no action to withdraw the counseling. Exhibit 15. Kallman testified that Okpala's counseling letter had a possible detrimental effect on Okpala's career with the City. Exhibit 2, Kallman, 31. Once again, Kallman has credibility problems. Kallman says she believed Cox over Okpala because she "had no reason not to believe Cox." Exhibit 2, Kallman, 109. Nevertheless, Cox's witnesses contradicted Cox's charges of profanity and use of a racial slur. Kallman testified that had Lara heard the profanity, it was likely Lara would have remembered it. Exhibit 2, Kallman, 29. Kallman also testified that Goode would have been sensitive to the use of racial slurs. Exhibit 2, Kallman, 27.1 Kallman's suggestion at deposition that Okpala had used profane language and racial slurs towards Cox "before and continues to do so" is non-sense. Exhibit 2, Kallman,

30-31. When asked if there were witnesses or statements to substantiate a suggestion of continual abuse by Okpala, Kallman replied: "No, I'm not aware of that." Id. According to Cox's memo, the alleged use of profanity and racial slur by Okpala occurred 8/10/94. Exhibit 11. Cox's letter was dated 8/24/94. Id. Okpala was not given a counseling letter until 11/9/94. What happened during the approximately 60 days between 8/24/94 and 11/9/94 is significant. On 11/1/94, Okpala filed EEOC charge number 330-95-0339. Exhibit 16. According to her testimony, Kallman likely was aware of the EEOC charge when it was filed. Exhibit 2, Kallman, 22-24. In deposition Kallman could not give a satisfactory explanation why it took 60 days to discipline Okpala. Exhibit 2, Kallman, 24. "I was very much involved in directing the consulting work. I did not have sufficient time to ... to prepare this adequately." Id.].

Retaliatory Denial of Promotion

Okpala was denied promotion to two different positions of Principal Planner. Position No. 55621 was given to Goode. Position No. 52388 was given to Imoisi. see Position No. 55621, Exhibit 17, and Position No. 55388, Exhibit 18.

Position No. 55621

Kallman selected Goode over Okpala for Position No. 55621. Kallman, who did not participate in the interview process, testified she selected Goode over Okpala based on the recommendation of the interview team and Goode's experience. Exhibit 2, Kallman, 57, 78. K a l l - man's deposition testimony establishes the following:

1. Educational Degrees: Okpala holds the Bachelors degree in Architecture and the Masters degree in City Planning. Exhibit 2, Kallman 65-68. Goode holds the Bachelors degree in Afro-American Studies and the Masters degree in Transportation planning and management. Id. According to Kallman, Okpala's Bachelor's degree, with-

out experience, "is obviously more relevant.,, Id., 66. As to the Masters degree, Kallman testified: "I'd have to say they're about the same." Id., 68.

2. Post Education Study: Okpala has two years of law school. Although Kallman noted law school was not a requirement, Kallman testified that Okpala's training in law was valuable in the work Okpala did in the area of eminent domain in the Neighborhood services Division with Gigi Chan. Exhibit 2, Kallman, 68-69.

In addition to his law training, Okpala is certified by the American Institute of Certified Planners ("AICP"). Exhibit 19. Imoisi, who got Position No. 52388, described the criteria for AICP certification as requiring graduation from an accredited school program, work experience and examination. Exhibit 20, Imoisi, 1011. Okpala's immediate supervisor, Madan Mangal ("Mangal"), described AICP certification as a "high professional credential." Exhibit 21, Mangal, 11. Goode has no legal training. Exhibit 22. Nor does Goode have AICP certification.

3. Tenure: At the time of the promotion, Okpala had in excess of eight years of City employment. Exhibit 19, 22; Exhibit 2, Kallman, 69. Goode had approximately four years of City employment. Exhibit 22.

4. Senior Planner: Goode had 2-1/2 years in the position of Senior Planner. Exhibit 2, Kallman, 83. Okpala's entire tenure was as Planner. The job posting does not call for Senior Planner experience. Exhibit 17. Nor does the posting indicate that Senior Planner experience is preferred. Exhibit 3, Garcia, 92. John Jackson, for example, was a Planner who was hired as a Principal Planner. Exhibit 2, Kallman, 15. Unlike Okpala, Jackson did not file an EEOC charge. Exhibit 2, Kallman, 108.

Okpala often did the actual work of a Senior Planner, as for example, replacing Scott Neitzel. Exhibit 2, Kallman, 46, 47; Exhibit 6.

5. Experience: One of the requirements for the position was "management skills and the ability to supervise. 11 Exhibit 17. Beyond her work as a Senior Planner, Goode

Exhibit 17. Beyond her work as a Senior Planner, Goode appears to have had little other experience in management. Other than Senior Planner, Goode lists on her resume work with the Texas Southern University ("TSU") Alumni and work at Research Associate Center for Transportation & Research and Center for Urban Programs ("Research Associate Center"). Apparently, Kallman did not consider the TSU student employment. Exhibit 2, Kallman, 72. Kallman was at a loss to explain Goode's tenure at the Research Associate Center or how the work related. Exhibit 2, Kallman, 72-73. Further, Kallman testified such specifics about the Research Associate Center position would not have been available to Kallman when Goode was selected. Id., 73. Goode's resume also lists employment with travel agencies, which Kallman agreed was not relevant to the promotion decision. Id., 73.

Kallman testified that experience prior to being employed by the City that included responsibility for hiring and supervising employees would be a plus for the candidate. Exhibit 2, 76. Okpala's resume reflects he had more than two years employment with Integrated Engineering & Material Services in charge of Project Design, which involved hiring and supervising technical support staff. Exhibit 19. When asked if such experience was included in the hiring decision, Kallman replied, "I may not have." Exhibit 2, Kallman, 76-77. Nor did Kallman consider the fact that Okpala appointed a 24-person administrative staff in a community organization in which he is involved. Id., 77. Kallman argued such experience was volunteer and not applicable as management experience. Id.

6. Quality of work: Although Goode's quality of work is not criticized and is praised, such praise lacks specificity. On the other hand, Okpala's record does have specificity. Because of his on-going litigation, Okpala only received one completed written job evaluation between 1989 and 1996. Exhibit 1. Relevant herein is the 1989 review of Okpala by Madan Mangal, who was Okpala's supervisor. Mangal rated Okpala above standard and eligible for

sition Mangal was asked: "Do you know of any reason, other than his filing lawsuits and EEOC charges, why in six years Mr. Okpala has never been promoted?" He replied: "I don't know." Exhibit 21, Mangal, 34.

As part of his duties in Utilities, Okpala drafted one of the chapters of what was to become the larger document, "Public Utilities Profile. " Exhibit 2, Kallman, 5 0. Okpala's chapter was of such quality that it became the model for the other chapters in the report. Exhibit 23, Memo, Kallman to Bob Litke, Deputy Director, Planning and Zoning, 7/27/93.

Summary Okpala v. Goode

Based on the record, Okpala's qualifications exceed those of Goode in the area of education, both as to degrees and posteducation study. Okpala's tenure with the City is double that of Goode. Although Goode was a Senior Planner for 2-1/2 years, such position is not a prerequisite for the promotion. For example, John Jackson, who was not in the protected group, moved from Planner to Principal Planner under Kallman. Okpala's experience prior to employment by Houston exceeds that of Goode. For example, for more than two years, Okpala was responsible for hiring and firing employees. Kallman designating Okpala's Utilities chapter as a model for the larger "Public Utilities Profile" document exemplarizes the quality of Okpala's work.

Position No. 52388

Garcia, Assistant Director for Neighborhood Services, selected Imoisi over Okpala for Position No. 52388. Exhibit 3, Garcia, 20. Garcia reported directly to Bob Litke ("Litke"). Exhibit 3, 10. In circa. 1991-1992, Litke had ordered all "foreigners" taken off the public speaker's agenda for the Planner of the Day Program. Exhibit 1; Exhibit 20, Imoisi, 16-18. In part as a consequence of such national origin discrimination, Okpala filed an EEOC charge. Exhibit 1. Imoisi chose not to file an EEOC charge against Litke. Garcia testified that he was aware of Okpala's prior lawsuit involving employment discrimination. Exhibit 3, Garcia, 42-43.

Garcia testified that he primarily selected Imoisi on the basis of Imoisi's work for Garcia at the City. Exhibit 3, Garcia, 27-28, 30. Garcia and Imoisi's depositions establish the following.

1. Tenure: Senior Planner: Okpala worked for the City in his present job since 1987. Exhibit 1. Imoisi began with the City in 1991. Exhibit 20, Imoisi, 22. Garcia was very emphatic that he did not consider experience as a Senior Planner, per se, necessary for promotion to Principal Planner. Exhibit 3, Garcia, 15, 16, 21, 33-34. In fact, Garcia's testimony in response to the City's deposition questions refutes the implication that the Senior Planner position involved significant supervisory responsibilities. ["The Senior Planner ... does more tasking, more work-related programs and functions as opposed to supervisory functions.." Exhibit 3, Garcia, 58.]

2. Education: Garcia rated Imoisi's Masters degree above that of Okpala, apparently solely because Garcia has a negative opinion of TSU, where Okpala got his degree. Exhibit 3, Garcia, 36. [Imoisi's degree was from University of Texas at Arlington. Id.] Garcia was aware that of the candidates, only Okpala had AICP certification. Exhibit 3, Garcia, 24-28.1

3. Post Degree Studies: In addition to AICP certification, Okpala had two years of law school. Exhibit 1. Imoisi had no law school training. Exhibit 3, Garcia 39. Garcia gave only minimal consideration to Okpala's legal training. Id.

4. Work Experience: Houston: As noted, Garcia limited judgment of Imoisi to the work Imoisi did under Garcia in Houston. Garcia primarily referred to Imoisi's work on the Hiram Clark area project wherein Imoisi was successful in conflict resolution. Exhibit 3, Garcia, 56-57. Garcia acknowledged that Imoisi had not listed specifically the

Hiram Clark experience on Imoisi's application for promotion. Exhibit 3, Garcia, 85. Garcia had high praise for Imoisi's work on the Hiram Clark project.

Imoisi attempted the same exam with Okpala for certification by AICP but failed the exam. Exhibit 20, Imoisi, 10.

Despite playing down Okpala's legal training, Garcia praised Okpala's work in the area of eminent domain. Exhibit 3, Garcia, 112. At the time that Okpala was working in the area of eminent domain, Garcia had suggested to Okpala that Okpala should apply for a transfer to work under Garcia. Id. Garcia acknowledged that Okpala's legal training was helpful in the work on eminent domain done by Okpala. Exhibit 3, Garcia, 49.

5. Prior Work Experience: Garcia acknowledged that in hiring for the position of Principal Planner, the City took into consideration work and management experience prior to employment with Houston. Exhibit 3, Garcia, 86, 87. Imoisi was deposed concerning his resume. Exhibit 24. Imoisi's deposition established that:

a) Immediately prior to coming to Houston, Imoisi was an Associate Planner and reported to a Planner. Exhibit 20, Imoisi, 26. Also, between 1989-1991 for a time, Imoisi worked as a facility planner making sure contractors went "by specs." Exhibit 20, Imoisi, 25-26.

b) Prior to 1989, Imoisi worked other jobs, such as taking soil samples. Exhibit 20, Imoisi, 28.

c) Imoisi summarized his professional work experience prior to coming to Houston in 1991 as: "My primary activities were really implementation." Exhibit 20, Imoisi, 30.

Okpala testifies that during his interview, Garcia told Okpala that community managerial skills were transferable to the job for which Okpala was interviewing. Exhibit 1.

In deposition Garcia was reluctant to acknowledge making the statement, but finally, when asked if he may have, replied, "Perhaps." Exhibit 3, Garcia, 52. One of Garcia's problems was that the City did not preserve Garcia's interview notes. Exhibit 3, Garcia, 22, 85. Okpala's resume reflects that he has considerable management type experience, both for other employers and in community activities. Exhibit 19. For example, Garcia acknowledged Okpala's management experience in such areas as:

a) Work in Houston Housing Authority, 19861987. Exhibit 3, Garcia, 50.

b) Planner Intern, graduate internship under the Federal urban Development Action Grant program. Id.

c) Integrated Engineering & Material Services, 1982-1984. Exhibit 3, Garcia, 50-51, 59-90.

Garcia also acknowledged that Okpala's work listed on Okpala's resume as being a member of a three-person planner team responsible for formation and support of the "In-service To The Public" citizens' participation group, et cetera, was an example of management duties. Exhibit 3, Garcia, 87-88.

Okpala also was responsible for a $250,000.00 investment portfolio, a 20-person administrative staff for the community organization Ndi-Ichie Cultural Club, Inc., Houston. Exhibit 19. Additionally, Okpala was responsible for appointing a 24-person administrative staff as Executive President of the Igbo Peoples Congress. Id. Such community activities were within the transferable managerial skills discussed above.

Summary: Okpala v. Imoisi

Okpala was employed by the City four years longer than Imoisi. Garcia did not consider it necessary for the candidate to have been a Senior Planner to be promoted to Principal Planner. Garcia appears to have had a bias against TSU degrees, which hurt Okpala. Okpala had more study beyond the Masters degree than Imoisi, including two years of law school and AICP certification. Garcia was impressed with Imoisi's work in Hiram Clark conflict resolution but cited few other specifics for the selection. Garcia was impressed enough with Okpala's work on the eminent domain project that Garcia suggested Okpala transfer to Garcia's area. Okpala's work history in management prior to being employed by the City far exceeds the work record of Imoisi prior to Imoisi's employment by the City. [In the extreme, Okpala hired and fired, while Imoisi took soil samples.] Okpala's community activities involved transferable managerial skills, which Garcia recognized but, perhaps because of Litke, ignored when Imoisi was selected over Okpala.

LAW
Summary Judgment

In the interest of space and economy, Okpala does not set out the well known standard for summary judgment that has evolved since Celotex Corp. v. Catrett, 106 S.Ct. 2548 (1986), and Anderson v. Liberty Lobby, Inc., 477 U.S. 242 (1986). Okpala does note that summary judgment is not favored as a "tool for resolving claims of employment discrimination, which involve nebulous questions of motivation or intent." Thornbrough v. Columbus and Greenville R. Co., 760 F.2d 633, 640 (5th Cir. 1985). Additionally, the Court is asked to note that in an age discrimination case styled Rhodes v. Guiberson Oil Tools, 75 F.3d 989, 994 (5th Cir. 1996), the Court held:

> In tandem with a prima facie case, the evidence allowing rejection of the employer's proffered reasons will often, perhaps usually, permit a finding of discrimination without additional evidence. Thus, a jury issue will be presented and a plaintiff can avoid summary judgment and judgment as a matter of law if the evidence taken as a whole (1) creates a fact issue as to whether each of the employer's stated reasons was what actually motivated the employer and (2) creates a reasonable inference that age was a determinative factor in the actions of which Plaintiff complains. (Emphasis added).

Once the employee establishes a prima facie case, the Fifth Circuit holds that:

> A jury may be able to infer discriminatory intent in an appropriate case from substantial evidence that the employer's proffered reasons are false. The evidence may, for example, strongly indicate that the employer has introduced fabricated justifications for an employee's discharge, and not otherwise suggest a credible nondiscriminatory explanation. Id., 994.

Retaliation

Title VII prohibits an employer from discriminating against an employee because the employee has alleged that the employer engaged in unlawful employment practices. Carter v. South Cent. Bell, 912 F.2d 832, 842 (5th Cir. 1990). To prevail in a retaliation case under Title VII, the employee must establish that: (1) he was engaged in an activity protected by Title VII; (2) an adverse employment action occurred; and (3) there was a causal connection between the participation in the protected activity and the adverse employment decision. Id'., 842-843.

In retaliation cases, direct evidence is virtually impossible to produce. In the ordinary retaliation case, all the proof will be circumstantial. Schlei and Grossman, Employment Discrimination, 2nd Ed. (1983), p. 558, citing Gates v. Georgia-Pacific Corp., 326 F.Supp. 399 (D. Ore. 1970), aff'd. 492 F.2d 292 (9th Cir. 1974). Once the plaintiff in a retaliation case has established a prima facie case, the employer has the burden of producing some legitimate nondiscriminatory reason for the adverse employment decision. McDaniel v. Temple Independent School District, 770 F.2d 1340, 1346 (5th Cir. 1985). If the employer satisfies this burden, then the employee must prove that such reason was a pretext for retaliation. id. In order to prevail in a retaliation case, the plaintiff ultimately must establish that "but for" the protected activity, he would not have been terminated. Id. See also, Jack v. Texaco Research Center, 743 F.2d 1129, 1131 (5th Cir. 1984).

Remoteness

In an unclear passing comment, the City seems to argue that the counseling of 9/1/94 was somehow too remote to be actionable. The City acknowledges that Okpala filed an EEOC charge 5/23/94, about four months prior to the alleged unwarranted counseling. City motion, p. 11. Okpala was not tried until April 1995. Exhibit 1. The City cites Clark v. Chrysler Corp., 673 F.2d 921, 930 (7th Cir, 1977), as its authority with regard to remoteness. In Clark, the plaintiff alleged that she was retaliated against by not being hired because of an EEOC charge her husband filed. The plaintiff filed three charges 15, 28 and 31 months after her husband's charge. The plaintiff in Clark did not establish that the employer had notice of the three charges. Further, the Court found that she was not qualified for the position in question and that the employer had hired her two children. The Court made a very limited finding that based on the facts of the case (i.e., alleged retaliation for a third party's filing of an EEOC charge, the charging party not being qualified for the job, and the employer not having notice), the "time lapse of two years between the filing of the charge and the allegedly retaliatory action is sufficient on these facts to negate any possible inference of retaliatory motive.,' Id., 930. There is no issue in the instant case of the employer not having notice of the instant lawsuit. There was not a two-year lapse between filing the lawsuit and termination. At all times, Okpala was qualified for the job as Principal Planner. Finally, Okpala, not a third party, filed the EEOC charges.

Statute of Limitations

The instant case is a Title VII case. The limitations period is governed by 42 U.S.C. Section 2000e-5(e). Because Texas is a deferral state, the limitation is 300 days from the act of discrimination. <u>Silver v. Mohasco Corp.</u>, 602 F.2d 1083 (2nd Cir. 1979). Okpala's charges are timely on their face. See City's exhibit A, incorporated herein by reference. Fed. R. Civ. P. 10. It is not necessary to refile on every retaliatory act done while a charge is pending. <u>Barrow v. New Orleans S.S. Ass'n.</u>, 932 F.2d 473, 479 (5th Cir. 1991), citing <u>Gupta, supra</u>.

Protected Group

In order to be in the protected group, an individual must be covered by 42 U.S.C. Section 2000e-3, which states:

> It shall be an unlawful employment practice for an employer to discriminate against any of his employees ... because he has opposed any practice made an unlawful employment practice by this subchapter, or because he had made a charge, testified, assisted, or participated in any manner in an investigation, proceeding, or hearing under this subchapter.

There is no ambiguity in the statutory language. The City offers no authority for its contention that Goode (African American) and Imoisi (Nigerian) are in the protected group for a retaliation claim, thereby negating one of the elements needed by Okpala to establish a prima facie case of retaliation Okpala's complaint does not allege racial or national origin discrimination. Okpala alleges retaliation. The City admits in its motion for <u>summary</u> judgment that "Imoisi and ... Goode, had not filed EEOC charges or a civil rights lawsuit.... " City's Motion, p. 18. The City's claim that Goode and Imoisi are in the protected group for retaliation must fail on its face. Such an argument is frivolous and in bad faith.

Conclusion And Prayer

Okpala established his prima facie claim of retaliation. There exists a genuine issue of material fact whether Goode or Imoisi were as qualified for the position of Principal Planner as Okpala. Retaliation beyond denial of promotion is actionable or, in the alternative, is admissible to establish intent and motivation.

Okpala prays that the City's motion for summary judgment be denied in all things, and that this case continues to trial.

Respectfully Submitted,
Patrick J. Gilpin
Federal Admissions No. 1545
Texas Bar No. 0796300

APPENDIX C

🙢🙠

Chronological (Docket) record of court proceedings covering the first lawsuit against the City of Houston

U.S. DISTRICT COURT
SOUTHERN DISTRICT OF TEXAS (HOUSTON)
CIVIL DOCKET FOR CASE #: 92-CV-1867

Okpala v. Lanier, et al
Proceedings include all events.4:92cvl867
Benneth E Okpala , filed. (hs) [Entry date 11/10/92]

01/25/93 12   FIRST AMENDED COMPLAINT by Benneth E Okpala, (Answer due 2/4/93 for Bob Lanier, for Houston City Of, for Dept Plan Develop, for Marina Sukup, for Charles Settle, for Marlene Garfrick) amending (1-1) complaint adding J Hal Caton, Bob Litke, Patricia Rincon-Kallman, Chris Ballard, filed. (hs) [Entry date 01/26/93]

01/25/93 ---   SUMMONS issued for Chris Ballard, Patricia Rincon-Kallman, Bob Litke, J Hal Caton and Donnah Kristaponis (hs) [Entry date 01/26/93]

01/26/93 13   RETURN OF SERVICE executed as to Patricia Rincon-Kallman 1/25/93 filed Answer due on 2/14/93 for Patricia Rincon-Kallman (ph) [Entry date 01/28/93]

01/26/93 14   RETURN OF SERVICE executed as to Dept Plan & Develop 1/25/93 filed Answer due on 2/14/93 for Dept Plan & Develop (ph) [Entry date 01/28/93]

01/26/93 15   RETURN OF SERVICE executed as to Chris Ballard 1/25/93 filed Answer due on 2/14/93 for Chris Ballard (ph) [Entry date 01/28/93]

01/26/93 16   RETURN OF SERVICE executed as to Bob Litke 1/25/93 filed Answer due on 2/14/93 for Bob Litke (ph) [Entry date 01/28/93]

02/08/93 17   MOTION [to strike (12-11 amended complaint by Houston City Of, Motion Docket Date 2/28/93 (17-11 motion), filed (hs) [Entry date 02/10/93]

02/10/93 18   RETURN OF SERVICE executed as to J Hal Caton 1/28/93 filed Answer due on 2/17/93 for J Hal Caton (hs) [Entry date 02/11/93]

02/12/93 19   AMENDED ANSWER to Complaint by Houston City Of: amends (7-11 answer), filed. (hs) [Entry date 02/16/93]

02/16/93 20   MOTION [to withdraw (17-11 motion to strike [12-11 amended complaint by Houston City Of et al, [motion Docket Date 3/8/93 (20-11 motion] , filed (hs)

03/29/93 21   EXPERT WITNESS LIST by Benneth E Okpala, filed. (nd) [Entry date 03/31/93]

04/23/93 ---   Recld letter from Dr Bartholomew C Okonkwo , Ref-copy of correspondence of 4/16/93 , frwd to CRD. (hs) [Entry date 04/26/93]

04/30/93 22   MOTION [for leave to serve more than 30 interrogs.1 by Bob Lanier, [motion Docket Date 5/20/93 (22-11 motion) filed (hs) [Entry date 05/03/93]

04/30/93 23   DESIGNATION OF EXPERT WITNESSES by Houston City Of filed. (hs) [Entry date 05/03/931]

04/30/93 24   OPPOSED MOTION [to require Plaintiff to submit to a metal examination by Houston City Of, [Motion Docket, Date 5/20/93 [24-11 motion , filed (hs) [Entry date 05/04/93]

05/03/93 25   MOTION [for leave of ct to serve more than 30 interrogs by Benneth E Okpala, [Motion Docket Date 5/23/93 (25-11 motion] filed (hs) (Entry date 05/04/93]

05/11/93 26   MOTION [to quash], and [for protective order by Benneth E Okpala, [Motion Docket Date 5/31/93 (26-11 motion, 5/31/93 [26-21 motion] , filed (hs)(Entry date 05/12/93]

05/11/93 27   MOTION [for extension of deadlines to permit the completion of discovery, dispositive mtngs, and all other mtngs by Benneth E Okpala, [Motion Docket Date 5/31/93 (27-11 motion, filed (hs) [Entry date 05/12/93]

05/14/93 ---   Recld Copy of correspondence of 5/12/93 to Judge Werlein.(hs) [Entry date 05/17/93]

05/14/93 28   OPPOSED MOTION [for protective order], or in the alternative [to dismiss by Bob Lanier et al, [Motion Docket.Date 6/3/93 [28-1) motion, 6/3/93 [28-21 motion] filed (hs) [Entry date 05/17/93]

05/14/93 29   UNOPPOSED MOTION [to extend time to taking defts depositions by Bob Lanier et al, (Motion Docket Date 6/3/93 (29-11 motion] , filed (hs) [Entry date 05/17/93]

05/14/93 30   RESPONSE by Houston City Of et al to [27-11 motion for extension of deadlines to permit the completion of discovery, dispositive mtns, and all other mtns, [26-11 motion to quash, filed (hs) (Entry date 05/17/93]

05/18/93 31   SUPPLEMENTAL (26-11 motion to quash, [26-21 motion for protective order by Benneth E Okpala [Supplemental Motion Docket Date 6/7/93 (26-11 motion to quash, 6/7/93 [26-21 motion for protective order] , filed. (hs) (Entry date 05/19/93]

05/18/93 ---   Recld letter from Dr Bartholomew C Okonkwo, Ref. deposition of the 9 defts frwd to CRD. (hs)(Entry date 05/19/93]

05/28/93 32   OBJECTION to Pltf's Untimely Filed Discovery by Defts City of Houston, etal, filed. (ks) [Entry date 06/02/93]

06/09/93 ---   **Terminated document (20-1] motion to withdraw [17-1] motion to strike (12-11 amended complaint, (17-1] Motion to strike (12-11 amended complaint - Doc #20 renders #17 Moot; no opposition filed to #20 - now moot (case)

06/08/93 33   MOTION [to quash notice to take deposition by Houston City Of, [Motion Docket Date 6/28/93 (33-11 motion] , filed (hs) [Entry date 06/10/93]

06/09/93 ---   Motion(s) referred: (29-11 motion to extend time to taking defts depositions referred to Magistrate Frances H. Stacy, [27-1] motion for extension of deadlines to permit the completion of discovery, dispositive mtns, and all other mtns referred to Magistrate Frances H. Stacy, [26-11 motion to quash referred to Magistrate Frances H. Stacy, [26-21 motion for protective order referred to Magistrate Frances H. Stacy, (25-11 motion for leave of ct to serve more than 30 interrogs. referred to Magistrate Frances H. Stacy, (22-11 motion for leave to serve more than 30 interrogs. referred to Magistrate Frances H. Stacy, [24-11 motion to require Pla to submit to a metal examination referred to Magistrate Frances H. Stacy (ph) [Entry date 06/11/93]

06/11/93 34   RESPONSE by Benneth E Okpala to [28-11 motion for protective order, (28-21 motion to dismiss , filed (hs) (Entry date 06/14/931

06/15/93 35   MOTION [for discovery conf] by Bob Lanier et al, [Motion Docket Date 7/5/93 (35-11 motion), filed (hs) (Entry date 06/16/93]

06/17/93 ---   Motion(s) referred: (35-11 motion for discovery conf, referred to Magistrate Frances H. Stacy, [33-11 motion to quash notice to take deposition referred to Magistrate Frances H. Stacy (hs)

06/15/93 36   ORDER granting (29-11 motion to extend time to taking defts depositions, [defts depositions due by 9/30/931 entered; Parties notified. (signed by Frances H. Stacy (hs) (Entry date 06/17/93]

06/23/93 37   REPLY by Houston City Of Houston et al to response to [28-1) motion for protective order, [28-21 motion to dismiss , filed (hs) (Entry date 06/24/93]

06/28/93 38   RESPONSE by Benneth E Okpala in opposition to defts' [24-11 motion to require Plaintiff's spouse to submit to a mental examination , filed (fs) [Entry date 06/29/93]

06/28/93 39   RESPONSE by Benneth E Okpala in opposition to defts' motion to deem request for admissions admitted, filed (fs) (Entry date 06/30/93]

07/01/93 40   RESPONSE by Benneth E Okpala to [35-11 motion for discovery conf, filed (mh) [Entry date 07/02/93]

07/01/93 41   MOTION [for summary judgment by Houston City Of, [Motion Docket Date 7/21/93 (41-11 motion], filed (mh) (Entry date 07/02/93]

07/01/93 ---   Recld discovery material and return it to Bartholomew C Okonkwo. (hs) [Entry date 07/06/93]

07/06/93 42   REPLY by Houston City et al of Pltf response to Defts Motion to Deem Request for Admissions Admitted , filed (hs) [Entry date 07/08/931

07/09/93 ---   Recld discovery material and return it to Bartholomew C Okonkwo. (hs) (Entry date 07/14/93]

07/09/93 43   MOTION [to withdraw (24-11 motion to require Pltf to submit to a metal examination by Houston City Of et al, [Motion Docket Date 7/29/93 (43-11 motion] , filed (hs) (Entry date 07/15/93]

07/14/93 44   RESPONSE by Pltf Benneth E Okpala to Defts (41-11 motion for summary judgment, filed (ea) (Entry date 07/15/93]

07/21/93 45   RESPONSE by Benneth E Okpala to Defts Motion to Limine, filed (ph) [Entry date 07/26/93]

07/21/93 46   SUPPLEMENTAL ANSWER by Benneth E Okpala to Motion Opposing Defts Motion to Deem Request For Admission Admitted, filed. (ph) (Entry date 07/26/93]

07/21/93 46   RESPONSE by Benneth E Okpala to Defts Counter Response to Pltfs Motion Opposing Defts Motion to Deem Request For Admission Admitted, filed (ph) (Entry date 07/26/93]

07/28/93 47   RESPONSE by Houston City Of to Pltfls [46-11 supplement answer to Deft's Mtn to Deem Request for Admission's Admitted , filed. (hs) (Entry date 07/29/93]

06/15/93 48   MOTION [to deem request for admissions admitted by Houston City Of, [Motion Docket Date 7/5/93 [48-11 motion], filed (hs) [Entry date 08/02/93]

07/30/93 49   MEMORANDUM AND ORDER granting in part, denying in part Deft's (28-11motion for protective order granting in part, denying in part (28-21 motion to dismiss granting Deft's [43-11 motion to withdraw [24-11 motion to require Plan to submit to a metal examination denying Pltfls [25-11 motion for leave of Ct to serve more than 30 interrogs. denying Deft's (33-11 motion to quash notice to take deposition denying Pltfls [26-11 motion to quash denying Deft's [22-11] motion for leave to serve more than 30 interrogs. denying Deft's Deft's [35-11]motion for discovery conf , entered. Parties notified. (signed by Judge Ewing Werlein Jr.) (hs) [Entry date 08/02/93] [Edit date 08/08/93]

08/12/93 ---   **Terminated document [26-21] motion for protective order, [24-11] motion to require Pla to submit to a metal examination; ruled on by Order previously entered (case)

08/16/93 50   SUPPLEMENTAL [41-11 motion for summary judgment by Houston city of [supplemental Motion Docket Date 9/5/93 [41-11 motion for summary judgment , filed. (hs) [Entry date 08/17/93]

08/16/93 51   SUPPLEMENTAL [41-11] motion for summary judgment by Houston City of [Supplemental Motion Docket Date 9/5/93 [41-11]motion for summary judgment filed. (hs) [Entry date 08/18/93]

08/31/93 --- Referral of Motion #27 withdrawn from Magistrate Judge. (case)

08/30/93 52 MOTION [for reconsideration of (49-11 memorandum and order], or in the alternative [to withdraw or amendment of the Ct.'s [49-11 memorandum and order] and [for extension of to permit completion of discovery I by Benneth E Okpala, Motion Docket Date 9/19/93 (52-11 motion, 9/19/93 (52-21 motion, 9/19/93 [52-31 motion], filed (hs) [Entry date 09/01/93]

08/31/93 53 MOTION [to consider their pending opposed mtn to require pltf to submit to a mental examination by Bob Lanier et al [Motion Docket Date 9/20/93 [53-11 motion], filed (hs) (Entry date 09/01/93]

09/01/93 54 Proposed PRE-TRIAL ORDER by Houston City Of, Benneth E Okpala et al , filed (hs) [Entry date 09/02/93]

09/01/93 55 SUPPLEMENT to Joint[54-11 pre-trial order by Houston City Of et al , Benneth E Okpala . filed. (hs)(Entry date 09/02/93]

09/02/93 56 MOTION [to enlarge time to respond to defts supplement todefts summary judgment motion by Benneth E Okpala, [Motion Docket Date 9/22/93 (56-11 motion], filed (original Response attached to Motion and filed) (ph) (Entry date 09/09/93]

09/02/93 57 RESPONSE by Benneth E Okpala to Defts [51-11 Supplement to [41-11 motion for summary judgment, filed. (ph)

09/07/ 93 58 FIRST AMENDED RESPONSE by Benneth E Okpala to the [57-1] Response to the [51-11 Supplement to defts [41-11 motion for summary judgment, filed. (ph) [Entry date 09/10/93]

09/08/93 59   MOTION [to strike Pltfs, [58-11 first amended response to defts summary judgment by Bob Lanier, Houston City Of, Dept Plan & Develop, Marina Sukup, Charles Settle, Marlene Garfrick, J Hal Caton, Bob Litke, Patricia Rincon-Kallman, Chris Ballard, [Motion Docket Date 9/28/93 [59-11 motion filed (ph) (Entry date 09/10/93]

09/08/93 60   OBJECTION to the [54-11 final joint pre-trial order by Bob Lanier, Houston City Of, Dept Plan & Develop, Marina Sukup, Charles Settle, Marlene Garfrick, J Hal Caton, Bob Litke, Patricia Rincon-Kallman, Chris Ballard, filed. (ph) [Entry date 09/10/93]

09/09/93 61   RESPONSE AND STATEMENT OF OPPOSITION by Houston City Of to Pltf's [52-11 motion for reconsideration of [49-11 memorandum and order, (52-21 motion to withdraw or amendment of the Ct.'s (49-11 memorandum and order, (52-31 motion for extension of to permit completion of discovery filed (hs) (Entry date 09/13/93]

09/20/93 62   REPLY by Benneth E Okpala to defts, response to (52-11 motion for reconsideration of (49-11 memorandum and order, [52-21 motion to withdraw or amendment of the Ct.'s [49-11 memorandum and order, (52-31 motion for extension of to permit completion of discovery, filed (nd) (Entry date 09/22/93]

09/24/93 63   NOTICE and MOTION [for leave to file pltfs request for production, and Ito compel defts to producer by Benneth E Okpala, motion Docket Date 10/14/93 (63-11 motion, 10/14/93 (63-21 motion filed. (ph) [Entry date 09/27/93]

09/24/93 64   RESPONSE by Benneth E Okpala to Defts (60-1] Objection to the Final (54-11 Joint pre-trial order , filed. (ph) (Entry date 09/27/93]

09/24/93 65   RESPONSE by Benneth E Okpala to Defts Objections to Pltfs Exhibits, filed. (ph) (Entry date 09/27/93]

09/24/93 66   RESPONSE by Benneth E Okpala to Defts [59-11 motion to strike Pltfs' (58-11 first amended response to defts summary judgment , filed (ph) (Entry date 09/27/93]

09/27/93 --- **Terminated document (48-11 motion to deem request for admissions admitted GRANTED at #49 (case)

09/27/93 67 ORDER [Motion hearing set for 11:00 10/15/93 for [63-11 motion for leave to file pltfs request for production, for (63-21 motion to compel defts to produce, for [59-11 motion to strike, for [56-11 motion to enlarge time to respond, for (53-11 motion to consider their pending opposed mtn to require pltf to submit to a mental examination, for [52-11 motion for reconsideration of [49-11 memorandum and order, for [52-21 motion to withdraw or amendment of the Ct.'s (49-11 memorandum and order, for (52-31 motion for extension, for [41-11 motion for summary judgment, for (27-11 motion for extension of deadlines], [terminated deadlines , entered; Parties notified. signed by Judge Ewing Werlein JR) (ph) [Entry date 09/29/93]

10/12/93 --- Recld discovery material and return it to Danita Roy Wiltz. (Entry date 10/13/93]

10/08/93 68 RESPONSE by Defts Bob Lanier, Houston City Of to Pltfs Memorandum of Points And Authorities and Motion to Strike Defts Pleadings, filed. (ph) (Entry date 10/15/93]

10/12/93 69 MOTION [to compel answers to-interrogatories and request for production by Houston City Of, Bob Lanier, Motion Docket Date 11/l/93 (69-11 motion], filed. (ph) (Entry date 10/15/93]

10/12/93 70 SECOND MOTION in limine by Houston City Of, Bob Lanier, [Motion Docket Date 11/l/93 (70-11 motion], filed. (ph) (Entry date 10/15/93]

10/12/93 71 OBJECTIONS to Pltfs Trial Exhibits, by Houston City Of, Bob Lanier , filed. (ph) (Entry date 10/15/93]

10/14/93 72 MOTION [for leave to file second amended answer by

Houston City Of et al, [Motion Docket Date 11/3/93 (72-11 motion], filed. (hs) (Entry date 10/18/93]

10/14/93 73   SECOND AMENDED ANSWER to Complaint by Houston City et al Of, amends (19-11 answer, filed. (hs) (Entry date 10/18/93]

10/14/93 74   REVISED OBJECTION to Pltfs Trial Exhibits by Houston City of et al , filed. (hs) (Entry date 10/18/93]

10/19/93---   **Terminated document (27-11 motion for extension of deadlines to permit the completion of discovery, dispositive mtns, and all other mtns (hs)

10/15/93 75   Minute entry: Motion Conf held on 10/15/93; App: Okonkwo and Sherman for pltf. Wiltz and Acosta f/ defts. denying (59-1] motion to strike Pltfs, [58-11 first amended response to defts summary judgment; denying (56-11 motion to enlarge time to respond to defts to defts summary judgment motion; denying [52-1] motion for reconsideration of 149-11 memorandum and order; denying (52-2) motion to withdraw or amendment of the Ct.'s [49-11 memorandum and order; granting [52-31 motion for extension of to permit completion of discovery (41-11 motion for summary judgment; taken under advisement granting [27-1] motion for extension of deadlines to permit the completion of discovery, dispositive mtns, and all other mtns Ct . The Ct will allow cnsl to take depositions during this month. Reporter: Reed (hs) (Entry date 10/20/93]

10/16/93 76   ORDER DENIED as mooting Defts (20-1] motion to withdraw[17-11 motion to strike (12-11 amended complaint; denying Pltfs [52-11 motion for reconsideration of [49-11memorandum and order; denying Pltfs [52-21 motion to withdraw or amendment of the Ct.'s (49-1] memorandum and order and granting Pltfs (52-31 motion for extension to permit completion of discovery [set discovery due for 11/30/93]; denying as Moot Defts [53-11 motion to consider their pending opposed mtn to require pltf to submit to a mental examination; DENYING as mooting Pltfs (56-11 motion to enlarge time to defts supplement to defts summary judgment motion [59-1) motion to strike Pltfs, (58-11 first amended to defts summary judgment:; Denying as mooting Pltfs [63-11 motion for leave file pltfs request for production; Denied as mooting Pltfs (63-21 motion to compel defts to produce; denying Defts [69-11 motion to compel answers to interrogatories and request for production , entered; Parties notified. (signed by Judge Ewing Werlein Jr.) (hs) (Entry date 10/20/93]

10/28/93 77   ORDER striking (72-11 motion for leave to file second amended answer. Motion does not comply with LR6, No statement of opposition or non-opposition. No statement of conf between counsel. , entered; Parties notified. (signed by Judge Ewing Werlein Jr.) (hs) [Entry date 11/01/931 (Edit date 02/24/94]

05/20/94 ---   **Terminated deadlines (case)

05/25/94 78   ORDER denying Defts' (41-11 motion for summary judgment entered; Parties notified. (signed by Judge Ewing Werlein Jr.) (hs) (Entry date 05/27/94]

05/31/94 79   ORDER referring case to Mediation, entered. Parties ntfd. Gabrielle Kirk McDonald is added as mediator; mediation shall occur no later than 90 days from the date of this order; if one or more ins COs must be involved in a settlement of the case a representative from each ins co. with authority to negotiate a settlement shall be present during the mediation; (signed by Judge Ewing Werlein Jr. (mk) [Entry date 06/01/941

06/20/94 ---   CASE reassigned to Judge Vanessa D. Gilmore
06/30/94 80   JOINT STATUS REPORT by Benneth E Okpala, Houston City Of filed. (hs) [Entry date 07/01/94]

07/19/94 81   ORDER [reset docket call for 1:30 3/31/95 before Judge Vanessa D. Gilmore] [entered; Parties notified. (signed by Judge Vanessa D. Gilmore) (hs) (Entry date 07/20/94]

07/21/94 82   OBJECTION to [80-11 joint status report by Benneth E

Okpala filed. (hs) [Entry date 07/22/941

08/01/94 83   RESPONSE by Houston City Of, et al to Defts' [82-11 objection, to (80-11 joint status report , filed. (hs) [Entry date 08/02/94]

08/11/94 84   REPLY to Defts' [83-1] response, to Pltfls [82-11 objection, (80-11 joint status report by Benneth E Okpala filed. (hs)

10/14/94 85   ORDER that Defts' Motion in Limine and Second [70-11 motion in Limine are DENIED WITHOUT PREJUDICE; All Motion in Limine may be urged after docket call and prior to the start of trial, entered; Parties notified; (signed by Judge Vanessa D. Gilmore) (ks)

07/09/93 86   MOTION [in Limine by Houston City Of, [Motion Docket Date 7/29/93 (86-11 motion, filed. Docketed this date per Judge Gilmore's instruction as it does not appear on the docket sheet. (ck) (Entry date 10/20/94]

10/14/94 ---   CRD recvd faxed copy of document stating that mediation was unsuccessful. Document frwd to file. vh (ck) (Entry date 10/20/94]

12/20/94 ---   **Terminated document [86-1] motion in Limine , per #85. (hs (Entry date 12/21/94]

02/09/95 ---   Recld letter-from Bartholomew C Okonkwo, fwd to CRD. (hs) (Entry date-02/10/951

02/09/95 87   MOTION [to vacate (76-21 order regarding request for admissions by Benneth E Okpala, Motion Docket Date 3/l/9S (87-11 motion], filed. (hs) [Entry date 02/13/95] [Edit date 02/23/95]

02/21/95 88   MOTION [for protective order staying discovery by Houston City Of, motion Docket Date 3/13/95 (88-1] motion . filed. (Part 1 of #88) (la) (Entry date 02/22/95]

02/21/95 ---   RESPONSE by Houston City Of to Pltfls [87-11 motion to vacate [76-21 order regarding request for admissions filed. (Part 2 of #88) (1a) (Entry date 02/22/95]

03/02/95 89   MOTION [for protective order staying discovery by Houston City Of et al, [Motion Docket Date 3/22/9S [89-11 motion , filed. (hs) [Entry date 03/03/95]

03/10/95 90   RESPONSE by Benneth E Okpala to Defts' [88-11 motion for protective order staying discovery , filed. (Part I of #90) (la) (Entry date 03/13/951 (Edit date 03/13/95]

03/10/95 91   MOTION [to compel the City of Houston's answers to the questions contained in Plaintiff's subpoena, and [for sanctions against the City of Houston for contempt of court [by Benneth E Okpala, [Motion Docket Date 3/30/95 [91-11 motion, 3/30/95 [91-21 motion , filed. (la) [Entry date 03/13/95]

03/10/95 92   MOTION [to compel Ms. Danita Roy Wiltz's answers to the questions contained in Plaintiff's subpoena] and [for sanctions against Ms. Danita Roy Wiltz by Benneth E Okpala, [Motion Docket Date 3/3,0/95 (92-11 motion, 3/30/95 (92-21 motion], filed. (la) (Entry date 03/13/95]

03/10/95 93   MOTION [to compel Ms. Constance K. Acosta's answers to the questions contained in the Plaintiff's subpoena, and [for sanctions against Ms. Constance K. Acosta] by Benneth E Okpala, [Motion Docket Date 3/30/95 (93-11 motion, 3/30/95 [93-21 motión], filed. (la) [Entry date 03/13/95]

03/10/95 94   MOTION [for sanctions against the City of Houston and its attorneys for failure to disclose potential for conflict of interest, conspiracy, etc, [to strike all the city's pleadings] and [for attorney fees] by Benneth E Okpala, [Motion Docket Date 3/30/95 [94-11 motion, 3/30/95 (94-21 motion, 3/30./95 (94-31 motion , filed. (la) (Entry date 03/13/95]

03/10/95 95   MOTION [for hearing and conference by Benneth E Okpala, [Motion Docket Date 3/30/95 [95-11 motion], filed. (la) (Entry date 03/13/95]

03/10/95 90   REPLY by Benneth E Okpala to defts' response to Pltf's

(87-11 motion to vacate (76-21 order regarding request for admissions , filed (Part 2 of #90) (la) [Entry date 03/13/95]

03/15/95 96   OPPOSED MOTION [to amend exhibit list by Houston City of, et al, [Motion Docket Date 4/4/95 (96-1] motion filed. (la) (Entry date 03/17/95]

03/15/95 97   MOTION [to compel answers to the questions contained in Plaintiff's subpoena, and for sanctions by Benneth E Okpala, [Motion Docket Date 4/4/95 (97-1] motion, 4/4/95 [97-21 motion, filed. (hs) (Entry date 03/20/95]

03/10/95 90   RESPONSE by Benneth E Okpala to [87-1] motion to vacate [76-2] order regarding request for admissions, filed. (hs) [Entry date 03/21/95]

03/22/95 98   REPLY by Houston City Of to response to [89-11 motion for protective order staying discovery, filed (hs) [Entry date 03/23/95]

03/22/95 ---   RESPONSE by Houston City Of et al to [95-11 motion for hearing and conference, [94-11 motion for sanctions against the of Houston and its attorneys for failure to disclose potential for conflict of interest, conspiracy, etc, [94-2] motion to strike all the city's pleadings, [94-31 motion for attorney fees, [93-11 motion to compel Ms. Constance K. Acosta's answers to the questions contained in the Plaintiff's subpoena, [93-21 motion-,for sanctions against Ms. Constance K. Acosta, (92-11 motion to compel Ms. Danita Roy Wiltz's answers to the questions contained in Plaintiff's subpoena, [92-21 motion for sanctions against Ms. Danita Roy Wiltz, (91-11 motion to compel the City of Houston's answers to the questions contained in Plaintiff's subpoena, (91-21 motion for sanctions against the City of Houston for contempt of court , filed. (hs) (Entry date 03/23/951

03/24/95 99   OPPOSED MOTION [to amend exhibit list, and for sanctions by Benneth E Okpala, motion Docket Date 4/13/95 (99-11 motion, 4/13/95 (99-21 motion, filed. (hs)

03/24/95 100 OBJECTION to Defts mentioning or alluding or offering any portion of Benneth E Okpala's deposition into
evidence by Benneth E Okpala , filed. (hs)

03/24/95 101 MOTION [for sanctions against attorney Benjamin
Hall by Benneth E Okpala, [Motion Docket Date
4/13/95 [101-11 motion, filed. (hs)

03/24/95 102 Exhibit list by Benneth E Okpala filed (in brown folder)

03/24/95 103 MOTION [to bifurcate trials], and [transfer trial issues
from the jury docket to the Ct docket] by Houston City
Of et al, [Motion Docket Date 4/13/95 (103-11 motion, 4/13/95 [103-2] motion], filed. (hs)

03/27/95 104 ORDER [reset docket call for 8:30 4/4/951; this case
is subject to being called for trial on short notice during the month of April, 1995, entered; Parties notified.
(signed by Judge Vanessa D. Gilmore) (ck) [Entry date
03/28/95]

03/28/95 --- CRD gave pltf, through secretary Yvonne, telephonic
notice that docket call is reset to 4/4/95 at 8:30 a.m.
(bj) (Entry date 03/29/95]

03/29/95 105 RESPONSE by Houston City Of to Pltf following motions: (101-11 motion for sanctions against atty Benjamin Hall, (99-21 motion for sanctions, [97-21 motion
for sanctions, (94-11 motion for sanctions against the
City of Houston and its attorneys for failure disclose
potential for conflict of interest, conspiracy, etc, [93-2]
motion for sanctions against Ms. Constance K. Acosta,
(92-21 motion for sanctions against Ms. Danita Roy
Wiltz, [91-21 motion for sanctions against the City of
Houston for contempt of court, [99-1] motion to
amend exhibit list , filed. (hs) (Entry date 03/30/95]

04/02/95 106 ORDER granting Defts (88-11 motion for protective
order staying discovery and denying Pltfs (87-1] motion to vacate [76-21 order regarding request for admissions , entered; Parties notified.(signed by Judge

Vanessa D. Gilmore (hs) (Entry date 04/03/95]

04/03/95 107 ORDER granting Deft (89-11 motion for protective order staying discovery. The following Pltfs motions are DENIED. denying (97-11 motion to compel answers to the questions contained in Plaintiff's subpoena denying (97-21 motion for sanctions denying (95-11 motion for hearing and conference denying (94-1] motion for sanctions against the City of Houston and its attorneys for failure to disclose potential for conflict of interest, conspiracy, etc denying [94-21 motion to strike all the city's pleadings denying [94-31 motion for attorney fees denying [93-11 motion to compel Ms. Constance K. Acosta's answers to the questions contained in the Plaintiff's subpoena denying (93-21 motion for sanctions against Ms. Constance K. Acosta denying [92-11 motion to compel Ms. Danita Roy Wiltz's answers to the questions contained in Plaintiff's subpoena denying (92-21 motion for sanctions against Ms. Danita Roy Wiltz denying [91-11 motion to compel the City of Houston's answers to the questions contained in Plaintiff's subpoena denying (91-21 motion for sanctions against the City of Houston for contempt of court denying (99-1] motion to amend exhibit list denying (99-21 motion for sanctions denying [101-11 motion for sanctions against atty Benjamin Hall , entered; Parties notified. (signed by Judge Vanessa D. Gilmore) (hs)

04/01/95 108 ORDER denying Defts (96-11 motion to amend exhibit list entered; Parties notified. (signed by Judge Vanessa D. Gilmore) (hs) (Entry date 04/03/95]

04/03/95 109 ORDER denying Defts [103-21 motion transfer trial issues from the jury docket to the Ct docket, entered; Parties notified. (signed by Judge Vanessa D. Gilmore) *(hs)*

04/04/95 110 Pltf's Supplement to Proposed JOINT PRE-TRIAL ORDER by Benneth E Okpala , filed (hs) [Entry date 04/05/95]

04/04/95 111 Minute entry: Docket Call held; App: Okonkwo and

Wiltz and Acosta. Case set for trial on standby status for the month of April. Ett: J - 1 week. [terminated deadlines, Pltf is set for trial in 125th district Ct [set trial date 4/17/95] Ett 2 weeks. Deft has witness problems lst 2 weeks in April. Ct Reporter: Edward Reed (hs) [Entry date 04/05/95]

04/06/95 112   Calculation of damages by Benneth E Okpala filed (hs) [Entry date 04/07/95]

04/10/95 ---   Recld and fwd to CRD: Pltfls revised jury charge/interrogatories w/floppy disc attached (ym) [Entry date 04/11/95] (Edit date 4/11/95]

04/10/95 113   Pltf's Revised Proposed Jury Charge Instruction by Benneth E Okpala , filed (hs) (Entry date 04/12/95]

04/13/95 ---   "On 4/12/95 and 4/13/95, CRD gave telephonic notice to pltf's & defense cnsl, respectively, that the case is on standby for trial beginning 4/19/95. They will be advised of their trial status on 4/17 or 4/18/95.11 vh (hs) [Entry date 04/14/95]

04/14/95 ---   **Terminated document (103-1l.motion to bifurcate trials (hs (Entry date 04/17/95]

04/17/95 ---   "CRD gave cnsl telephonic notice that the case is set for jury selection & trial on 4/19/95 at 10:00am. Cnsl shall, however, appear at 9:30 to discuss any pretrial matter-" vh (hs) (Entry date 4/18/95]

04/19/95 114   Minute entry: Final Pretrial Conf held; App: C Okonkwo and Wiltz. Cnsl hear re: Issues to be tried. The Ct will not strike instrument #110. The copy received in the clerk's office may be filed and tabbed. Deft's first motion in limine is DENIED. Defts' 2nd motion in Limine is granted in part and denied in part. Trial to begin immediately. [terminated deadlines Ct Reporter: W Farris (hs)

04/19/95 115   1st Day Jury trial held before Judge Vanessa D. Gilmore Ct App: Okonkwo, Ekoh and Wiltz. Reporter: W. Farris voir dire begins. Jury impaneled and sworn. (Lunch) Opening statement made. Testimony begins. Ct adjourned until 9:00 on 4/20/95. (hs) (Entry date 04/20/95]

04/20/95 116   2nd Day Jury trial held before Judge Vanessa D. Gilmore Ct Reporter: W Farris App: Okonkwo, Ekoh, Wiltz and Acosta. Rule invoked by the pltf. Ct rules on pltf's motion to vacate. Ruling dictated into the record. Testimony resumes. Ct adjourns until 9am on 4/21/95 (hs) (Entry date 04/24/951 (Edit date 04/24/95]

04/21/95 117   3rd Day Jury trial held before Judge Vanessa D. Gilmore App: Okonkwo, Ekoh, Wiltz & Acosta. Ct Reporter: W Farris Testimony resumes. Ct adjourns until 9am on 4/24/95. (hs) (Entry date 04/24/95]

04/24/95 118   Day 4 of Jury selection and trial held before Judge Vanessa D. Gilmore: Testimony resumes; Testimony continues; Jury excused for the day at 4:55am; Parties shall not submit duplicate exhibits to the Jury; Court adjourned until 9:00am on 4/25/95; Appearances: Same as day 1; Ct Reporter: Willa Farris/ Yvette Perry (la)[Entry date 04/26/95]

04/25/95 119   Day 5 of Jury trial held before Judge Vanessa D. Gilmore Ct Reporter: Yvette Perry App: Okonkwo; Ekoh, Wiltz, Acosta. Testimony resumes. Pltf rests. Jury excused for the day at 4:25pm. Defts move for a directed verdict. The Ct will rule on 4/26/95. Ct adjourned until 8:45 on 4/26/95. (hs) (Entry date 04/27/95]

04/28/95 120   ORDER Parties shall withdraw from the Clerk their evidence and shall maintain it for purposes of appeal , entered; Parties notified. signed by Judge Vanessa D. Gilmore (hs) [Entry date 05/01/95]

05/01/95 121   FINAL JUDGMENT entered. Parties ntfd. (signed by Judge Vanessa D. Gilmore) (hs)

05/01/95 ---   Case closed (hs)

04/26/95 122   6th Jury trial held before Judge Vanessa D. Gilmore Ct Reporter: Y Perry App: Okonkwo, Wiltz and Acosta. (hs) (Entry date 05/01/95]

04/28/95 ---   Recld Proposed Pretrial Material and fwd to CRD . (hs) (Entry date 05/02/95] [Edit date 05/02/95]

04/28/95 123   JURY VERDICT , filed (hs) (Entry date 05/03/95]

04/28/95 124.   1'A Exhibit list by Houston City Of filed (hs) [E n t r y date 05/03/95

04/28/95 125   7th Day Jury trial held before Judge Vanessa D. Gilmore App: Okonkwo, Ekoh, Wiltz & Costa. Ct Reporter: Y Perry Testimony resumes. Defts rest. Ct adjourned until 8:00 am 4/28/95. (hs) (Entry date 05/03/95]

04/27/95 126   8th Day Jury trial held before Judge Vanessa D. Gilmore CtApp: Okonkwo,Wiltz, and Acosta. Reporter: Y Perry Chargingconf. Ct charges the jury. Closing arguments. Jury deliberations being at 11:45am.Verdict returned for the defts at 3:43 pm. Jury polled at request of pltf. Jury released from jury service. The Ct will enter a judgment. Ct adjourned. (hs) (Entry date 05/03/95]

04/28/95 127   Certification of Trial Exhibits for Jury Deliberations by Benneth E Okpala, filed (hs) [Entry date 05/03/95]

04/28/95 128   Jury instructions, filed (hs) [Entry date 05/03/95]

05/03/95 129   AMENDED FINAL JUDGMENT: pltf shall take nothing from deft, entered. Parties ntfd. (signed by Judge Vanessa D. Gilmore)(ck) [Entry date 05/04/95]

04/28/95 130   Exhibit list by Benneth E Okpala filed (hs)[Entry date 05/12/95]

05/12/95 131   MOTION [for new trial, [vacation of judgment, and [making of new findings and conclusion of law] by- Benneth E Okpala, [Motion Docket Date 6/l/95 [131-11 motion, 6/l/95 [131-21 motion, 6/l/95 [131-31 motion], filed. (ck) (Entry date 05/15/95]

05/25/95 132   RESPONSE by Houston City Of to [131-11 motion for new trial, (131-21 motion vacation of judgment, (131-31 motion making of new findings and conclusion of law, filed. (hs) (Entry date 05/26/95]

06/08/95 133   AMENDED MOTION [for new trial], [to vacate [121-11 order, [129-11 order], and [making of new findings and conclusions of law] by Benneth E Okpala, motion Docket Date 6/28/95 (133-11 motion, 6/28/95 (133-21 motion, 6/28/95 (133-31 motion], filed. (mac) [Entry date 06/13/95]

06/08/95 134   REQUEST by Benneth E Okpala for hearing filed. (mac) [Entry date 06/13/95)

07/03/95 135   SUPPLEMENTAL RESPONSE by Chris Ballard, Patricia Rincon-Kallman, Bob Litke, J Hal Caton, Marlene Garfrick, Charles Settle, Marina Sukup, Dept Plan & Develop, Houston City of, Bob Lanier to pltf's amended [133-11 motion for new trial, (133-2] motion to vacate [121-11 order, [129-11 order, [133-31 motion making of new findings and conclusions of law, filed. (bj) (Entry date 07/07/95)

TOASTING THE BRIDE
MEMOIRS OF MILESTONES TO MANHOOD

Order Today
$19.95

Purchased by: _____

Address: _____

City: _____ State: _____ Zip Code: _____

Telephone #: _____

SHIP TO:

P U R C H A S E   O R D E R

CODE	QUANTITY	DESCRIPTION	UNIT COST	TOTAL
		Shipping/Handling		
		TOTAL:		

Benneth E. Okpala
Phone: (713) 270-8746
E-Mail: bennethokpala@hotmail.com

Christiana Okechukwu
Phone: (301) 340-7701
E-Mail: eaglepalm1@juno.com